Social History, Popular Culture, and Politics in Germany
Geoff Eley, Series Editor
(Continued)

State of Virginity

State of Virginity

Gender, Religion, and Politics
in an Early Modern Catholic State

Ulrike Strasser

The University of Michigan Press   *Ann Arbor*

First paperback edition 2007
Copyright © by the University of Michigan 2004
All rights reserved
Published in the United States of America by
The University of Michigan Press
Manufactured in the United States of America
♾ Printed on acid-free paper

2010   2009   2008   2007   5   4   3   2

A CIP catalog record for this book is available from the British Library.

Library of Congress Cataloging-in-Publication Data

Strasser, Ulrike, 1964–
      State of virginity : gender, religion, and politics in an early
modern Catholic state / Ulrike Strasser.
         p. cm. — (Social history, popular culture, and politics in
Germany)
      Includes bibliographical references and index.
      ISBN 0-472-11351-8 (alk. paper)
      1. Munich (Germany)—Church history.   2. Christianity and
politics—Catholic Church—History.   3. Marriage—Religious
aspects—Catholic Church—History of doctrines.   4. Women in the
Catholic Church—Germany—Munich—History.   5. Munich
(Germany)—Politics and government.   6. Christianity and
politics—Germany—Munich—History. 7. Marriage—Germany—
Munich—History. 8. Catholic women—Germany—Munich—
Social conditions. I. Title. II. Series.

BX1539.M8 S83   2004
943'.304—dc21   2003012775

ISBN-13: 978-0472-03215-0 (pbk. : alk. paper)
ISBN-10: 0-472-03215-1 (pbk. : alk. paper)

Title page illustration:
Raising the Pillar of Mary in 1638. Original in Stadtmuseum, Munich.

To Ulrich Strasser, my Father

Contents

Illustrations

Acknowledgments

This book and I owe a great deal to people and institutions on both sides of the Atlantic. They saved us from many things, even if not from all errors. My first thanks go to my professors at the University of Minnesota, Gianna Pomata, James Tracy, Mary Jo Maynes and Ann Waltner, for their multifaceted support and inspiration when this project was still a dissertation. I am equally indebted to Professor Heide Wunder at the Gesamthochschule-Universität Kassel in Germany. She too enabled me to write a dissertation and imagine its future as a book.

The generosity of several financial benefactors created the logistical preconditions for the book's completion. A research fellowship from the city government of Munich made it possible to spend enough time in German archives to carry out the necessary research. A fellowship from the Women's Studies in Religion Program at the Harvard Divinity School gave me both the leisure and the intellectual stimulation needed to write most of the manuscript. I was able to tie up loose ends and finish the book thanks to a faculty career development award from the University of California, Irvine. I am very grateful to these institutional sponsors.

I am also thankful for the professional advice of archivists and the kindness of the staff at the following institutions: Stadtarchiv München, Bayerisches Hauptstatsarchiv München, Diözesanarchiv des Erzbistums München-Freising, and Bayerische Staatsbibliothek. In addition, I am profoundly appreciative that the Franciscan sisters of Kloster Reutberg and the Englische Fräulein from the Institute in München-Nymphenburg were willing to open their doors and archives to me.

Many more people made this book better and me happier and I would like to record my gratitude to them. At Harvard, I benefited immensely from conversations with Ann Braude, Ann Mongoven, Susan Sered, Gail Sutherland, and Amy Hollywood (who has continued to make me think hard). Other friends and colleagues from the United States and Germany also nurtured this book and me: Stefan Breit, Susanna

Burghartz, Silvia Evangelisti, Otto Feldbauer, Valentin Groebner, Daniela Hacke, Paul Hoser, Sabine John, Thomas Krüßmann, Amy Leonard, Helmut Puff, Ulinka Rublack, Angela Stascheit, and Merry Wiesner. At UCI, I have been lucky to enjoy the support of wonderful colleagues, especially Elizabeth Allen, Sharon Block, Natalka Freeland, Marcia Klotz, Leerom Medovoi, Dave Newman, Annette Schlichter, and Heidi Tinsman. Lynn Mally and Bob Moeller deserve special thanks for their perceptive reading of the entire manuscript and for their warm friendship.

The two anonymous readers for the University of Michigan Press had excellent advice while Geoff Eley had unflagging faith in the project, Robert Frame read very closely and made incisive editorial suggestions. My research assistants, Rebecca Nykwest, Amy Rowe, and Anne Wohlcke, had lots of skills and a sense of humor. Thank you all.

Final thanks go to my family. I want to thank Frank Biess for making the coffee every morning and much more. I also want to thank my parents, Henrike and Ulrich Strasser, for moral and financial support at key moments and for providing me with a home to return to in Germany. During the many years that it took me to finish this book, my father fought a difficult battle with a debilitating illness. I am especially grateful for the opportunity to tell him that this book is done and dedicated to him.

Introduction

In 1638 two rather different spectacles took place in the city of Munich: one on the central market square and in the presence of a festive, spirited crowd, the other in front of a small, sober audience and within the confines of the civic court. If one had followed, on Sunday, November 7, the sound of religious hymns reverberating from the Schrannenplatz, where vendors offered their goods on ordinary days, a sumptuous, baroque ceremony would have come into view. Elector Maximilian I, Bavaria's most staunchly Catholic prince and leader of the Catholic League during the Thirty Years' War, was fulfilling a religious promise. The capital of his principality and seat of his court had been spared from being sacked by Gustavus Adolphus's Protestant Swedes. On this Sunday in 1638 Maximilian repaid the spiritual debt he felt he owed to the Virgin Mary for the deliverance. In the course of elaborate festivities, a large golden statue of the Virgin was raised in the very heart of Munich, giving the city its distinctive landmark: the Mariensäule or pillar of Mary.[1]

The choice of location and religious imagery mirrored the larger sociopolitical currents that were sweeping through Bavaria during the confessional age. From the sixteenth century onward Bavaria's center of political power, spearheaded by the ruling Wittelsbach dynasty, embarked upon a program of systematic centralization and expansion of its bureaucratic apparatus at the expense of local governments and their liberties. Located next to the city hall, the central square was in the purview of Munich's civic government. In placing the Mariensäule literally before the city fathers' eyes, the Elector erected a monument to his determination that his authority would be greater than that of the magistrate.[2]

While Bavaria's court regularly discovered in Catholic renewal and Counter-Reformation a site for political self-aggrandizement, this absolutist agenda nonetheless went hand in hand with an earnest commitment to religious reform. The Mariensäule thus also symbolized Maximilian's religious fervor and his special dedication to the Virgin Mary. As a boy he had already vowed to follow her dictates in a letter written to her with his own blood.[3] Later on, as prince, he dubbed the Virgin Mary the patroness of his territory, fought battles, and burned witches in her name. Because she stood at the same time for the holiness of female virginity and for the cult of the saints, the Virgin Mary embodied perfectly the spirituality that the Council of Trent (1545–63) had proclaimed to differentiate its theology from Protestantism. Maximilian's patronage of the Virgin was one highly visible component of what the Wittelsbachs defined as their duty toward God—to transform their territory into a showcase of the old faith and their subjects into model citizens of a Catholic polity.[4]

The towering Virgin was meant to change the religiopolitical topography of Bavaria. Once her image stood in the heart of Munich, all distances in the principality had to be measured in reference to this religious icon.[5] State-sponsored Marian devotion functioned as a set of religious practices that extolled the Wittelsbachs as the defenders of orthodoxy. At the same time, it extracted compliance from the dynasty's subjects and habituated them to observance of these religious norms that legitimated state rule. Among other things, Maximilian's "Marian program of the state" entailed that every man and woman in Bavaria, from the highest ranking government official to the poorest domestic, had to carry a rosary. They had to go down on their knees to utter the Ave Maria three times a day at the sound of church bells.[6]

Marian devotion decreed from above found an echo in popular piety. Women in Munich who intended to enter a religious house began to pre-ambulate or drive in a carriage around the statue three times before they embraced the virginal life of the cloister.[7] Through their actions, they asserted a connection between the example of the Divine Virgin and their chosen way of life. Mary's virginity prefigured and thereby authorized their decision to remain unmarried and chaste.

Female virginity also featured as a leitmotif in the second—albeit less public—spectacle that occurred in Munich in 1638, only a few footsteps away from the Schrannenplatz. Again a woman named Mary took center stage. Yet it was not her virginity, but rather the loss thereof, that drove this event. Maria Jaus, the unmarried daughter of a citizen, appeared before Munich's highest civic judge to bring suit against Hans Renner, a journeyman.[8] Hans, Maria explained to the judge, had vowed to marry her before he deprived her of her "virginal honor" and impregnated her. She implored the judge to force the young man either to keep his promise or to provide her with proper financial compensation for the costs accrued.[9]

Maria's demands bespoke courage. For the high judge, far from being a disinterested arbiter, was the very same civic official in whose charge Elector Maximilian had placed the prosecution of so-called profligacy (*Leichtfertigkeit*). This referred to the crime of nonmarital sex, especially among men and women who lacked sufficient means to set up a joint household. The judge delivered regular reports to the city council and court about his progress in eradicating this particular criminal offense.[10] With the same Counter-Reformation spirit that gave impetus to raising the Mariensäule, Maximilian pursued the religious and moral restoration of civic order by purging the city of all sinful acts. He agreed with ecclesiastical and urban authorities that sexual transgressions carried the particularly disturbing twin dangers of social disruption and of incurring God's wrath. The Elector's ardent aversion to nonmarital sexuality—in particular women's sexual activity outside of marriage—was the flip side of his glorification of virginity.[11]

With her lawsuit against Hans Renner, Maria Jaus automatically directed judicial attention to the carnal act that had been consummated between the two unmarried people. The success of her case therefore depended on the credibility of her assertions about the marriage promise and the attendant loss of virginity. It comes as no surprise that Hans Renner, in his turn, sought to tarnish Maria Jaus's reputation. While he admitted to intercourse with her, he denied that she had been a virgin, implicitly casting her as a lewd woman. The case hovered in the gray area between profligacy, a serious offense in Counter-Reformation Bavaria, and the traditionally accepted courtship practice of making a marriage promise and consummating it prior to official solemnization. Maria Jaus remained insistent on the marriage promise and her initial virginity, a token she had given with the legitimate expectation of emotional and economic returns. It was up to the judge, the representative of state authority, to adjudicate the exact meaning of Maria's lost virginity: was it part of legitimate courtship or evidence of the illegitimate nonmarital sex that threatened to tear the fabric of Catholic society?

**In the Shadow of Max Weber: Narratives of State Formation
in Early Modern Europe**

This book contends that the virginity of both Marias, or, differently put, holy and human female virginity, was constitutive of the development of a modern-style, centralized government and the emergence of a public sphere in Germany's first absolutist state. Modern conceptions of politics proceed from a sense of deep disjuncture between a secular space of public institutions and a private domain of religious morality. We have only recently begun to explore how the modern state worked to constitute a depoliticized conception of privacy and domesticity against which notions of the politi-

Der Marckt zu München.

Fig. 1. Pillar of the Virgin Mary in the seventeenth century. Note the worshippers on their knees as they pray in "The Market of Munich." (Original in Bildarchiv, Bayerische Staatsbibliothek, Munich.)

cal could be defined as an essentially male sphere. In light of the growing body of feminist scholarship on the state, it now seems plausible that gender was integral to state building.[12] But the importance of female virginity in the formation of the modern state has yet to be recognized.

The political nature of virginity and its importance to the functioning of the polis was generally accepted in early modern culture. In more than one way the virginal body represented a crucial resource and reservoir of power for state and society. Communities often called upon sacred virgins for protection in times of warfare, plague, or other social ills. A firmly entrenched topos in political discourse, female virginity allowed theorists to fashion myths of political purity.[13] In times of peace, polities were imagined as feminine and virginal to reflect the community's self-understanding as free and honorable. In times of war, the defense of the body politic was subsequently likened to the defense of an inviolate and intact female body, its conquest compared to the dishonoring ravishing of a virgin.[14]

Virginity as master metaphor and (some) women's destiny also served to elaborate ideas about good governance and a functioning society. Aegidius Albertinus, counselor of Maximilian I and one of Bavaria's most popular and widely read writers,[15] thus began his main treatise on the preservation of public order and the state with a long section on the female virginal estate and its benefits.[16] The virginal estate, his choice indicates, was deemed indispensable in the society of estates (Ständestaat) that preceded more modern forms of government.

Neither female virginity nor Catholicism, which upheld and mobilized virginity as a potent ideal and underwrote the state's reconfiguration of marriage, sexuality, and public order, plays a prominent role in existing accounts of state formation in Western Europe. They are at best secondary plotlines in the story of the state or peripheral characters belonging to the premodern past that modernity superseded. By locating female virginity at the center of governmental evolution in Bavaria, this book aims to advance a more complex history and to expand our vision of the relations among politics, religion, and gender in early modern Europe. Its goal is to rethink the meaning of modernity by focusing on the female virginal body and religion, since both at first appear inessential, even inimical, to the modernizing project and hence prove to be particularly illuminating objects of inquiry. Along the same line, this study concentrates on the case of Bavaria, model of a Catholic state within the Holy Roman Empire until the end of the confessional age. Catholicism has long epitomized the purported backwardness or medieval quality of religious belief in Western history. A close look at Bavaria's early modern history is especially effective in revealing the degree to which Catholicism operated with the modernizing state and not in antithesis to it.

The study of state formation, more than any other object of historical analysis, is linked to the origins of the historical profession itself. Inspired by movements of national self-determination, the first professional historians, many of them directly involved in state government, made the state's network of political institutions the subject of their inquiry. These institutions offered a tangible locus of power and historical agency traceable over time, and they literally held the key to the archival sources needed to reconstruct their workings and the origins of the state apparatus that cohered in the nineteenth century. The story of the fluctuating fortunes of political institutions hence became the historical profession's first assignment, its original—in both senses of the word—master narrative.

If the historian's primary task was born of political allegiance, its accomplishment was aided by another offspring of the nineteenth century: the social sciences. Max Weber's sociology furnished historians with the main analytical tools to translate their archival data about state politics into the story of the state in Western Europe. This tool kit has become all too familiar by now: formation and rationalization of a unified staff of bureaucrats; monopolization of legitimate violence by the state; governmental autonomy—fiscal and otherwise—from dominant social groups; and the capacity to set an agenda for an entire territory and the people within it.[17]

Weber's understanding of the modern state was intimately connected to his conception of the psychological makeup of the modern state subject. Weber's modern man (and he is male) is a profoundly rational and self-disciplining creature who submits willingly to the regimen of state power and of the state-sanctioned capitalist market. What accounts for his voluntary surrender is the formative power of Protestantism. According to Weber, religion shapes and resides in, first and foremost, the individual psyche. In other words, the subjectivity of the state subject is the primary portal through which religion enters the otherwise markedly secularized scene of state power.[18]

Protestantism played at once too great and too small a part in Weber's tale of progressive rationalization of state power. Too great, because the Weberian view credits Protestant doctrine, a set of beliefs neither unified nor unambiguous, with the force to single-handedly propel the inhabitants of the medieval world of ritual and magic into a modern universe of reason, hard work, and capital accumulation. Too little, because Protestant religion, in the Weberian scheme of things, has its strongest impact in its least religious guise—as the ideological cement of the secular state, a system of belief whose distinctive hallmark and greatest accomplishment is the overcoming of religion itself.[19]

More recently, researchers tracking the genesis of the modern state in early modern Europe have begun to move beyond Weber's thesis linking Protestantism with rationalization and modernization in the West. A key paradigm of this newer work is the study of confessionalization. Confessionalization theorists—Heinz Schilling and Wolfgang Reinhard in the case of Germany—have credited *each* religious confession with similar transformative power. They have downplayed theological differences and emphasized instead the parallel nature of socioreligious and political change in all the German territories: the emergence of bureaucratic forms of government and the state's appropriation of religious concepts and sentiments for purposes of centralizing and of creating a "uniform body of princely subjects."[20]

Although this theoretical move lifted the weight Weber had placed upon Protestantism and redistributed it equally across the confessions, confessionalization theorists have at times unwittingly reinscribed some of the presumptions of Weber's highly influential approach to state formation. Above all they continue to operate within a framework of progressive rationalization, in which religion remains an ideological tool of governmental expansion, and modernization implies the increasing marginalization of religion by a state gaining in strength and sovereignty.

By contrast, this book argues that religion did not simply fall by the wayside during the metamorphosis of the early modern into the modern state. The case of Bavaria suggests that the triumph of modern statehood is better understood not in terms of the state's ability to overcome religion but rather of its ability to absorb desirable religious influences and to push the undesirable ones into a newly created sphere of individual morality and privacy. Religion took on changed trappings, traversed different sociopolitical arenas, or was disguised as personal or cultural. In a political sleight of hand, the state in effect coded parts of religion as in the general public interest and therefore essentially "of the state," thus making invisible religion's precise contribution to the formation of its own power. A particular notion of religion was produced simultaneously with a particular notion of politics.

In the Shadow of Friedrich Engels: Stories about Gender and the State

The nineteenth-century origins of the study of the state constrained the scholarly imagination in other respects as well. The preoccupation with institutional politics encouraged a procrustean treatment of various social and cultural forces that have shaped the fate of states. Only with the ascendancy of the new social history in the 1960s and women's history in the 1970s did some historians begin to consider a more decentered and nuanced model of the state in which power and agency are diffused throughout the social whole. Poststructuralist theorists, above all Pierre Bourdieu and Michel Foucault, reinforced this approach by calling attention to the everyday micropolitics of state power.[21]

As a result, the study of gender and the state in Western Europe has developed slowly and unevenly. Theorists of confessionalization have yet to take into account fully and systematically the pivotal role that the reconfiguration of gender relations played in the making of modern rule. They have investigated the phenomena of confessional state building on various sociopolitical levels and they have even considered some of the disciplinary effects of the marriage reforms and sexual regulation that followed the Reformation.[22] It remains to be seen, however, how gender and sexuality were constructed in the first place and how this very construction—and not just the attendant regulation—was constitutive of governmentality. Along analogous lines, the conjugal household still needs to be studied as the smallest *political* building block of early modern rule rather than viewed as a quasi-private space inhabited by unruly subjects who await disciplining by the advancing forces of confessionalization.

Many historians of women and gender, on the other hand, have engaged in the traditionally "masculine" inquiry into the history of the state in an effort to answer feminist scholarship's cardinal question: how and why did patriarchy originate? Work of this type unfolded against the epistemological background of another nineteenth-century figure: Friedrich Engels. Following Engels's lead in his seminal *The Origin of the Family, Private Property, and the State,* feminist scholars interpreted women's oppression as a product of the historical development of private property and an outgrowth of state formation.[23]

This approach contributed greatly to denaturalizing both state power and gender inequality and encouraged the contextually situated study of gender and the state. At the same time it inadvertently imported yet more nineteenth-century assumptions into modern scholarship on the state.[24] Engels's theoretical lens, analytically precise and perceptive in many ways, was nonetheless tainted by the Victorian presumption of "separate spheres" as a perennial fact of human life. While he dismantled the supposed naturalness of the state, Engels firmly anchored the public/private divide and the sexual division of labor in nature—as if they were a precursor rather than a product of the historical development of the state. Even in the matriarchal and egalitarian society of ancient times that he described, reproductive capacities and exclusion from the male public sphere are the paramount markers of womanhood.

Such static understandings of gender roles neither elucidate women's role in state formation in non-Western areas (as anthropologists and historians of these areas have demonstrated in recent decades)[25] nor do justice to political developments within Western Europe itself. We need to historicize more fully understandings of public and private in the European context and incorporate studies of gender and the state in early modern Europe into the increasingly sophisticated analyses that exist for the nineteenth century.[26] In the polities of sixteenth- and seventeenth-century Europe, such as Bavaria, the categories of public and private had yet to be constituted as binary opposites and aligned with the gender and political system that launched society into the world of "separate spheres."

The early modern society of estates, recent scholarship has shown, still considered the household a part of the public sphere. The married couple heading the household represented officeholders of sorts. Unequal in reference to internal household hierarchies, husband and wife nonetheless equaled one another in their distinct yet complementary participation in the making of a public order for which both were held responsible by the authorities. Public order flowed directly from the Christian values that the Church expounded and that state governments strove to implement in collaboration with members of various estates, including the matrimonial estate. Privacy, as we have come to know it, was inconceivable in the early modern world of overlapping collectivities just as conceptions of individual rights were unimaginable before the modern conception of the private person as the counterpart to public state power.[27]

It was eighteenth-century civil society that ushered in a different set of sociopolitical arrangements and assignments of civic duties, adumbrating the "separate spheres" of the nineteenth century with their formative influence on the twentieth century. Once the state constituted its bureaucratic apparatus independent from and capable of ruling society without the latter's consent or complicity, it simultaneously began to institute a new boundary between men and women in the shape of a public/private divide. Whereas men were designated as citizens whose rights and duties ran the gamut from participation in the political public to protection of their private sphere, women became citizens' wives and mothers whose second-class, ancillary status expressed itself in political exclusion and a lack of private protection. Women were made the male citizens' exclusive private property. Their "privatization" for the benefit of husbands paralleled the "privatization" of religion for the benefit of the state. A secularized notion of the public good emerged alongside the idea of the good of the private individual whose religious beliefs ideally informed his moral judgments and deeds.[28]

Writing this public/private divide back into the early modern past eclipses women's participation in premodern modes of political governance and hence their role in the creation of modern rule. During the early modern period, women's involvement in governance took place through the public and political space of the household and not through the political mechanisms of republican and princely rule; these later superseded and supplanted the system of household governance to become the main, male-coded modes of modern governance.[29]

In analyzing the household and its connection to political power in early modern Europe, feminist historians by and large have treated this space of governance as a site of female subordination, where fundamentally unequal civil laws and gender norms forced women into subservient positions, marriage, and motherhood.[30] Lyndal Roper has explained the success of the Protestant Reformation in Augsburg as the result of a fortunate convergence of male interests in household governance. City and guild elites found common ideological ground in Protestantism, for it sacralized a sociopolitical vision they both held dear: a commonwealth composed of patriarchal households. Roper rejects Weberian portrayals of the Protestant Reformation as a harbinger of modernity on the basis of the fundamental conservatism of the gender vision of its supporters, who advocated "domestication" as the norm for all female lives.[31]

Similarly, Sarah Hanley has contended that early modern French state building centered on patriarchal households and female subordination reinscribed within the family. According to Hanley, two congruent sets of interests fueled political centralization: the royal need for an administrative elite and this elite's concern with its families' social advancement. The legal offspring of the alliance between king and elite families—what she calls "the family-state compact"—was legislation that aimed at greater patriarchal and magisterial control over family formation and reproduction, which had an especially negative impact on women. Women, Hanley concludes, had a role in French state building because political centralization hinged on the restructuring of elite familial relationships and progressive control over female sexuality and reproduction.[32]

The Bavarian case confirms as well as complicates these narratives of gender and politics in early modern Europe, allowing us to push research on gender and the early modern state in new directions. As elsewhere, strengthening the position of male heads of households expedited centralization efforts in Bavaria. Through changes in family, marriage, and inheritance law, the Bavarian state built alliances with male heads of households. Governing authorities strove to turn these men into bureaucratic representatives of the state in order to acquire control over subjects on a political level that was otherwise not easily accessible to the central government. Based on a strong belief in the stabilizing capacities of an orderly household and the social benefits of channeling sexuality into marital life, the Bavarian state also embarked upon the prosecution of sex outside of marriage and the prevention of illegitimate offspring.

Not surprisingly, much of this happened to the detriment of women, for whom respectability became irrevocably tied to life in a patriarchal household. With respect to marriage, Catholic women in Bavaria in fact experienced a type of social change stunningly reminiscent of the Protestant developments about which we know so much more. The Bavarian state's conception of public order, marriage, and gender relations could very well be summarized in analytical shorthand coined initially in a Protestant context: "a new morality of sedentariness,"[33] a redefinition of marriage as a "locus of purity,"[34] or a social vision constructed around "the holy household."[35] In a sense—to paraphrase Joan Kelly's answer to her famous question about women's Renaissance—Bavaria's married Catholic women also had a Reformation, but just not during the Reformation.[36]

The parallels in the Protestant and Catholic approaches to marriage have barely been recognized or commented on in the historiography, since studies on the Counter-Reformation have traditionally concentrated on religious life.[37] Scholarly literature associates Protestantism with matrimony, whereas Catholicism is linked with the convent. While the Tridentine emphasis on the superiority of the chaste life and the Protestant introduction of clerical marriage warrant this correlation between the confessions and the institutions of marriage and cloister, these standard foci of analysis nonetheless overlook the other half of the story in each context. Marriage was no less vital to the functioning of Catholic society. In fact it experienced a growing valorization during the sixteenth century. Convents, in turn, were such an integral part of the fabric of social life that Protestants experienced severe difficulties in their attempts to abolish female monastic houses.[38] In short, the standard correlation of Protestantism with the marital life and Catholicism with the celibate life blocks from our view similarities between the two confessions. These similarities evolved in a context of ongoing confessional rivalry that drove the escalation of moral politics until the end of the Thirty Years' War and gave German developments their distinct character.[39]

Even though the Bavarian state did "domesticate" women in patriarchal households in a manner comparable to Protestant polities, this change did not occur because state formation was a development carried out by men against women. Control of female reproduction and the "domestication" of women were certainly expressions but not necessarily the intent of state formation. Rather, gender as a relationship of power served as a primary mechanism by which the early modern state, a heterogeneous and partially ineffectual entity, could propel itself into greater coherence and efficiency. To the extent that women were implicated in this mechanism and in the patriarchal household order set up to administer normative gender relations, they were, undoubtedly, participants in the process of political centralization.

Yet this notion of women as participants in state formation needs to be qualified in significant respects. First, not all women participated equally in political rule through the sphere of the household, and we should not mistake the status of a participant with the status of a beneficiary. Second, the politically convenient dictate of marriage and biological reproduction for some women implied the dictate of chastity for others, namely, the permanently unmarried. State formation meant conscripting both virgins and wives in the service of a centralizing project.

What was at stake was not only control of marriage and the household, but also the need to regulate who could and who could not have sex. State sexual regulation was a means to reconfigure the social order as well as to establish heterosexual monogamy as the norm.[40] While these shifting constructions of sexuality had far-reaching ramifications for both men and women, this book hones in on women's bodies.[41] Female virginity occupied a determining position in the confessional discourses on sexuality, and women as a social group were a privileged object of state and church regulation. State formation entailed producing the female body as a sexualized body, defined primarily by either sexual reproduction or renunciation of sexuality for the sake of social reproduction.

Because the formation of the Bavarian state occurred on the bedrock of economically stable households of monogamous couples, it was politically mandatory to curtail sexuality outside of marriage, in particular, the sexuality of the lower classes. The state began to require a public marriage ceremony and to restrict the issuing of marriage licenses to those with a modicum of property. Once the novel legal markers for legitimate marital sexuality were in place, the sexual unions of the poor automatically fell into the category of illegitimate nonmarital sex. Although this change had implications for both lower-class men and lower-class women, the women, much more so than their male counterparts, bore the brunt of the new regulatory efforts. State legislation ultimately demanded that lower-class women uphold the boundaries of the new social and sexual order by avoiding sexual relations altogether and thus preventing sexual unions and procreation among the lower social strata.

Not only the virginity of some laywomen but also the virginity of religious women mattered greatly to the state. In the course of Catholic confessionalization the Bavarian state implemented the monastic reforms outlined by the Council of Trent in a manner that appropriated the spiritual power of nuns and harnessed it to the state's own ends. Sacred virginity bestowed sacred—anthropologists might say magical—power upon state representatives and legitimated their policies of expansion at home and abroad. Religious women in the Bavarian capital recited daily prayers on behalf of the ruling dynasty, offered spiritual counsel to members of the court, and prophesied the births of male successors to the princely throne. Religious women also assumed leadership positions in the newly emerging field of state-sponsored female education.

The virginity of Bavaria's religious women, who were mainly of the upper classes, was valued differently than that of lower-class women, as one would expect. Nuns still were among the most powerful and influential women of the early modern state; because of the Counter-Reformation's preoccupation with chastity and the Virgin Mary, some rose to greater prominence than they had previously enjoyed. The opposite held true of the poor women whom state legislation defined out of the pool of those considered eligible to engage in sexual acts and enter marriage. These women belonged to a more disenfranchised segment of society already; the state's regulatory efforts in matters of sexuality pushed them further in that direction and penalized any resistance on their part.

The valences of virginity finally varied not only according to class but also across time. In the aftermath of the fundamental criticism that Protestant reformers leveled at the Catholic ideal of chastity, the debates about continence in Catholic polities changed their content and tenor. Female virginity—and male celibacy for that matter—were unquestioned possibilities and norms of clerical life prior to the Reformation, even if these ideals were not always honored in practice. Physiologically grounded understandings of continence that precluded any sexual experience coexisted with spiritualized interpretations of chastity as a moral and mental attitude one could embrace regardless of prior sexual experience. For women, moreover, the virginal life represented a powerful vehicle for overcoming gender barriers and espousing masculine as well as feminine self-articulations.[42]

The Protestant Reformers reset the terms in which virginity and celibacy were conceptualized by insisting on a natural and irrepressible sex drive. Although the Protestant insistence surely authorized old as well as new demands for a sexually satisfying life, its liberating effects must be weighed against its repressive results. Once nature itself required the fulfillment of sexual needs, it became impossible to imagine continence as something other than sexuality's corollary. Abstinence from sexual relations represented either a vain (from a Protestant perspective) or a heroic (from a Catholic viewpoint) disavowal of the dictates of corporeality. Subsequently, even Catholics, in talking back to Protestants, found themselves speaking of the continent life in increasingly and more often exclusively sexual terms—a discursive shift that foreshadowed the modern equation of the avoidance of sexual activity and repression. This shift was especially consequential for women, since the sexualized body became their primary marker, while female virginity took on the much more restrictive meaning of physiological intactness.

State of Virginity: Bavarian State Formation and the Transformation of Munich

To capture large-scale changes in their complexity and trace the shifting meanings of virginity in everyday life, this book centers its analysis on developments in Munich, the state capital. Bavaria's rulers viewed and treated Munich as a model of a Counter-Reformation metropolis and the place from which the centralizing government could extend its reach; accordingly, Munich's history opens a window on the much larger political and religious trends that characterized Catholic state building. While the Wittelsbachs may not have been able to shape every distant corner of their territory,[43] their vision of a Catholic polity left an indelible mark on the state capital where the forces of confessionalization gained their greatest momentum. It was no coincidence that the city's transformation from *Bürgerlicher Stadt* (the city of burghers) to *Residenzstadt* (the city of residence) of Bavaria's rulers began with the religious upheavals in the sixteenth century and reached its conclusion with the end of the Thirty Years' War.

Throughout the Middle Ages, Munich enjoyed a kind of self-rule often associated with imperial cities. It had its own charter and far-reaching market privileges, both of which German emperors confirmed with regularity.[44] Like numerous German cities, Munich experienced inner turmoil in the fourteenth century when civic guilds revolted and vied with the old elite for political control. After a brief period of guild governance, a constitutional compromise was struck in 1403. This so-called Wahlbrief of 1403, forging a tight connection between the city government and Munich's guilds, remained in force well into the eighteenth century.[45]

Once political calm had returned to the city, Munich entered a century-long period of prosperity. These were the golden days of Munich's patricians whose goods sold very well in trade centers across Europe.[46] The patriciate's economic fortunes were flourishing to such an extent that the ducal court relied heavily on the resourceful burghers. The court's economic dependence on the city brought with it close contact between civic society and court society. Burghers and courtiers attended the same dances, tournaments, and public baths. Burghers furthermore provided the court with loans as well as the necessities of life: food, textiles, and other services.[47] In this climate of prosperity, the city reached its economic and political zenith. By 1500 it had developed into Bavaria's largest urban center with a population of approximately 10,000.[48]

The year 1506 marked the beginning of a new era in the city's history. The bloody Bavarian War of Succession (*Landshuter Erbfolgekrieg*) resulted in the unification of Upper and Lower Bavaria, and Munich became the capital of the enlarged duchy. Henceforth Bavaria's rulers paid a new kind of attention to the city they designated to be the center of their administration. As the court enlarged its bureaucratic apparatus with university-educated officials and its personnel with independently hired servants and artisans, the social ties to the urban community loosened. The tables turned, and Munich's burghers had to seek court services instead of providing invaluable services to the court. From its new position of independence and strength, the court began to intervene in the city's political affairs.[49] The Bavarian dukes, members of the proud, powerful, and pushy dynasty of the Wittelsbachs, had had their eyes set on centralization since the late Middle Ages. Claiming to represent the entire territory, they gradually extended their rule into areas under the control of competing local and ecclesiastical authorities.[50] As in other European polities, the court of the Wittelsbachs acted as the main vehicle for the progressive takeover of administrative, executive, and judicial functions.[51] The most serious obstacle to the court's centralizing efforts were the estates, who jealously guarded their liberties and on whose approval of taxes the notoriously bankrupt Wittelsbachs depended.[52] The confessional conflicts that followed Luther's challenge to the Catholic Church at last provided Bavaria's rulers with ample opportunity and justification for more systematic expansion of their government and, ultimately, the defeat of the estates.

The Wittelsbach dukes were among the earliest defenders of the old faith in the German empire; they immediately enforced the Edict of Worms in their lands. Taking advantage of the phlegmatic attitude of Bavaria's episcopate, the Wittelsbachs assumed the lead in ecclesiastical reform. Ironically, their proactive involvement was reminiscent of the Protestant notion of "emergency bishops," since the Wittelsbachs too viewed it as incumbent upon princes to step in and take over if the episcopate proved incapable of initiating reform measures. With the approval of the papacy, the dukes successively eroded the ecclesiastical monopoly over the disciplining of religious houses and interfered with the education and disciplining of the clergy. Already a fact of political life, state control over religious reform in Bavaria became a constitutional fixture in 1583 with a landmark concordat between church and state.[53]

Confessional strife also created an occasion for the Wittelsbachs to disempower Bavaria's nobility, or at least the faction most resistant to state rule. A powerful faction of noblemen under the leadership of

Pankraz of Freyberg and the Count of Ortenburg, who ruled one of the few free imperial enclaves of the duchy, claimed the right to clerical marriage and communion of both kinds granted to Protestants by the imperial Augsburg Interim of 1548. Duke Albrecht V, his hands tied by fiscal worries, at first made several concessions to this so-called Chalice Movement. During the 1550s, no less than 20 percent of court council members were known to receive communion of both kinds and to subscribe to the Protestant Confessio Augustana.[54]

In the winter of 1563–64, however, Albrecht took the county of Ortenburg by force. There he discovered letters that proved very useful in making a case for a noble subversion. The subsequent suppression of the Chalice Movement ended all independent political and religious action on the part of the Bavarian nobility. From this point on, officeholding in the duchy became tied inextricably to both confessional and Wittelsbach allegiance. By 1569 the court mandated outright that all officials, teachers, and priests in Bavaria swear an oath to uphold the Tridentine *confessio fidei* before they could assume office or become members of the government structure.[55] A series of duchywide religious tribunals followed between 1567 and 1571, purging the territory of religiously suspect subjects by forcing them into exile and making religious conformity the basis of political cohesion.[56]

As elsewhere in German territories, Protestant ideas found a particularly fertile ground in Bavaria's cities. The printing press disseminated these ideas to the reading public, and well-traveled journeymen spread the word about reformed communities in the artisans' shops. Such was the case in Munich, where the Protestant movement flourished in the 1520s and then again in the 1550s and 1560s. During the first wave of Protestantism the printer Hans Schobser distributed Luther's writings in unusually large quantities in the Bavarian capital. The destruction of the products of Schobser's printing press was one of several court measures against unorthodoxy. The court also imprisoned and interrogated a circle of patrician Lutherans, including a number of women. In the late 1520s Bavaria's rulers ordered the execution of several Lutheran journeymen and a larger group of Anabaptists. After the extirpation of the Anabaptist community, attacks on the old faith subsided for decades in Munich.[57]

The second wave of Protestantism hit the capital in conjunction with the duchywide Chalice Movement around 1550. Adam Bartholomäi, preacher at Munich's cathedral, actually advocated communion of both kinds as a fulfillment of Christ's commands. Burghers would invoke such reasoning in their defense when they received the lay chalice in neighboring Protestant areas or when they demanded from the court an opportunity for receiving the chalice in their city. There were other signs of the return of

Luther's ideas. Lutheran hymns interrupted Catholic masses, and his texts were once again stacked on the shelves of Munich's bookstores. This time Protestantism's main supporters came from the patriciate.[58]

The magistrate did virtually nothing to stop this resurgence of Protestantism. When the duke ordered the city fathers to take action against a group of patrician women running Protestant gatherings in their households, the councilors investigated the matter yet found the women not guilty.[59] Their leniency reflected Protestant leanings within governing circles and also the kinship ties between the accused and the patrician city fathers.

Precisely this blend of religious unorthodoxy and political power made Munich's Protestants a worthwhile target for the court. In 1567 Duke Albrecht V, still riding the wave of success after his suppression of Bavaria's Protestant nobility, turned his attention to Munich's burghers. He decreed that access to citizenship and officeholding in the capital be limited to Catholics; only the most reliable Catholics were allowed to run for election. The same year, the duke charged council members with interrogating a long list of alleged Munich Protestants. Displeased with the results of the civic commission, Albrecht then conducted his own tribunal and exiled groups of Protestants. In 1571 the duke ordered one last religious tribunal. Although he again entrusted the council with the proceedings, Albrecht assigned a Jesuit to the interrogation team. When the inquisition pronounced its final judgment, more people were expelled from the city, and some of the city's wealthiest patricians were among the exiles. The Protestant movement was practically dead, the magistrate chastened and undermined in its sovereign government, and the Counter-Reformation truly began with the introduction of Tridentine regulations in the 1580s.[60]

If Albrecht V became the first architect of confessional state building, his son Wilhelm V and his grandson Maximilian I furthered Albrecht's project of engendering a centralized Catholic territory. Wilhelm V and his successors represented a new generation of princes who rejected the indulgence of Renaissance courts in favor of austere self-discipline.[61] They derived ideological justification for their incursions on ecclesiastical and civic privileges from the patriarchal concept of the *Landesvater*. Patterned after the head of the household who rules his dependents with a strong but loving hand, the father of the land considered himself called by God not only to protect true religion but also to restore paternal authority among his subjects for the sake of the common good.[62] The more recent bourgeois virtues of the head of the household, such as economic shrewdness, hard work, and caring for the weaker members of the community, were added to the older catalog of princely virtues, such as maintaining peace and order.[63]

The process begun by Albrecht V to disempower Munich's magistrate came to completion during the reign of Maximilian I (1598–1651), who denigrated the city's highest political body to a mere "recipient of orders."[64] Relying on his fiscal discipline and his political acumen, Maximilian I acquired the long-desired financial capacity for independence from the Bavarian estates. After the estate assembly of 1612, the prince never called upon these corporate bodies for the remaining thirty-nine years of his reign. He was the first true absolutist ruler in the Holy Roman Empire.

Maximilian's success derived, in no small part, from his remarkable ability to exploit the shared interests of the privileged classes and to play dominant social groups against one another, thus accumulating power in his central government. He variously formed alliances with the upper social strata against the lower strata and with one dominant class against another. For instance, Maximilian's expansive recruitment of university-trained burghers into state service created a counterweight to the noble officials and councilors, who in the past had dominated the highest levels of government. The growing strength of the bourgeoisie forced the nobility into a position of competition for prestige and power that weakened its influence on state affairs over time.[65]

A central area in which the interests of the privileged converged was the prohibition of marriages among the servant population. Constant complaints about the unsatisfactory supply of servants and calls for enforcing marriage restrictions could become the basis for an integrative political program—one that united propertied peasants, guild masters, and noble estate holders under the banner of state-sponsored control of the lower-class population.[66] Wittelsbach initiatives against lower-class marriages dated back to the mid–sixteenth century, in the reign of Albrecht V, but reached new levels of systematization and intensity as part of Maximilian's centralizing efforts.

Treating his capital as the test case for restructuring other Bavarian communities, Maximilian I interfered in Munich's affairs more aggressively than in other places. He first of all changed the nature of civic government in order to increase his influence on the ruling body of Munich, a city that by 1600 housed approximately 20,000 people.[67] An already profoundly oligarchic polity, in which only 2,000 people enjoyed full civic rights and no more than nineteen families staffed the ranks of the patriciate,[68] the urban community became even more top-heavy under the guiding hand of the prince.[69] Maximilian reduced the number of mayors and gave lifelong tenure to all civic councilors. He also established a separate collegium for the mayors, the Kammerrat, and entrusted it with special tasks, most notably the reform of Munich's bureau of marriage, which enforced marriage prohibitions against domestics (among others).

Under Maximilian's forceful rule, stricter control of urban government combined with the issuing of a flurry of police ordinances and mandates to make inroads into civic power in the Bavarian capital. Moral politics were also the politics of centralization, since the area of "good police" was the only legal arena in which state law automatically overrode urban legal codes. This legal proviso opened the city to state encroachment and made virtually every aspect of urban life—from the study of the catechism and the treatment of beggars to the pricing of local products and the celebration of weddings—an object of regulation from above.[70]

The Thirty Years' War further advanced Maximilian's project of political centralization within his territory and also the consolidation and growth of Bavaria's power in the empire at large, where a constitutional disadvantage hampered Wittelsbach expansionist designs. Since the Bavarian Wittelsbachs were not among the designated imperial electors (*Kurfürsten*) who enjoyed the privilege of selecting the emperor, their position vis-à-vis the Habsburg and—to a lesser extent—the other electoral princes was inevitably precarious. Well aware of this structural impediment, Maximilian took advantage of the emperor's military and political needs in the beginning years of the Thirty Years' War, bargaining Bavaria's much-desired and formidable military aid in return for the promise of admission to the imperial electorate (among other things). By 1623, when the Catholic and imperial forces seemed to be triumphing, Maximilian achieved his goal with the promotion of Bavaria to the status of an electoral principality (*Kurfürstentum*).

On the home front, the Thirty Years' War and the initial Catholic successes also fueled Wittelsbach self-aggrandizement. Applying the same logic of divine retribution as his Protestant foes, Maximilian set his mind on sweeping reform measures against any form of misconduct so that he could avoid God's wrath and secure abiding divine support for the Catholic cause.[71] This trend of accelerating state regulation was most pronounced in the Bavarian capital and also most effective because it interlocked with the magistrate's regulatory responses to massive socioeconomic shifts and political upheaval. As Munich was ravaged by warfare and torn apart by internal strife in the 1620s and 1630s, the city's political leaders became ever more willing to surrender their sovereignty to a central territorial authority that promised the restoration of peace, order, and prosperity.[72] And so they did. In 1641, when a German emperor confirmed Munich's privileges one last time, the act constituted a nostalgic invocation of the medieval past rather than a reflection of early modern political realities.[73]

Against this backdrop, the beginning of Catholic confessionalization in the second half of the sixteenth century and the first decades of the Thirty Years' War, characterized by heightened confessional rivalry between Germany's Protestants and Catholics, emerge as two decisive phases in the formation of the Bavarian state. During the earlier phase (Part I, chaps. 1 and 2), the state's efforts to centralize and the Church's attempts to reform began a process of complex interaction that required the reconfiguration of gender relations by legal and institutional means. It was not until the 1620s, however, that warfare coupled with socioeconomic crisis brought about the transformations of gender, religion, and politics for which the legal groundwork had been already laid in the second half of the sixteenth century. These transformations are the focus of Part II (chaps. 3, 4, and 5).

More specifically, the first two chapters explore the converging ecclesiastical and secular reform initiatives of the sixteenth century for their attempts to draw more sharply defined boundaries between the sacred and the profane (particularly in its sexual manifestations) and for the gender-specific implications central to these mutually reinforcing boundary drawings. The Council of Trent put a premium on creating order in church and society through the control of women and gender relations. Following a long-standing tradition of cultural and ecclesiastical misgivings about women's allegedly lesser moral capabilities, the council fathers decreed a twofold remedy against female fallibility: either cloister walls or a husband should guard every woman (*aut-murus-aut-maritus*). Catholic state building in Munich implied that the Bavarian fathers of the land selectively codified the reform measures of the Tridentine council in policy. Within this developing legal context, women—in particular lower-class women and women in uncloistered religious communities—found themselves burdened with the primary responsibility for upholding novel boundaries and maintaining a public order whose mainstays were distinctions of class and gender.

Chapter 1 explores the place of marriage reform in the respective agendas of the Tridentine church and the centralizing state. The social articulation of attitudes toward marriage and sexuality in Catholic Bavaria occurred at the intersection of two juridical discourses that simultaneously stabilized and undermined each other. An ecclesiastical discourse of matrimony as a sacrament and right of every Christian capable of consent and consummation existed alongside a secular discourse of matrimony as a socioeconomic partnership and privilege of the propertied members of the body politic. Decrying the unions of the poor as the kind of sex that pollutes public order and brings God's wrath upon the Catholic commonwealth, state law required that future spouses bring proof of property before they engage in sexual relations and set up their own household as husband and wife. Where state and church authorities found common ground was in condemning sexuality outside of marriage and introducing a public marriage ceremony as the norm. Their reform efforts also reinforced one another in strengthening patriarchal rule within households.

Female virginity was a key component of both ecclesiastical and secular reforms of marriage and sexuality. Within the sacramental frame of reference, the virginity of the bride aided in sanctifying matrimony and marital intimacy. When it came to state law, female abstinence from premarital sexuality helped safeguard the transmission of property among the wealthy, while lower-class women's lifelong renunciation of sexual relations could be marshaled in support of preventing sexual unions and procreation among the poor.

The stakes of these new legal and institutional trends were particularly high for some women. Chapter 2 investigates the ramifications of the growing valorization of male-headed households and marriage for those women who either did not wish to or were not able to integrate into the patriarchal household system of propertied Catholics: vagrant and poor women, unmarried women, and women in various religious communities. Early modern culture classified convents, brothels, and female-headed houses under the same rubric: they were *Frauenhäuser,* or houses of women. As male-headed households rose to greater prominence and prestige, and as Catholics argued with Protestants over the boundaries between the sacred and the sexual, these so-called houses of women, religious and secular, inevitably experienced the repercussions.

Tracing the history of Munich's common brothel, this chapter documents the progressive sexualization of its inhabitants and their identification with lower-class women. By the time of the Protestant Reformation, the brothel had turned into the sole site of officially sanctioned sex outside of marriage in the Bavarian capital, mirroring developments in Protestant areas. After the state shut down the brothel in the late sixteenth century, prostitutes could theoretically be everywhere. Governing authorities subsequently were more and more likely to view lower-class women who could not meet the property requirements for marriage as similar to prostitutes if these poor women engaged in any form of (nonmarital) sex. The lower-class prostitute began to represent the social and sexual pollutant par excellence.

The chapter parallels the story of Munich's brothel with the history of its female religious houses. Like the prostitute, the nun was increasingly defined by her sexuality (even if only in its renunciation). The Protestant discourse about the dissolution of convents and the Catholic discourse about the enclosure of convents pivoted on the same trope of the nunnery as brothel or open house. In this light, Tridentine enclosure was an attempt to differentiate houses of religious virgins from the morally dubious secular houses of unmarried women. It also carried a class bias since a contemplative life behind cloister walls was costly and only women of financial means and social standing would be able to buy their way into a Tridentine nunnery. At least in the Bavarian capital, the nun became identified with an upper-class virgin whose purity (and class) symbolized the immunity of the Catholic commonwealth against social, sexual, and spiritual pollution. Given that few honorable alternatives to matrimony existed for Munich's women, the greater exclusivity of convents further reinforced the class discrimination of marriage laws.

The tenacity of traditions is a recurrent theme of the book's first part, and so is Catholicism's abiding rivalry with Protestantism as the primary agent of change.[74] Many reform initiatives of this first phase of Catholic confessionalization, even though this period saw crucial shifts in legal discourse and significant reconstruction of the institutional landscape, did not translate into tangible sociopolitical and cultural change until the Thirty Years' War when confessional competition reached its apex. Destruction, disease, hunger, and social unrest were read as signs of God's discontent with the Catholic polity, an interpretation that justified and facilitated considerable expansion of state regulation in Munich. The war furthermore mobilized powerful images of virginity and purity. In light of these representations, women appeared to embody the integrity of government and were therefore primary objects of state control.

Chapter 3 resumes the analysis of the nexus between state formation and control of marriage and sexuality in the charged context of the Thirty Years' War. During the 1620s, civic and state authorities seized on the regulation of sexual behavior as a general panacea. Secular authorities embarked upon the eradication of profligate marriages, or unions between partners of low economic standing contracted without official approval, which, in their view, undermined both human morality, the guarantor of divine benevolence, and economic stability, the guarantor of public order. As secular legislation against profligacy wedded attempts at *sexual* purification to attempts at *social* purification, Tridentine mores became fitted to a secular agenda of creating a community of economically reliable burghers. The ecclesiastical understanding of matrimony as a sacramental right lost institutional significance in Catholic Munich.

This adaptation of theology to political practice had a twofold effect. It progressively criminalized sexual unions of the lower classes, and it deepened preexisting gender inequalities within the lower classes. Men, in particular lower-class men, could invoke these more restrictive attitudes and laws to avoid their obligations toward women. Good citizenship was in fact tantamount to rejecting not necessarily sexual involvement outside of marriage, but rather certain women as permanent partners. Inversely, lower-class women who lacked the economic means to turn their relationships into marriages were at increasing risk of being stigmatized or left without support for a child if they engaged in sexual relations outside of marriage (even if their lovers had made a marriage promise). Such risk was best avoided by abstaining from sexual relationships altogether. Good citizenship, in the case of these women, spelled lifelong chastity.

It was no coincidence that the state's campaign against profligate women occurred simultaneously with the state-sponsored drive to preserve the virginity of religious women by subjecting them to strict cloister. Chapter 4 takes a close look at the reform of two Munich convents in the 1620s and highlights the parallels between marriage reform and monastic reform. The history of nuns, often understood and told mainly in terms of religious history, appears as an integral part of an overarching story of gender, sexuality, and political centralization. Women's religious communities were re-created in the image of male-headed households, with the added component of confinement. Just as secular patriarchs had a stake in controlling their female dependents' behavior, so did the male guardians of nunneries. They too guarded women in their care from improper public exposure that could jeopardize female honor and, in this case, the societal resource of sacred virginity.

Munich's religious women resisted the reforms imposed from above in creative ways, even though they had to accept a regime of strict enclosure and contemplative practice (chap. 4). Cloistering at first weakened the female convents by disconnecting them from their traditional power base in the urban community. But sequestration enabled the nuns to acquire a new and more prestigious kind of power in the second half of the seventeenth century and expand it during the eighteenth century. Not only did it foster closer ties between the convents and the state, whose patronage benefited the communities, but it also raised the social and symbolic value of the women's virginal bodies in Catholic society by supplying them with the "additional hymen"[75] of cloister walls. The women understood how to capitalize on both state patronage and the power associated with their virginity.

Chapter 5 takes a close look at a group of women who succeeded in forging a new female identity: the honorable, uncloistered single woman engaged in social service in society at large. During the 1620s—when nuns suffered enclosure and lower-class women persecution due to mounting fear of unbridled female sexuality—the English woman Mary Ward and her followers established the Institute of English Ladies in Munich. Contrary to Tridentine norms, the women were neither married nor behind cloister walls, but they nonetheless claimed to champion the Counter-Reformation through female education. It was not entirely surprising that the papacy ordered the suppression of the Institute of English Ladies in 1631.

The English Ladies, however, survived this attack on their institution thanks to the Bavarian Elector, whom they convinced that their educational work was highly relevant to public order. In order to obtain state support, they had to give up many of their pedagogical and intellectual aspirations, along with their goal of obtaining official recognition as a religious order. Yet the very existence of the English Ladies, their educational work, and the manner in which they subverted state control also meant that some women were able to move outside the sociopolitical grid of male-headed households. Respected virgins in the world, they paved a new path for the future.

Part I

Discursive and Institutional Foundations, 1550–1600

CHAPTER 1

Which Public Matters Most?
Rites of Marriage Formation

Secret Deals with the Vicario? Reconfiguring Courtship, Custom, and Law

In July 1599 Katharina Rieger, a Munich resident, turned to the civic court for help. She explained to the secular judge how the artisan Hans Vorster had promised her marriage so that she "finally acted according to his will." They had intercourse and she became pregnant, yet Vorster did not keep his word. Rieger now asked the civic judge to make Vorster fulfill his promise and take her as his wife. Called to testify on his behalf, Vorster admitted that he had taken her virginal honor and impregnated her, but he adamantly denied the marriage promise. Even if had made a promise, the defendant pointed out, "such a clandestine union could not hold up according to the Council of Trent and the laws of Bavaria." At most Vorster was willing to make economic compensation for the losses Rieger suffered. His former lover did not consider this sufficient, arguing that "she had not had any intercourse with him until he promised marriage [and therefore] did not want a settlement; he should rather keep what he had promised." With both parties digging in their heels, the judge's attempts to achieve an arbitration were to no avail. He terminated the lawsuit with a referral to the church court in Freising, the center of the diocese to which Munich belonged. Only an ecclesiastical court, according to the judge's rationale, could make a decision about the validity of marriage promises.[1]

By 1600, however, Vorster and Rieger were back in the civic court-room—except that this time around they had switched the roles of plaintiff and defendant. Vorster took Rieger to court in an effort to impose silence upon the woman. Apparently the ecclesiastical judge had concurred with Vorster's view of the marriage matter and absolved him of any obligation to wed the woman. Still, Rieger did not let go of Vorster. She kept spreading rumors about an alleged marital bond with Vorster. Questioned by the civic judge as to the reasons for her behavior, Rieger explained:

> Because he [Vorster] had promised marriage to her, and took her honor this way, and now he did not keep anything [he had promised], she could not find him an honest person. She did not care what was negotiated between them in Freising since she did not get a proper hearing there. Vorster might have struck a secret deal with the Vicario [the ecclesiastical judge] . . . for they listened to him but not to her, she intended not to let him get away and if it were going to take the rest of her life, she would get in his way in matrimonial matters wherever she could.[2]

The legal dealings of Katharina Rieger and Hans Vorster bring into view the field of social, political, and cultural forces that constrained sexual relations between men and women in Counter-Reformation Munich. Rieger's arguments evoked a context of customary courtship, in which exchanges of promises and sex created mutual obligations.[3] If the judicial system failed to recognize the binding nature of this reciprocal contract, the world outside the courtroom, familiar with the rules of the game, was likely to listen and to support her cause. It was for good reasons that Vorster wanted her to stop gossiping about their relationship.

Not custom and community sanction, but law and the power of state and church subtended Vorster's case.[4] He cited the most recent regulations for the formation of a proper marriage, Bavarian state law and the marriage doctrine decreed at Trent, in an attempt to pull the rug out from Rieger's claim. Regardless of what happened between them, he reminded the court, the traditional manner of forming a marital union now stood in unequivocal violation of the law. A refusal to honor clandestine marriage promises, this line of reasoning suggested, was tantamount to honoring secular and ecclesiastical authority—without doubt a compelling argument in front of an authority figure.

But Munich's secular judge wavered. He too was caught between the pulls of traditional courtship practices and contemporary legal trends. He knew firsthand, since he had watched it happen often, that Munich's residents understood marriage as a process that went through a series of stages, promises and intercourse included, and could very well originate in a completely personal setting. On the other hand, he was cognizant of the state's police ordinances against clandestine marriages and premarital sex, which overrode city law and urban customs.[5] One easy way to resolve this tension was to refer the litigants to the ecclesiastical judge and let him decide on the basis of canon law. This strategy had the added advantage of honoring a long-standing division of labor, recently confirmed by the Council of Trent, that placed validity disputes in the purview of church courts.

What the civic judge could not anticipate was that he would have to face the parties again because of Katharina Rieger's refusal to accept a negative verdict from the ecclesiastical court. He tried to put an end to the case once and for all by mandating that Vorster deposit money to compensate the woman for her losses and some extra cash "for better peace" in the civic court. Rieger was given three months to claim the deposit and ordered to quiet down unless she wanted to "be punished, with severity, as an example to others."

How had things become this complicated in the first place? And what did it all mean for men and women like Rieger and Vorster who entered into sexual relationships after Trent? This chapter shows that the social articulation of attitudes toward marriage and sexuality in Catholic Bavaria took place at the intersection of two juridical discourses at once overlapping and at odds. First, there was an ecclesiastical discourse of matrimony as sacrament and sole rightful forum for sexual activity. This discourse both reinforced and undercut a second, secular discourse that constructed marriage as socioeconomic partnership and sexuality as a privilege of the propertied.

The Counter-Reformation Church reasserted the superiority of celibacy to marriage since the chaste and sacred body represented a primary marker of difference vis-à-vis Protestantism. Its marital doctrines, however, were clearly influenced by Protestant discussions. Tridentine Catholicism fashioned the marital estate as the primary institutional site for the salvation of the laity, a haven of beneficial sexuality and nursery of divinely ordained gender hierarchies. The state of matrimony thus underwent a new valorization within Catholicism as well, reflected (among other things) in the greater emphasis on sexual reproduction within marriage coupled with a more forceful condemnation of sexuality outside of marriage.[6] Every Christian capable of forming the sacramental bond of marriage and of engaging in legitimate sexual relations was assured of his or her right to do so but ordered to maintain a state of virginity prior to entering the sacramental union. Inversely, Tridentine Catholicism dictated that those incapable of forming a marital bond and those called to the religious life remain in a lifelong state of virginity.

This ecclesiastical vision of marriage found its complement in secular measures to outlaw nonmarital sexuality and to strengthen patriarchal governance in marriage. Like the Church, the state also sought to secure a state of virginity at the time of marriage. Unlike the Church, however, the Bavarian state treated matrimony not as an a priori right of every Catholic citizen capable of entering the sacrament but rather as a privilege of the propertied members of the body politic. Marriage in this political scheme of things represented the institution that should regulate access to social adulthood with its attendant rights and responsibilities. Subsequently, sexuality itself also constituted a privilege of the propertied because the state took legal steps to confine sexual activity to economically viable unions, and it criminalized sexuality outside of marriage. Hence state authorities, in notable contrast to ecclesiastical authorities, strove to impose continence on all members of the lower classes.

Traditional practices stood in the way of ecclesiastical as well as secular attempts to regulate the state of matrimony and relegate certain social groups to a state of sexual abstinence. Medieval marriage formation unfolded in stages and in the context of smaller networks of family and kin. This sphere was carved out and dominated by custom and private law; medieval canon law, specifically the doctrine of consent, placed it beyond the firm grasp of official authorities. Yet if medieval ecclesiastical doctrine accorded privacy to marriage formation, the marital reforms decreed at Trent, especially the novel requirement of a public marriage ceremony for the validity of a union, now opened marriage formation up to public access and state regulation. As soon as the Bavarian state had consolidated its power sufficiently in the second half of the sixteenth century, it took advantage of Tridentine doctrinal tools to run aggressive interference in marriage formation and to regulate the sexual lives of Bavaria's people.

From Feast to Bed and Bath: Marriage Prior to the Council of Trent

As in other early modern European polities, the forming of a marital bond in medieval Munich unfolded as a process whose centerpiece was the physical consummation of the spouses' promise to one another. Priests or secular officials were, at best, marginal figures in a rite of passage that was orchestrated by peers, family, and kin, and was grounded firmly in a medieval culture of feasting. When two spouses and their respective families decided to tie their fortunes together, festive acts framed and marked each stage along the way toward permanent ties. Depending on the economic means and the social standing of the spouses, these stages could be more numerous and the rituals accompanying them more elaborate. After negotiating the specifics of a marriage contract—the legal basis of the betrothal—future kin sealed their agreement with a ritual *Weinkauf* or

Lovelbier, a drinking bout.[7] Entertainment likewise took place during the time of the betrothal in the form of sumptuous ceremonies.

While betrothal ceremonies at times drew in parts of the wider public, familial interests nonetheless held sway. For example, betrothals occasionally occurred in churches or town halls,[8] but the choice of location often showed the involved families' preference for neutral ground and not necessarily submission to either ecclesiastical or secular authorities.[9] If any authorities were present, they were more likely to be notaries than clergy. Judging from the linguistic kinship between betrothals (*stulfeste*) and public scribes (*stulschreiber*), the ceremony was closely associated with a notarial act.[10]

After the betrothal, further festivities advanced the joining of spouses and families. Any number of "breakfasts, evening drinks, day or night carousals" might take place during the time leading up to the wedding.[11] A special preparatory ritual for the bride customarily took place on the day before the wedding: the so-called Brautbad (bridal bath), an act of ritual cleansing open to guests.[12] The weddings themselves were often held at the time of carnival, slipping easily from private celebrations into public extravaganzas on these occasions of communal merrymaking. Wealthy citizens could stage dances in Munich's streets. Less fortunate burghers had to confine the festivities to the street of their residences.[13] It was also common for the wedding party to attend a public bath after the festivities. City law characterized the sequence of events as follows: "to the feast, to the bed, to the bath."[14] A final collective drinking ritual in honor of the newlywed spouses, the *Ansingwein,* put the finishing touches on the drawn-out celebrations, as it cheered the two on to the conjugal bed.

Among the three ritual steps "to the feast, to the bed, to the bath," the marital bed was the crucial rite of passage. Kin ushered bride and bridegroom into their bedroom where they covered the two with a blanket. The ritual tucking in by family members, in its anticipation of copulation, signified the legal beginning of the marriage.[15] The customary blessing of the marital bed, at times in conjunction with priestly solemnization in the bridal chamber,[16] illustrates the pivotal role that successful physical consummation played in establishing a marital bond and also speaks to the centrality of the family setting regardless of the presence of a priest.

It was the Church's own law that underwrote this process-oriented and consummation-centered model of marriage formation and relegated officials, ecclesiastical or secular, at best to a position of marginal importance. Since the twelfth century, the Church had subscribed to a marital doctrine that declared the freely exchanged consent of spouses to be the constitutive element of marriage. Every Christian capable of freely expressing consent and physically consummating his or her promise enjoyed the right to enter the sacrament of matrimony.[17]

The doctrine of consensualism is a complicated issue that has generated a substantial body of historical and contemporary literature. Formulated by Pope Alexander III, this medieval doctrine brought to a close a long-standing debate within the Church over essential and inessential elements in the formation of the sacramental bond between husband and wife. On one side of the issue, Gratian and his followers (mainly from the University of Bologna) argued that both consent and physical consummation established matrimony. On the other side, Lombard (with the backing of the University of Paris) outlined a doctrine of marital validity as deriving exclusively from "words of present consent" (*sponsalia per verba de presenti*). Lombard furthermore offered a distinction between "words of present consent" as constituting marriage and "words of future consent" (*sponsalia per verba de futuro*) as the exchange of informal vows amounting to a betrothal.[18]

Alexander III's resolution of the question of marital validity favored Lombard's position, yet it altered this position based on Gratian's viewpoint. Although Alexander III decreed that the exchange of present consent was the sole requirement for a valid marriage, he also ascribed binding power to the exchange of future consent, if such consent was then expressed by physical consummation.[19] Promises and betrothals followed by physical consummation were ruled "valid and indissoluble."[20] In essence, Alexander embraced Lombard's distinction between "words of present consent" and "words of future consent," but declared the former sufficient in and of itself, while he required that the latter be backed up with sexual intercourse. Last but not least, these doctrinal decisions had a consequential side effect. Even "words of future consent" that lacked sexual consummation exerted some binding power upon the consenting parties: clandestine betrothals were dissoluble but they were not easily dissolved.[21]

From the twelfth century onward, the validity of marriage thus hinged on consent alone. This legal definition produced a number of social and political quagmires. Since a public ceremony was recommended but not required,[22] many couples took merely private vows and sealed their union through physical consummation before they underwent a public rite of passage, if they did so at all. There was no clear-cut distinction between married and nonmarried people and between sex outside of marriage and intimate marital relations, making it extremely difficult for governing officials, including church officials, to have a definitive say in the course of events.[23]

Not only did the consensual doctrine script the exclusion of ruling authorities from the process of marriage formation, it also limited the influence of families. Because the Church privileged the freely given exchange of consent between future husband and wife, it sided with the children, whose free will in the choice of spouses it validated regardless of their parents' and kin groups' marital schemes. The consensual doctrine gave the young powerful ammunition against the wishes of their elders and destabilized familial relations by declaring the "free and individual" bond between future spouses to be sufficient in strength for the establishment of a marriage.[24]

This is not to say that secular authorities did not undertake numerous legal efforts to introduce an element of parental and seigneurial control in the process of marriage formation. Notably, Germany's oldest secular marriage laws are statutory laws mandating parental consent.[25] Yet the doctrine of consent remained beyond the grasp of secular rulers. It represented more than a theological abstraction because the highly developed system of church courts could reinforce consensual marriage formation in social practice.

Significantly, the medieval doctrine of consent and the ecclesiastical courts upholding it appear to have served women more often, if not better, than men. Women accounted for the majority of plaintiffs in cases of contested marriage promises, and female litigants were much more likely than their male counterparts to win lawsuits before an ecclesiastical judge. Success could consist of the successful evasion of an undesirable marital union that parents sought to impose upon their daughter without respect for her consent.[26] Success could also amount to getting the husband of one's choice. In the late Middle Ages, ecclesiastical courts exerted moral pressure on men to fulfill marriage promises with predictable regularity, in particular if a promise had been followed by physical consummation and resulted in a pregnancy.[27]

Doctrinal obstruction of parental and seigneurial controls over marriage formation helps account for the great success with which Protestants could thematize the issue of secret marriages and the putative social evils resulting from clandestine unions.[28] Starting in the fifteenth century, secular authorities began to take a more interventionist interest in marriage as their bureaucratic apparatus expanded. Given the Catholic Church's monopoly on the question of marital validity, however, they lacked the ideological wedge to insert themselves fully into the process of marriage formation and to subject the process to secular sanction. What traditionally occurred in a personal realm circumscribed by canon law and popular practice first of all had to be redefined as belonging in the purview of public concern. Protestant challenges to medieval canon law, especially the reformers' attack on the sacramental nature of marriage, at last permitted such a redefinition.

In the imperial city of Augsburg, Munich's powerful neighboring town, the Reformation found the backing of the ruling elite, which recruited heavily among powerful guild members, because its theology of matrimony proved to be compatible with their conception of married life as the backbone of social, economic, and political order.[29] Declaring marriage a "worldly thing" and calling for parental approval as a precondition for entering matrimony, Protestants freed the institution from the fetters of ecclesiastical control and justified greater regulatory efforts on the part of secular authorities. Secular authorities suddenly found values they had long held dear sacralized by Protestant theology, and they willingly seized on the resulting opportunities for sociopolitical reform. The Reformation's triumph in 1537 in Augsburg was accompanied by the installment of various public controls over marriage. A city-run marriage court tried all matters pertaining to married life, including those that church courts had handled in the past, such as cases of broken marriage promises. The secular court's duties included the enforcement of a newly introduced requirement of parental consent for marriage formation; if marital unions were contracted in opposition to parental wishes, the court ruled them invalid.[30]

Although the Reformation did not take hold in Munich, it is telling that the first supporters of Protestantism were connected to the world of the guilds. The ethos of marriage formation that these sympathizers of Luther promoted was one that not only predated Protestant ideas, as it did in Augsburg, but also outlasted the swift disappearance of Protestantism from the Bavarian capital. Half a decade after the Bavarian court virtually extirpated Protestant leanings in Munich, the Catholic magistrate passed a New Wedding Ordinance in 1535 that echoed the paternalistic tone and reformatory zeal of concomitant regulatory efforts in Protestant Augsburg.[31] The ordinances dubbed the *stuelfest,* or betrothal, which customarily entailed notarial authentication of a marriage contract, the "day of marriage"[32] and thus marked the public registry of the union as the crucial element in its making. This was but one way in which the council set itself up as arbiter of the proper rite of passage. It also strove to whittle down the complex wedding ritual and regulate the number and behavior of participants, ostensibly for the sake of public order and civic peace. A cap was put on the number of guests that could attend both betrothal and wedding celebrations; the bridal bath and *Ansingwein,* as well as any other festivities with the potential for unruly or amoral conduct, were outlawed.[33]

Clearly, Protestant and Catholic authorities alike strove to readjust the scales between the personal consent of couples and the public scrutiny thereof. Where the confessions parted ways was in their choice of the specific mechanism of control over illicitly contracted marriages. While the Protestant answer to the problem of clandestine marriage was to declare marriage a "worldly thing" and make parental consent a prerequisite of marital validity, Catholic marriage reform ultimately took a different route toward the goal of securing public supervision of marriage formation. The new Protestant discourse on marriage and sexuality set crucial parameters for the Catholic discussion without determining its final outcome.

Increasing the Small Knot of the Faithful: The Sacramental View of Marriage and Sexuality

Marital doctrine was among the most controversial issues Catholic clerics debated during the general council that convened in the Italian city of Trent in 1545 in an effort to reform the Catholic Church and confront the spread of the Protestant movement. Marriage represented the boundary around which the difference between the laity and the clergy was organized in the Catholic taxonomy of sacredness and sexuality. Because Protestantism made clerical marriage the major signifier of breaking with the old faith, marking and upholding this particular boundary became more symbolically charged and politically important than ever. The council fathers at Trent carried out parallel discussions that treated the question of marriage reform simultaneously with the question of clerical concubinage and the issue of abuses in monastic communities. These boundary drawings were part and parcel of the same overarching effort of establishing, or in some respects reestablishing, firm distinctions between the holy and the profane.

Consequently, the council fathers reaffirmed the sacramental and consensual definition of matrimony and held up the married life as the laity's path toward salvation,[34] the superiority of the virginal life notwithstanding.[35] Yet while these issues remained uncontested, the problem of clandestine marriages sparked heated debate among the delegations. French and Spanish cardinals championed the introduction of normative parental consent as the remedy for clandestine marriages, offering an uncanny resemblance to Protestants in the choice of means as well as in the choice of arguments. The opposing theological faction was made up of those who were convinced that the requirement of parental consent for a marriage's validity was a doctrinal impossibility. The result of this clash between two diametrically opposed groups was the agreement articulated in the Tametsi decree of 1563.[36]

Tametsi dictated that future spouses, prior to physical consummation and cohabitation, have their parish priest announce their intention to the community. He had to make his announcements during mass, allowing ritual time for intervention by community members.[37] The decree also encouraged bride and bridegroom to attend confession and partake in communion three days before the wedding. This encouragement underlined the sacramental nature of marriage and sought to ground the process firmly in the ritual life of the parish.[38] A final moment of possible intervention occurred when the parish priest at last solemnized the union "in facie ecclesiae."[39] Vows had to be exchanged in the presence of the priest and of two or three witnesses. At the end of the day, the priest was obliged to enter the names of spouses and witnesses in his church book, an entry that froze the decisive moment in time for future reference.[40] Solemnization in private homes, even if the parish priest conducted the ceremony, was strictly prohibited.

While the council fathers thus denied parents a veto in marital matters, another mechanism of public control was simultaneously introduced, namely, supervision through the parish community represented by the parish priest. In other words, the doctrinal definition of validity stood on two legs after Trent: consent and publicity. What had once been a potentially prolonged, obfuscated process, involving as few as two people, was to become a structured rite of passage witnessed by and embedded in the parish community. The oral exchange of consensual promises between two individuals gave way to a parish-centered matrimonial rite and its textual articulation in the parish registrars. In this manner, an elusive and potentially entirely personal process could be transformed into a publicly witnessed moment that one could revisit later through the written record. This allowed for a clear distinction between the state of courtship and the state of marriage, between problematic premarital sex and proper marital intimate relations—the boundaries of which had been obfuscated for centuries. Combined with the council's concomitant reiteration that premarital sex was a mortal sin, the novel conceptual distinction could function as a forceful tool for prosecuting sexuality outside of marriage.[41]

The paradoxical nature of the compromise decree of Tametsi, which reaffirmed private consent and mandated publicity in the same breath, was bound to result in varied patterns of local application. Studies from diverse European regions and the New World point to tremendous differences in Tametsi's application and impact on family relations. In Mexico the rulings of Trent gave doctrinal grounds to the young for opposing parental wishes, even though local Church officials tried to alert parents to matches they might disapprove of and allowed them to interfere.[42] In France, on the other hand, the state entered an alliance with upper-class families who had a strong interest in controlling their offspring's reproductive behavior and subverted the full implementation of Trent's marital doctrine. Secular authorities wrested judicial control over clandestine unions from church courts and insisted on mandatory parental consent to

Fig. 2.   Council fathers in deliberation at Trent. (By Nöel Cochin. Original in
Staatliche Graphische Sammlung, Munich.)

the point of forcing priests to procure proof of the parents' acceptance
from prospective spouses for the state's records.[43]

Where then did Tametsi leave its traces in Bavaria? First of all in the
ecclesiastical setting where clergymen sought to familiarize their parishioners with the new rules as soon as the guidelines of Trent reached
Bavaria in the early 1580s. Even though they operated on diametrically
opposed doctrinal assumptions, these local agents of Tridentine reform
sold a concept of marriage to their audience that had many chords in har-
mony with Protestant notions of married life. Like Protestant preachers
elsewhere, Munich's Catholic clergy spoke of marriage as constitutive of
Christian society and as the institutional enactment of god-given hierarchies between men and women.

The sermons of Geminianus Monacensis illustrate the point. What
the church fathers at Trent proclaimed in plain doctrinal language,
Munich's popular Counter-Reformation preacher made palatable to his

parish communities with metaphorical speech. Thus he began the marriage sermon he reserved for the Sunday after Epiphany by invoking the elaborate, opulent images that decorated the ancient temple of Jerusalem. The mural paintings, he explained, depicted a cherub as a beautiful young man surrounded by lilies and two palm trees. After Geminianus conveyed the richness of the temple's interior to his listeners, he went on to convey the imagery's spiritual richness.

> Enlightened by God, Salomon wanted to prefigure with his temple's adornments in what way the Holy Christian Catholic Church was going to be adorned with three kinds of estates: the first being the ecclesiastical epitomized through the Angel Cherub. . . . The lilies [next] are an image of the virginal [estate] and the chaste estate of the widow. . . . The third adornment of God's church is the holy estate of matrimony represented by the palm trees. It appears as if God created this plant for this very end as to be a mirror for the spouses . . . these plants have such love for one another they cannot bear fruit without each other . . . as soon as they get close to one another . . . their roots . . . intertwine to such degree that no human being can disentangle them. . . . In between these images of marriage Salomon placed the Cherub in order to explain: Who is it that must unite those two loving plants? The Angel that is [to say] the Priest: after this kind of union has taken place, the two plants can never be divorced again.[44]

By the metaphor of the Cherub, the lilies, and the two palm trees, Geminianus communicated several abstract doctrinal points by making them understandable and palatable for his audience (as is the hallmark of successful metaphors). In the ensuing sermon Geminianus approached these points over and over again: the sacramental nature of marriage distinguishing Catholic orthodoxy from the "heresies" of the time and the imperative presence of the priest embodying the authority of Christ and the Church (even though the "two loving plants" would unite naturally). He also added and elaborated a few others, such as the purpose of marriage in salvation history or how the relationship between bridegroom and bride ought to resemble the one between Christ and his Church.

Interestingly, when Geminianus took it upon himself to explain to his listeners how and why Christ first transformed marriage into a sacrament, he spoke about social survival rather than individual salvation. Abandoning the traditional Pauline pitch for marriage as a highly effective buffer against the temptations of the flesh, the Munich priest instead offered an argument for the centrality of sexual reproduction.[45] Christ, he asserted, installed matrimony as a sacrament in order for "the number of faithful people [to] prevail and increase, otherwise the small knot of the Holy Church [would have] perished soon."[46]

Even though Geminianus invoked the dangers of the old Church's extinction and the life-saving benefits of marriage in the past, the typological relevance of his reasoning to the present time of confessional conflict with Protestants was unlikely to be lost on his Munich audience. In this perspective, as many Catholics as possible ought to be married: more than a spiritually desirable state, which every Christian capable of consent had the right to enter, matrimony became a virtual duty of a Counter-Reformation Catholic—and so did sexual reproduction.[47]

In the wake of Trent, Munich's priests indeed were required to remind future spouses that the first reason for getting married was the necessity of multiplying Christians before they could proceed and solemnize the union.[48] This message echoed the message that Protestant preachers, such as Johannes Mathesius in Saxony, sent to their parishioners.[49] The parallels come into even starker relief in the gender-specific behavioral code that was intertwined with the exhortation to marry and the exaltation of married life. During the marriage ceremony, Munich's priests also impressed upon bride and bridegroom the wondrous resemblance of the union they were about to enter to the union between Christ and his Church;[50] they asked future spouses to honor this resemblance by emulating the sacred relationship in their actions.

According to Geminianus, this meant that men had to aspire to Christ's protectiveness and unfailing patience; equally key to imitating Christ was awareness of the need for firm admonition and stern punishment of one's bride. To the women, in turn, the Counter-Reformation preacher held up a model of the Church, depicting the latter as industrious, humble, and ever striving to please the divine spouse.[51]

In expressing their will to become husband and wife during the actual ceremony, men and women had to utter distinct words that corresponded to the dissimilar roles they were about to embrace and into which the ritual transported them. Whereas the groom announced his willingness to "honor /love/nourish/and protect her like [his] own body," she promised to "exhibit honor and support/be submissive and obedient in all things decent and proper/like Sarah was toward Abraham."[52]

What Munich's clergy conveyed most strongly through the ritual means of a Catholic wedding ceremony, Protestant pastors communicated in the wedding sermon, the centerpiece of their rite. The means differed, but the message was the same. In either case, social norms for proper, gender-specific behavior insinuated themselves into a soteriological discourse on marriage to such an extent that they seemed to be derived from it—a true case of reification. The Protestant Mathesius extolled the complementary roles of husband and wife on the plane of salvation history and their spiritual equality, only to find in the higher meaning of married life a basis for justifying social inequality between men and women. The husband, Mathesius pointed out in numerous sermons, owed the wife nourishment, protection, and supervision. She in turn was supposed to honor her obligations toward him through housework, child rearing, and willing acceptance of his divinely authorized rule.[53]

The standard Catholic view of marriage, despite its insistence on the sacramentality of marriage, finally made room for and accommodated a secular understanding that veered close to the Protestant conception of marriage as a worldly thing. Geminianus insisted on a clear distinction between "two parts in the state of matrimony": a "civic contract/linking man and woman indissolubly for the education of children within marriage" and a "supernatural mystery . . . a replication of the indissoluble union between Christ and his Holy Church."[54] On the basis of this distinction between the sacramental nature and social function of marriage Geminianus reminded couples to balance the need for a modicum of property with awareness of the spiritual insufficiency of economics. He exhorted listeners to pay some heed to temporal goods—for "where there is nothing/with whom will you *hausen* (have a joint household)?"—but he put those who privileged economic considerations on a par with "beasts" and "pagans."[55]

One Bavarian marriage custom, however, indicates how the distinct features of Counter-Reformation Catholicism could come into play. Brides-to-be were able to borrow crowns of virginity from Bavaria's churches. The headgear was fashioned after the crown worn by the Virgin Mary herself, with local Marian statues serving as models for the artists.[56] Clearly, virginity as a Catholic religious ideal could be marshaled in support of the reaffirmed sanctity and even heightened valorization of matrimony. The virginity of the bride, in signifying the avoidance of premarital sexual relations, contributed to the sanctification of marriage. It is important to note, though, that this powerful symbolic mechanism, while it celebrated women's ability to confer divine grace upon matrimony, also placed a great social and moral burden on women, and not men, to secure a state of virginity prior to marriage.

In addition to teaching the sacramental and social meaning of marriage, Counter-Reformation clergy in Munich sought to familiarize their flock with the public wedding ceremony that Trent had made mandatory for the validity of a marriage. At least once every month, Munich's priests read to their communities word for word and explained "with diligence" the Tridentine process of forming a valid marriage.[57] Old customs, however, died hard. In 1597, the bishop of Freising sent a letter to Munich clergymen, urging them to put a stop "to the private solemnization in inns as well as other houses."[58] In 1625, the bishop was still complaining to Munich's parish priests. "The solemnization of weddings," he noted, "was commonly taking place in houses . . . and very rarely in churches."[59]

While solemnizations at home were popular among the people, church ceremonies enjoyed little respect. Apparently, many couples and their guests, if they arranged for a church ceremony at all, showed up too late for the occasion. Incensed by what he took to be "an irreverent act toward God and this holy sacrament," the bishop instructed his clergy that they "were no longer obliged to wait, but could go home without a hindrance," if the wedding party failed to be in church by 10:30 A.M. Although Munich's priests read this order from the pulpit on several occasions, the behavior of their parishioners showed little improvement. By 1634 the bishop decreed that couples lost their claim to solemnization altogether, if they had not made an appearance by 10:00, perhaps hoping that the earlier deadline would result in people's final appearance by 10:30. However, an abiding lack of punctuality necessitated yet another mandate in 1640.[60]

Ecclesiastical authorities in the Bavarian capital thus found their efforts to set a new standard foiled again and again. The ongoing popular resistance to ecclesiastical and secular moves toward greater public control over the formation of marital bonds did not lack a certain historical irony. When ecclesiastical authorities tried to gain a firmer grip on the creation of conjugal bonds, they were running up against (at least partially) their own successfully implemented policies from the past. What now appeared as tradition was nothing less than the historical creation of the medieval church. The Church's pre-Trent marriage doctrine with its emphasis on consensual promises had apparently achieved widespread acceptance in people's perceptions and practices—a fact clerics had to confront even in their own court system.

A lawsuit involving broken marriage promises tried before the ecclesiastical court in Freising in 1624 illustrates that traditional understandings persisted well into the seventeenth century. The plaintiff Ulrich Kobold relied on what he considered sufficient ground for marriage in making his case: the combination of promises and intercourse. When he outlined the evolution of his relationship with the defendant Renate Damianion to the ecclesiastical judge, Kobold highlighted the following elements.

In the presence of her cognates, their hands joined, they promised marriage to each other and he gave her a golden ring . . . On April 5th of this year [1625] the parties celebrated public sponsalia in Munich, and the marriage contract was fixed. . . . To corroborate the marriage promise, they exercised carnal copulation freely. . . . He prepared himself for the wedding, and he had already invited guests.[61]

Kobold's description shows the resilience of a process-oriented and consummation-centered concept of engendering the conjugal tie. Munich's people, in spite of the efforts of Geminianus and other Counter-Reformers, had not internalized the idea that physical consummation of a marriage promise was to follow, not to precede the promise's public declaration in church. The Church surely worked hard to clarify that the decisive moment marking "married" as opposed to "unmarried" was the priest's joining of the spouses rather than the public signing of a marriage contract that signified the beginning of the union in secular law. Only a few years prior to Kobold's statement in his court, the bishop of Freising in fact reminded his parishioners again that the true marital vows were those exchanged before a priest. "The promises or *stulfesten,*" he pointed out, "are sponsalia de futuro [words of future consent] and not matrimonia de presenti [a marriage in the present]."[62] Yet the message either did not get through to Kobold or he decided to ignore it.

If Church courts turned up ample evidence for the violation of the rules of Trent, they were at the same time the site of greatest leverage for ecclesiastical authorities bent on imposing a new regime of marriage formation. Here the exhortations from the pulpit could be backed up with the force of law. Adjudicating cases of contested marriage promises, ecclesiastical judges automatically also adjudicated the relative weight of new regulations and traditional practices.

There was leeway for both interpretation and implementation of the novel regulations. The Council of Trent had given ecclesiastical judges a set of formal guidelines and criteria, such as the presence of witnesses and of a priest, permitting an indisputable assessment of the binding nature of "words of present consent." Still, the council fathers had confirmed marriage's sacramental nature and the centrality of the consent between the two spouses in the sacrament's enactment. A promise of marriage, this assertion recognized implicitly, set in motion a process that was of immediate bearing on the state of one's soul and could thus not be dismissed in a spirit of levity. Even after Trent, there existed a theoretical possibility for deriving a legal claim from a clandestine exchange of "words of future consent," a legal loophole for validating customary courtship practices.[63]

This helps explain why Katharina Rieger, whose quest for justice opened this chapter, was so upset about the negative verdict in the bishop's court. Not only had she lost her case of broken promises, she obviously left with a deep sense of not having received "a proper hearing" in the first place. Rieger could not think of any good reason for her treatment other than "secret deals" between the judge and her former lover. Ecclesiastical judges had long listened to women and sided with female plaintiffs on the mere basis of their testimony.[64] If this judge could not hear her, he must have been deafened, as it were, by the defendant's deceptive words.

It is not necessary to share Katharina Rieger's suspicion of the ecclesiastical judge to recognize that Munich's women indeed encountered greater difficulties in winning suits of broken promises after Trent. At least unwittingly, the ecclesiastical judge changed from an advocate of women to an ally of men. Very few court cases have survived for the period between 1592 and 1631, but the extant sources nonetheless present a record of turning down female plaintiffs who were bent on enforcing marriage promises in the church court. Thirteen out of fourteen women suing for recognition of the binding nature of a marriage promise lost their case; the fourteenth verdict is missing. In effect, the ecclesiastical judge virtually always awarded economic restitution and never exerted pressure on a man to enter a marriage with a female plaintiff.[65]

If it had not been a tacit guideline of judicial practice already before then, the unfavorable treatment of women's suits of broken promises became official policy in 1618. At this historical juncture, the archbishop of Salzburg dispatched a letter to the ecclesiastical judges in his charge, including the court officials at Freising. The missive demanded a more aggressive judicial stance against the entire spectrum of courtship beyond public scrutiny, from "secret betrothals" to "promises made in dark corners" and "sponsalibus clandestinis between unmarried men and women folk around here." It provides an intriguing gloss on the conceptual filter with which ecclesiastical authorities could view the problem of clandestine unions after Trent.

The archbishop identified the root of the problem first of all in women's gullibility and their lack of moral discernment. He complained that "many women are seduced and swayed by the pretext of these kinds of marriage contracts . . . so that they continue living in . . . dishonor for several years without shame and without awareness of sin." If this practice in and of itself constituted a reason for concern, what made it even more troublesome in the eyes of the archbishop was the frequent abandonment of such a relationship by a disenchanted lover and the many cases of broken promises that resulted from it. Given the context, the archbishop undoubtedly spoke of men, although he does not specify them, when he bemoaned the unwillingness "to keep the promise given earlier." His ire peaked in recounting how these men "come to court and deny the promise with false oaths and assurances, with perjury free themselves from the betrothal they initiated, betray the judge, and burden their conscience not without damage to their salvation."

On the one hand, the episcopal analysis identified men's and women's individual psychologies as the cause of clandestine marriages and their attendant problems. On the other hand, the solution the archbishop proposed did not aim at remedying the shortcomings of individuals, for example, by forcing irresponsible men to keep their promises. Instead the cleric sought an institutional cure-all in a rigid application of Trent's publicity criteria, at the expense of Trent's affirmation of the binding power of consent. Extending the formal criteria outlined at Trent to betrothals and thus breaking with canonical respect for "words of future consent," the archbishop called for an abolition of all "sponsalia clandestine [*sic*]" and "marriage promises exchanged in dark corners." In the same breath in which he acknowledged their binding power, the archbishop decreed that even physically consummated promises were invalid "regardless of whether the sponsiones or promises united the contracting parties in their consciences."[66] It was only logical that the cleric, far from putting a stop to men's perjury in the courtroom, concluded by asking his subordinate judges "not to give a hearing to the parties, to take them away from the courts and tribunals and punish them . . . so that others will be deterred from the discussed [marriage] contracts."[67]

Trent was showing its darkest side in the archbishop's words, the side that used formal criteria to brand consensual relations without public approval as condemnable premarital sexuality. Posted on church doors and read from Bavarian pulpits, the archbishop's guidelines must have discouraged suits for broken promises. Those female litigants who did take the risk at the bishop's court and lost their cases could consider themselves lucky if they collected financial compensation and went unpunished.[68]

Trent's affirmation of marriage as a consensual and sacramental bond available to all Christians had no impact on the court's approach to marriage promises, whereas Trent's publicity requirements shaped judicial processes by making it very difficult for litigants to win in a case of breach of promise. If anything, Tridentine marriage doctrine might have raised people's expectations at the same time that Trent's novel formal criteria for valid marriage promises clearly worsened the prospects of enforcing a promise.

Women, who initiated the majority of these types of lawsuits, were directly and adversely affected by this trend. One way to respond to the restricted options was to seek recourse to traditional, noninstitutional means of social control: threats of curses,[69] disparaging gossip, and community pressure. This was what Katharina Rieger did by taking the case to the streets. Her former lover Hans Vorster was not alone in his effort to silence such female speech. The judge's stern threat of exemplary punishment for Rieger illustrates that the spreading of stories was a common and effective female stratagem.

While women turned to judges with the intention of compelling their male lovers to meet obligations, men resorted to the judicial system to fight a different battle. For them women's allegations of marriage promises presented a source of danger. In 1610, for example, Michael Kirchmayer asked the secular judge to silence his former lover Ursula Huber because "now that she has seen that he is about to enter an honorable marriage and also obtain civic rights, she has threatened him with wanting to approach him outside the church because of marriage."[70]

Along similar lines, Martin Airnschmaltz requested the imposition of silence upon Johanna Räder. He had made payments to her "in the presence of four honorable men" for impregnating her, and Räder had agreed to drop all claims regarding a marriage promise, the plaintiff explained to the judge. But when Airnschmaltz wanted to marry the daughter of an innkeeper's widow, Räder informed the bride's mother how she was planning "to approach [the plaintiff] outside the church regarding marital things and debts." Airnschmaltz wanted her to be quiet so she would not "obstruct the realization of the marriage he planned."[71]

Men like Kirchmayer and Airnschmaltz stood at an important threshold in their lives when women like Huber and Räder threatened to get in their way. Not only was marriage a decisive event in the lives of women, it also was a marker of important life changes for these early modern men. For the merchant Kirchmayer, it meant that he was headed to join the community of Munich's upstanding full male citizens, men who, as a rule, were married.[72] For Airnschmaltz, who was a soldier by profession, the impending wedding with the daughter of a widowed innkeeper held the prospect of an increase in status and money: as the man in the family, he would take over the inn at some point in time. Women's claims could unleash a perilous power during these transition moments in men's lives, moments that rendered men socially vulnerable due to intense scrutiny. Female interference could disrupt the consolidation of patriarchal social norms that linked masculinity, economic clout, and citizenship.

Judges and male plaintiffs clearly knew of the import of female gossip, how women could "get in the way of matrimonial matters." Even if the court system did not easily give credence to women's claims of clandestine marriage promise after Trent, popular perceptions of the binding power of consensualism apparently did. In this sense, traditional understandings tended to support women's claims whereas post-Trent definitions favored men in facilitating their avoidance of obligations. Men sought the secular judge's aid in countering female claims, claims whose perilous power stemmed from their deep roots in popular culture.

Approaching a man at the church's door with marital demands was a

particularly loaded act after Trent. Husband and wife were after all supposed to make public and thereby valid their marital intention *in facie
ecclesiae*. Showing up as the "true wife" at this very point in time meant
inserting oneself into a ceremony that allowed for no more than one husband and one wife, thus making the point that someone else was taking
one's place. Such appearance meant introducing a serious impediment and
a dishonorable past into present plans.

Ironically, the Council of Trent helped create this most opportune
moment for effective intervention and for the powerful assertion of the
binding nature of clandestine promises—the kind of promise it sought to
eradicate precisely by requiring the publicity of a church ceremony for a
marital union's validity. Telescoping the ritual process into one decisive
moment, Trent imbued this moment with great significance. Women simply need to step into it as the "true wife" and their marital claims, no matter how unfounded they might be in terms of Tridentine doctrine, could
become explosive. When women approached men with claims of private
marriage promises at the church door, the world of medieval consensualism pierced one last time, as it were, the Tridentine church's monopoly on
valid promises—a centuries-old understanding of marital bonds flaring up
briefly but glaringly in the very public forum that signaled its demise.

In sum, Tridentine Catholicism in the Catholic stronghold of Munich
mattered little where it differed most sharply from Protestantism—with
regard to the sacramental nature of marriage. The clerics who, in sermon
and ritual, praised marriage to the high heavens as a spiritually desirable
and even quasi-obligatory state might have enhanced the institution's
appeal among Munich's laity. But they were virtually powerless when it
came to the worldly business of lowering the greater economic barriers
that state authorities began to put in the way of their parishioners. The
ecclesiastical court was the sole arena in which church authorities were in
full control of the application of the marriage doctrine outlined by Trent.
Even there, however, the Tridentine emphasis on the sacramental obligations of consensual promises faded into the background of judicial decision making, whereas the enforcement of stricter sexual mores and the
publicity of marriage formation moved toward the center of regulatory
efforts.

Of Property, Progeny, and Profligacy: Marriage as a Privilege and Instrument of Public Order

The main legacy of the Council of Trent in Bavaria lay in the mandate of
a public ceremony and the attendant condemnation of sex outside of marriage. The Church bequeathed powerful tools to state authorities already

engaged in building a public order on the bedrock of economically stable households. Secular government conceptualized marriage legislation through the prism of economics and public order. Genuine bows to the divinely ordained state of marriage notwithstanding, the guiding principle of the secular arm was by and large the protection of property among those who had it and the prohibition of marital unions among those who had no property to begin with.

The state's primary interest consisted of strengthening propertied patriarchal householders and mobilizing household governance for political rule. Lacking the means of direct regulation of social life on the everyday level, early modern governments, at this stage of nascent centralization, needed the consensus and cooperation of traditional authorities outside of secular bureaucracies to advance their political agenda. Authority was dispersed throughout a network of traditional authorities, and centralization could be accomplished only by harnessing the regulatory powers and forces of these interlocking networks of rule to the goals of central administration.[73]

On the lowest level of governance this meant recruiting heads of household into service for the central government. Bavaria's state law hence displayed some of the same features that characterized contemporary legislation on sex and marriage in France, notably an increase of magisterial and patriarchal power.[74] Centralization in Bavaria also meant preventing men and women who were purportedly ill-suited for household governance from marrying and assuming the offices of *Hausvater* (father of the household) and *Hausmutter* (mother of the household), offices that entailed disciplinary responsibilities. Centralization further included the regulation of sexual relationships among the lower classes; this pronounced class bias set the developments in Catholic Bavaria apart from those in France.

The Ordinance of Good Police of 1553, issued ten years prior to the conclusion of the Council of Trent, gave key impulses toward strengthening patriarchal marriage and preventing lower-class sexual unions. The Bavarian state introduced punishments for intercourse between unmarried people, turning premarital sexuality into a criminal offense. It further castigated all clandestine unions as "aggravating profligate cohabitation of men and women outside of the marital estate ordained by God."[75]

Unlike the Church, the state threw its legal support behind parents and decreed stiff sanctions for the clandestine marriages of minors.[76] The Ordinance threatened daughters (under twenty-five) and sons (under thirty) with loss of dowry and even disinheritance should they fail to consult their parents about their marriage partners.[77] The high age set for minority placed children under parental control for a lengthy period of their lives, mirroring French law in overall intent as well as detail.[78] The same Ordinance of Good Police also introduced stricter distinctions between the inheritance rights of legitimate and illegitimate children, deliberately disadvantaging the latter so that "there is greater incentive for honorability and discipline."[79]

By 1616 the punishments for rule infractions regarding parental consent had undergone further specifications whereby the severity of the financial loss now depended on the choice of partner, the sex, and the age of the disobedient child. The worst possible case scenario was one where a child entered a clandestine union with a partner from a lower class and of dishonorable reputation.[80] The law granted parents of such malfeasants the right to disinherit their offspring entirely.[81]

If a child entered a clandestine union with a partner who was acceptable on moral grounds but below the family's station, the law still judged the offense unfavorably and meted out gender-specific punishments. A son forfeited rights to any parental support for his household as long as his parents were alive. He remained entitled to his inheritance, however, and could lay claim to these withheld payments at his parents' death.[82] Not so a daughter who had committed the equivalent transgression. She lost her right to a dowry temporarily (for her parents' lifetime), and her future inheritance was reduced permanently. It shrank to one half, the other half going to "her obedient siblings."[83]

Even if the partner came from the appropriate class and was of good character, the circumventing of parental consent had its costs. For sons under the age of twenty-one the punishment was imprisonment, the only nonpecuniary penalty on the list. Daughters under the age of twenty-five lost their dowries, and sons under the age of thirty were deprived of their equivalent rights to parental subsidies. But neither sons nor daughters were stripped of their inheritance in these cases, and they could reclaim their dowry portions at their parents' death.[84]

The different legal treatment of men and women highlights the different positions the two sexes occupied in the process of property transmission and in the Bavarian kinship system. Munich's women were dowered, but, unlike their counterparts in Italian cities, the dowry did not automatically entail the exclusion of a woman from inheritance.[85] Some Bavarian women could and did forgo their right to inheritance for a dowry upon marriage, engaging in the kind of trade-off that was normative for Italian women. This option was initially a prerogative of the nobility, but it was later extended to the patriciate as well.[86]

Comparable to inheritance practices in some regions of France, Bavarian children of both sexes received a form of parental support for their marriage.[87] A daughter received a dowry representing her contribution to the new household. Her husband had to match the value of this dowry through his *Widerleg* (matching). In addition, the husband bestowed upon his wife a *Morgengabe* (morning gift), the price paid for her virginity, which was rightfully hers after their first "having lain together."[88] Dowry, matching, and morning gift formed the bedrock for the couple's economic partnership.[89]

Although the spouses pooled their resources, the husband had the power to make crucial economic and legal decisions on behalf of his wife and children. Whatever the woman had brought into her marriage, including her clothes and jewelry, came into his "power."[90] She was not allowed to sell or donate any of her own or their joint property without his consent. Neither could the wife enter contracts or pursue legal action without her husband's permission.[91] If there were children, the husband's guardianship also encompassed their financial matters.

Bavaria's law took from Roman law the concept of *patria potestas,*[92] granting fathers nodal positions in the kinship system and defining fatherhood first and foremost in terms of property ownership and not biology.[93] A father was entitled to interfere in the financial transactions of his children (natural as well as adopted), and even of his sons' children. He served as their representative in court and held usufruct rights to the children's maternal inheritance and other property the children might have acquired through inheritance. Death or emancipation in court put an end to the "paternal power," and so did the child's establishment of a separate household. Otherwise sons and daughters remained in the father's power until they reached the age of twenty-five.[94]

Men's and women's complementary contributions to the new household community and the different roles they assumed in their economic partnership were reminiscent of the Church catalog of gender norms derived from the sacramental model of Christ and his ecclesiastical bride. Property rights and inheritance law placed women in a state of dependence on and subordination to their husbands. Obedience was a wife's primary obligation. In addition, the existence of the morning gift accorded special significance to the female virginal body by marking the bride's past sexual conduct as relevant. The morning gift was a reward for the only proper loss of the female state of virginity, namely, that within an officially sanctioned sexual union. There was no corresponding valorization of male virginity in this asymmetrical legal construction of gender roles.

The male head of the household, in turn, was defined by his power, which entailed unique privileges and duties. Ideally, he protected his dependents, including his wife, by guarding the property and representing the household in social and legal settings. He was also the main beneficiary of state efforts to protect familial property. The flip side, however, involved greater responsibility before the law and greater exposure to an expanding state bureaucratic apparatus.

Moreover, because paternal power was property-based, men without access to a modicum of economic means were by definition ineligible for patriarchal household governance. Instituting the rule of the father demanded that men without property in fact walk away from fatherhood and, at least in theory, also from sexual relations. At the very moment in time when the state first began to write mechanisms into law to protect family property and exclude extramarital children from the patrimony, state officials also embarked upon the prohibition of sexual unions among those without sufficient means. Secular authorities were most interested in tackling the problem of so-called *Leichtfertigkeit* (profligacy), a term that captured both economically irresponsible and morally reprehensible sexual behavior. Any unmarried person who entered a sexual relationship, especially one without a material base, was considered guilty of profligacy.

Even though religious language suffused the legal rhetoric on profligacy, this idiom should not obscure the underlying secular intention of curbing marriages among the lower classes and the servant population whose labor should remain available to householders. The already cited Ordinance of Good Police of 1553 contained an explicit clause against "domestics . . . who often get married in a profligate manner and without the establishment of a permanent household and without property."[95] The state issued an outright prohibition against marriages among servants in the same year.[96]

From the very beginning the state-orchestrated fight against premarital sexuality in Bavaria was thus inseparable from the attempt to confine the right to get married and engage in sexual acts to certain social groups and to establish patriarchal household governance. State officials feared that economic recklessness and lack of sexual restraint combined to launch a twin assault on a public order whose only reliable bedrock consisted of households of financially stable married couples. The underlying logic was one of a subsistence economy whose limited resources called for deliberate distribution and the regulation of all desires, including sexual desire. Impoverished families and their offspring threatened to burden community chests unduly through poor relief. In this respect, the state's agenda of avoiding profligate and clandestine unions and the agenda of propertied householders blended well.[97]

By defining profligate cohabitation as a matter of public order, the state was able to pursue offenders, even if they had the backing of parents or church officials. Already in 1557, still years prior to the conclusion of the Council of Trent and the issuance of Tametsi, the state authorized its officials to prosecute public profligacy whether or not couples in question had received a clergyman's stamp of approval. The trend reached a climax in a mandate of 1578 that made the consent of state authorities or their local agents obligatory for the validity of any marital union. Thereafter, systematic seigneurial control of marriage formation was the official order of the day.[98]

By the time Tridentine marriage doctrine filtered into Bavaria in the early 1580s, state authorities were already well positioned to adopt this doctrine as they saw fit. Parallel to creating a new legal apparatus, Bavaria's central government had long curtailed ecclesiastical jurisdiction. There was not going to be too much of a disjuncture between the theory and practice of marriage regulation. In 1583, state prerogatives in marital jurisdiction became a constitutional fixture in the so-called Munich Concordant. Pushed upon Bavaria's bishops by the state with the help of the papacy, this agreement between church and state authorities accounted for Bavaria's exceptional status among Germany's Catholic politics after Trent.[99] While other Catholic territories witnessed a deepening of the traditional division of labor between bishops' courts focused on validity disputes and secular courts dealing with criminal aspects of marriage or questions of property, Bavaria approached a "secularization of marital jurisdiction" usually ascribed to Protestant areas.[100]

Licensing Sexuality: Munich's Bureau of Marriage

The reform initiatives of the state swiftly reached the capital city, where they encountered support as well as opposition among Munich's residents. On the one hand, civic authorities shared the state's (and the church's) interest in moving marriage out of the familial sphere and under the auspices of officials. The stipulations of the New Wedding Ordinance of 1535, the first legislative landmark of the city fathers' more forceful intervention in traditional marriage-making discussed previously, were repeated and partially sharpened in succeeding legislation into the second half of the sixteenth century. On the other hand, these very reiterations bespoke the difficulties the magistrate had in going against the grain of marriage rites based on kin group. Tradition was tenacious. A major city ordinance (*Pueßordnung*) of 1587 still had to acknowledge the familial sphere as the primary site of matchmaking when it called at least for restraint during betrothal ceremonies in family homes.[101]

Another layer of complications consisted of the conflictual relationship between an urban government determined to maintain autonomy and a state government set on centralization. The overall trend of Bavarian state building implied a reshaping of Munich's judicial landscape along the lines of further centralization. Because the regulation of marriage and sexuality was one of the major initiatives of Bavaria's central authority, this political project, even where it meshed with civic agendas, always also spelled erosion of urban self-government.

The establishment of a new civic institution, the so-called bureau of marriage (*Hochzeitsamt*), in the last decades of the sixteenth century represents a case in point for the intersection between policing sexuality and centralizing politics.[102] Set up in connection with a new Ordinance of Marriage and Good Police,[103] the bureau represented an institutional link between civic and state government, a transmission belt for the import of state policies on marriage into the city. It was intimately connected to the city's political center of control through its two main officials, the lords of marriage (*Hochzeitsherren*). They were members of the inner and outer council respectively, at the same time that they served as a liaison with the court.[104] The highest court judge (*Hofoberrichter*) supervised the lords of marriage and kept the ruling dynasty up-to-date about the bureau's workings in his monthly reports.[105] Urban government was required to follow state rules on limiting admissions to civic rights, guild status, and the estate of matrimony.[106]

All in all, the bureau advanced the cause of creating a community of orthodox, honorable, and financially stable burghers centered on married households.[107] Its officials were there to secure public order in Munich through the exclusion of economically and morally undesirable people. They also scrutinized the religious reliability of any applicant who was a stranger to civic authorities, inquiring "above all things what his religion is, whether he ever was fond of another religion . . . and through which means he came to our religion."[108] Applicants had to visit a local priest in the company of a designated city councilor, receive religious instruction, go to confession, and proclaim Trent's statement of faith before their application was considered.[109]

Only those with a fortune of 100 to 150 Gulden or more were eligible to apply for the status of citizen. The lords of marriage charged various fees based on the applicants' wealth and their gender. A "full" male burgher paid 6 to 7 Gulden "burgher money" (so-called defense money after 1601), plus 3 Kreuzer, 6 Denari "small money," something akin to a processing fee.[110]

Being married (hence, performing reproductive sex) was a chief marker for the burghers of Catholic Munich, regardless of the Tridentine claims that chastity outshone matrimony in the eyes of God. Strangers who applied for civic rights were not admitted to their final plea in front of the city council until after they had held their wedding.[111] The sons of burghers obtained complete civic rights only at the time of their marriage, when their kin made the necessary payments on their behalf: the full male burgher was always a married man; his civic rights included the right to have sex.[112]

Couples who wanted to get married in Munich first needed to obtain a license at the bureau, which meant they had to bring proof that their joint property amounted to no less than 100 Gulden. Men needed to document a fortune of at least 60 Gulden, not counting the earning potential of their profession or their household goods. Similarly, women's assets needed to amount to at least 40 Gulden, independent of their personal belongings, such as clothing.[113] Short of such proof, the unions between men and women automatically fell into the category of "profligate marriages." Because profligacy constituted a serious defiance of the bureau's authority, it was punishable with expulsion from the urban community.[114]

"By far more wealth" was required if an applicant came from one of the poorer surrounding villages and had not worked as a servant in Munich.[115] Obviously greater financial power had to make up for the lack of social credit of less desirable applicants. In the same spirit, the initial practice of having all applicants swear an oath regarding the size of their fortune was soon abandoned in favor of a more selective practice that limited admittance to the oath to "credible," "honest and unsuspicious" people.[116] All others had to submit to an assessment of their wealth in the presence of a scribe (in the seventeenth century always a procurator)[117] and, ideally, they offered evidence of their economic standing in the form of cash.[118]

Most important, all applicants had to provide between four and six local guarantors who vouched for their reliability in economic matters. For a period of seven years, these guarantors were held liable to step into the breach should the applicants themselves ever be unable to make ends meet and thus become a burden to public welfare. The potential financial obligations of guarantors made for a limited pool of those who could take on the task. They had to have a "pretty good fortune" and, as a rule, could not give surety for more than three people.[119] Within these dimensions, the system of guarantors appears to have operated as a patronage system, filtering applicants and opening the city's gates to a limited number of clients. The system of mandatory guarantors also assured parents of having some say in marital matters. Just like other applicants, the unmarried children of burghers had to provide guarantors, who in all likelihood would include their kin.[120]

The lords of marriage finally assumed the function of police agents whose task it was to report violations against marriage ordinances to the city council. Among the various offenses, clandestine marriages (*Winkelheiraten*) and profligate marriages (*leichtfertige Heiraten*) stood out as undermining the very mission of the Hochzeitsamt. These terms referred to unions between people who were either too young or too poor in the eyes of the municipal government. State and civic government defined clandestine marriages as marriages that lacked not only ecclesiastical solemnization but, more crucially, the approval of secular authorities.[121] Profligate marriages, on the other hand, were those that bypassed the economic barriers to participation in the community of married burghers. The equivocal meaning of *leichtfertig* or profligate—connoting lewd as well as economically thoughtless behavior—is perhaps the most poignant illustration of the equation of nonmarital sexuality with the sexual unions of the propertyless no matter how stable or consensual such unions might otherwise be.[122]

Munich's bureau of marriage was established around the same time that clerics in the Bavarian capital first began to read and explain Tridentine marital doctrine to their parishioners. Tridentine attempts at sexual regulation thus existed alongside secular attempts at social regulation from the start. Not coincidentally, the city government at this point also threatened profligate servants and their families with exile "so that such young people will first think about how they will support themselves and their children before they get married."[123] The Tridentine messages about marriage as a sacrament and sole site of legitimate sexuality intersected with political measures against some marriages—those among people deemed too poor, or too young, or simply destined to serve. Over time Tridentine notions of marriage were going to be eclipsed by more class-bound conceptions and subsumed under the secular goal of prohibiting certain types of marriages. Instead of *sin* and *salvation,* the key terms became *wealth* and *poverty, sedentary* and *vagrant,* or *master* and *servant.*

When Munich's secular government formulated its policies against servants and economically disempowered groups, it looked to the magistrate of neighboring Augsburg for legislative models.[124] That the avowedly Catholic magistrate took its cue from the city fathers of a formerly Protestant stronghold and now biconfessional town indicates that doctrinal difference was of secondary importance in matters of marriage and sexuality. Much more crucial were considerations of public order driven by the logic of a subsistence economy. Governments of any religious persuasion grappled with the distribution of limited resources and the restraint of sexual activity that scarcity seemed to dictate. It was only through the political grappling with this logic that the inherently ambiguous and unstable meaning of religious doctrines became fixed in practice.

Scrutinizing the religious as well as financial reliability of applicants, Munich's bureau of marriage in effect worked to secure public order by excluding economically and morally undesirable people from the civic community. In so doing, it transposed a set of values that had evolved within the milieu of the guilds[125] and among patricians with a vested interest in protecting family property onto the civic community at large. When government officials defined profligacy as a problem, what they really defined was something else: profligacy became code for who did and who did not belong to the urban community. A bourgeois morality constituted itself up and against an entire social stratum, many of them from the surrounding countryside, as it criminalized their sexual unions. The new restrictions thus created an entirely new category of sexual disorder, and they might even have increased the tendency toward profligate unions, as more people found themselves unable to afford legal marriages and hence were forced to avoid them. Either way, the result was a deepening of already existing social divides.

In the Tridentine scheme of things, marriage set the laity apart from the clergy. In the urban universe, it also distinguished the haves from the have-nots. Whereas these legal and institutional trends augmented the rule of propertied husbands and fathers, they pushed men of lesser economic means to walk away from the obligations and privileges of marriage and fatherhood. The same trends heightened pressure on women to subordinate themselves to a male head of a household and to retain their virginity outside of marriage. As regards the sacramental nature of matrimony, the virginal female body played a key role in conferring sanctity upon marriage and marital sexual relations. As regards the secular construction of marriage as economic partnership and privilege of the propertied, the female virginal body played an equally important role. For wealthier social strata, virginity prior to marriage protected the transmission of property in an increasingly patrilineal kinship system. The virginity of lower-class women, on the other hand, promised to secure the state the prevention of sexual unions and procreation among the poor.

CHAPTER 2

Nuns and Whores: Houses of Women in the Male Public Sphere

For women the greater importance of male-headed households for public order meant that female respectability became tied ever more strongly to being under the supervision of a man at the helm of a household community. This development was especially consequential for women who did not wish to or were not able to integrate into the patriarchal household system of propertied Catholics. The fate of these "unassimilated women" lies at the center of the following discussion—poor women, religious women, prostitutes, and nuns. While we have learned to situate nunneries and brothels at opposite ends of the social, sexual, and moral spectrum, early moderns perceived them as belonging to the same institutional universe. They categorized the two institutions as "houses of women" (*Frauenhäuser*), their unmarried inhabitants set apart from male-headed households and not (yet) defined by the presence or absence of sexual relations.

The modern distance from this early modern association is itself a long-term result of the changes in female institutions triggered by the Reformation-inspired crisis over the relationship among sexuality, spirituality, and state power. This chapter highlights points of connection between the institutional histories of brothels and convents. It shows that the sixteenth-century reforms of these two all-female institutions worked toward producing a new public order or "state of virginity" in the Bavarian capital. Both the nun and the prostitute became more sharply defined in terms of their gender and their class. Whereas the prostitute began to embody the sexualized lower-class woman whose body threatened to pollute the Catholic community, the nun was destined to represent the upper-class virgin whose purity (and class) promised and symbolized the intactness of the same community and its immunity against social, sexual, and spiritual pollution.

Secular Houses of Women: Poverty, Promiscuity, and Paternalism in the Middle Ages

In 1597, at the initiative of the Wittelsbach court, Munich was the last major city in Germany to shut down its civic brothel (*gemeine Frauenhaus*).[1] The closing of Munich's brothel marked the completion of a century-long process of sorting out permissible and nonpermissible heterosexual activity through the definition and regulation of prostitution. At the beginning of this process, boundaries between married and nonmarried were porous, and there existed a cultural category—the *Frauenhaus*—to legitimate female lives that pivoted neither on sexual relations with men nor on the renunciation of these relations. During the Middle Ages any house inhabited by women and without a male head of household was called a *Frauenhaus*. A merely descriptive and value-neutral term, it referred to dwellings as varied in nature and function as female-headed households, houses associated with prostitution, or women's religious communities.[2] Not the absence or presence of men and/or sexual relations with them, but the primacy of female affiliation defined the *Frauenhaus*.

In the same vein, medieval attitudes toward female honor and sin were flexible and informed by sensitivity toward the social circumstances of sexual behavior. Governing authorities displayed an awareness of the connection between economic destitution and what they considered improper sexual deportment. While they did not condone promiscuity among the poor, they opted for a paternalistic and protectionist rather than an outright criminalizing and punishing approach to this "social problem."

Officials were especially cognizant of the perilous position of impoverished women whose meager options on occasion swayed them to barter their sexual honor in return for economic support. When Bavarian magistrates set up dowry foundations for poor women in the early fifteenth century, they underscored economics' impeding effects on moral behavior. The rationale was that "the daughter of a poor man often falls into impurity and loses the crown of her virginity because father and mother are so poor."[3]

A similar blend of protective paternalism and moral condemnation drove the contemporaneous establishment of civic brothels in Bavaria's towns. Like elsewhere in Europe, the founding of a common house of women in Munich expressed the need of local authorities to establish themselves as guardians of civic peace and public morality.[4] Munich's officials opened the brothel's doors in 1437 for two explicit reasons. First, they hoped that the existence of such a house would make it easier for the so-called common daughters (*gemaine dochterlein*) to remain in the city.

As the very label suggests, these women were considered a public charge as well as public property, which brings us to the second reason for their incorporation into the civic community. The magistrate also pinned its hope on the preventive function of a publicly sanctioned house of prostitution, arguing that "many things perpetrated on women and virgins could be prohibited."[5]

The institutionalization of prostitution, in other words, aimed at the protection of women. It was meant to shield the city's honorable women from a fall into dishonor by directing a socially disruptive and damaging form of male sexuality away from them. At the same time, the establishment of a civic brothel also offered a modicum of protection to the less reputable common daughters, apparently often vagrant women, by providing them with a permanent home and legal regulation. The magistrate put a civic official, the so-called master of women (*Frauenmeister*), in charge of affairs in the civic brothel and issued a special ordinance for him (*Frauenmeisterordnung*), which regulated his dealings with the women and which he vowed to observe upon taking office.

The ordinance stipulated how much the master could charge per customer, what kinds of services he owed to the women, and what rights the women enjoyed in turn. It also granted the master a certain amount of policing and corrective power, such as asking him to report suspicious customers to the city council and to make sure that the women under his care refrained from work on Church holidays and attended services instead.[6]

In official urban understandings of the late fifteenth century, life in the civic brothel represented a liminal state in two senses of the word. It relegated common daughters to the city's periphery, a geographic placement reflective of their marginal social standing. This life on the border, however, could also turn into a passage toward a more reputable existence: urban rituals, perceptions, and treatment of prostitutes as well as the social practices associated with the common house of women testify to this possibility of crossing over into respectable society.

During Munich's annual great fair (*Jakobidult*), for example, prostitutes competed in a public race for a piece of linen (*Barchant*), a material that was traditionally included in a woman's dowry.[7] The award of linen became of use for Munich's common daughters from 1488 onward, after the city council granted women in the brothel the right to get married.[8] Interestingly, the prostitutes' race took place on the fair grounds in close proximity to the convent of Poor Clares; a renowned pilgrimage to the cloister church customarily followed on the heels of the fair. The cloistered nuns and the common daughters, this illustrates, had an equally exposed and important symbolic position in the urban cycles of merriment and repentance.

If one could easily reverse the dishonor of temporary prostitution through marriage, it was equally possible to atone for the religious guilt that might be associated with this brand of nonmarital sexuality. Stories of former prostitutes turned saints proliferated in the late Middle Ages and enjoyed great popularity.[9] Together with the flourishing Mary Magdalen movement, which furnished ex-harlots with an institutional space and a religious vocation, this hagiography testifies to a flexibility of both cultural categories, that of the "prostitute" and that of the "female religious woman." In Munich, the renowned Franciscan preacher Capistrano persuaded several prostitutes with fiery sermons to change their ways and leave the life of sin in 1454. By the early sixteenth century, the magistrate resolved to make systematic efforts to promote the conversion of prostitutes and promised the brothel manager a financial award from the city's coffer whenever a woman in his charge turned her back on the common house of women.[10]

There are other indications that late medieval understandings of prostitution, while not free of discriminatory elements, were still malleable. The majority of female residents in Germany's civic brothels came from the lower social strata and were known as *Dirnen,* a label with multiple meanings ranging from "young woman" to "maidservant" to "harlot." Differently put, the life of a poor unmarried woman who might accept much-needed monetary gifts from a lover and the life of a woman who worked in the civic brothel for pay were situated on an economic and cultural continuum.[11] Promiscuity was part and parcel of the life of the poor, who lacked the financial means to turn a relationship immediately into a permanent, officially sanctioned partnership and set up household. This had negative as well as positive consequences for *Dirnen.* While it reinforced some medieval stereotypes linking poor women's sexuality with venality,[12] it inversely also made allowances for temporary sexual misconduct, as long as economics could be cited as an excuse and an improvement of one's financial situation promised a return to respectability.

Along the same lines, the medieval common house of women was not yet exclusively a center of commercialized sexuality provided by lower-class women. Rather, civic brothels were places of merrymaking where customers gathered in an often decidedly courtly ambiance to fancy themselves experiencing the pleasures of noble life, including unrestrained consumption of wine and food as well as the company of beautiful women. For the same reason, urban governments might even entertain important outside guests during their visits to the city by frequenting the brothel for food, drink, and conversation, but never for sexual pleasure.[13]

Finally, civic brothels were meeting points for urban unmarried youths, even places of courtship. Journeymen accounted for the majority of customers, and some of them indeed chose brides from among the women in the *gemeine Frauenhaus.* There was considerable common ground between journeymen and *Dirnen* to warrant such a choice. *Dirnen* too lived in a state of dependency on a master—in Munich literally the "master of women"—and they labored for wages under his supervision. *Dirnen,* like journeymen, knew the perils and burdens of the vagrant life and therefore were equally keen on settling. Throwing in their lot together, a journeyman and a *Dirne* might very well make it across the threshold of wealth that kept each of them from running a household of their own and joining respectable society. City fathers interested in rehabilitating fallen women willingly gave their approval.[14]

Sexualizing the *Frauenhaus,* Prostituting the Lower-Class Woman

Over time, a regime of seclusion and a reduction to sexual relations supplanted the culture of convivial interaction in the brothel and replaced the permeable borders between the world of the *Dirnen* and the larger urban community with rigid divides. This trend first arose from within the guilds in the course of the fifteenth century and in conjunction with a new value system. Stiffening competition for guild admission drove the emergence of a household ethic that stressed sedentariness, marriage, and patriarchal household governance and based its key concepts of honorability on marital sexual relations and legitimate births.[15] Journeymen, as they grew progressively more desperate to break into the closing ranks and become married guild masters, experienced pressure to embrace the mores of the desired circle, an ideological membership that could substitute for the unachievable social one. As a result, these young men felt the urge to distance themselves from the lower classes associated with a vagrant, promiscuous, and hence dishonorable existence.[16]

This was the larger context for the guild authorities' efforts to prohibit the association of journeymen and *Dirnen,* or at least to confine their involvement to sexual relations in the brothel itself. Members of Munich's blacksmiths' and wagoners' guilds, for instance, were ordered to stay away from common women, should they encounter them while enjoying a glass of wine in one of the city's taverns or during a guild gathering.[17] Journeymen of the cutlers' guild faced disciplinary measures should they be caught "lying in the house of women during day time."[18]

Such regulations touted a notion of the civic brothel and its inmates that contrasted with the more open-minded and protective attitude of the medieval magistrate. The common house of women, in this new view, was no longer a site of conviviality and honorable sexual relations. It had more limited use as a sexual safety valve for journeymen condemned to years of waiting for marriage and masterhood. In other words, it served their protection and that of their married male guild associates, who had an interest in keeping the younger men away from the women in their household. The women in the brothel, who were once redeemable sinners and possible candidates for marriage, were reduced to an outlet for young men's otherwise uncontrollable lust. It was but a short step from this development to blaming these involuntary objects of male desire for the acting out of desire itself.

Not coincidentally, the fifteenth century also witnessed a growing cultural differentiation between brothels and other houses of women based on the criterion of the dwelling's accessibility to men. What was supposed to set the brothel apart among houses of women was its unqualified and publicly sanctioned openness to men, earning it the distinction of being the so-called *offene Frauenhaus*. It was an "open house," and it is no accident that the term *öffentlich* (public) derives from *offen* (open). The etymology reflects the emergence of a particular kind of public sphere reserved for men. Women who ventured into this public risked being labeled not respectable. At the same time, and as a result of this redefinition, any other house of women that kept its doors open to men automatically moved closer to prostitution on the plane of social perception. By the end of the fifteenth century, the shift in the cultural understanding of houses of women was complete. No longer an encompassing and delineating label, *Frauenhaus* became a synonym for brothel, a sexualized and altogether pejorative term.[19]

The Reformation produced theological justification for the guilds' censure of brothels and rallied support among city fathers and the larger urban community for the abolition of this civic institution. The reformers conceived of sexual activity as a human need that was as natural and inescapable as the need for food or sleep. Perilously powerful if improperly handled, this need for sexuality was best met within the morally safe sphere of marriage.[20] Stressing the naturalness and sanctity of marital sexuality, the Protestant debates on sex and marriage broadened the concept of *Hurerei* (whoring or prostitution) to encompass the entire range of sexual relations outside of the divinely ordained estate of matrimony.[21] Commercialized sex figured as a social pollutant in this sexual discourse, the polar opposite of the purifying powers of marital intimacy. *Dirnen* embodied danger of the first order. Martin Luther's vitriolic tirades against "dreadful, scabby, stinking, loathsome, syphilitic [whores]," who ought to be "broken on the wheel and flayed," capture this conception of the *Dirne* as bearer of a social and sexual disease.[22]

Munich's magistrate, even though officially Catholic and patrician-dominated, nonetheless showed itself susceptible to the guild ideas about sexuality and marriage, on which the Protestant reformers elaborated.[23] The 1531 Ordinance Against Vices proves the point. After blaming the sins of individuals for the age's social ills, the magistrate proceeded to fulminate mainly against nonmarital sexual activity. Promiscuous women, married and unmarried alike, appear as the main culprits in the magistrate's moral tale of a social order going to pieces. Hence, the ordinance called for new disciplinary measures:

> Should they [promiscuous women] fall into the hands of the brothel manager (*Frauenwirt*), he shall have the power and authority to take them into the common house . . . and keep them there until they change their lives from sin and shame to penance and honor.[24]

The civic brothel, formerly a place of merriment and even courtship, appears as an institution for correction and confinement here. The ordinance's shaming tone highlights the transformation. The brothel manager was authorized to arrest and detain any woman who strayed from the path of normative sexuality for the purpose of deterring other women from following in her footsteps. If there had to be nonmarital sex, the city fathers were bent on restricting it to one location under the supervision of a civic correction officer.[25] It was only logical that the city fathers put two women into civic jail in 1532 after they attempted to escape from the confines of the brothel.[26]

The outcome of these disciplinary measures was a sharpening of the very definition of prostitution. During the first half of the sixteenth century, the common house of women was officially designated as the sole site of tolerable sex outside of marriage and dedicated exclusively to commercialized sexuality. As such, the reformed civic brothel offered a set of criteria by which the fuzzy medieval meanings of prostitution could be brought into sharp focus, turning it into the polar opposite of monogamous marriage. The *Dirnen* in the civic brothel, like wives in patriarchal households, were consigned to a status of subordination under their master; unlike wives, however, they were the property not just of one but of all men and hence by definition dishonorable.

The common women's deteriorating position soon led to their complete exclusion from the larger community. Munich's authorities abolished the traditional public prostitute race for a piece of dowry linen during the annual fair (*Jakobidult*) in 1562.[27] In 1597, the court initiated the abolition of Munich's brothel, and the magistrate obliged willingly. One half of the female inhabitants retired to a life behind convent walls; the other collected dowry money from the court and set out to find a spouse.

Munich's purification from prostitution thus occurred on two levels: on a collective level, through the closing of the brothel; and on an individual level, through funneling its inhabitants into the honorable institutions of cloister and marriage. The celibate life and the married life, as the twofold institutional destiny of these women illustrates, were the new places of purity in the post-Trent urban community.

It was not merely a chronological coincidence that the court entrusted Munich's highest judge with the task of prosecuting profligate unions in the city around the time it ordered the closing of the brothel.[28] The abolition of publicly sponsored prostitution belongs within the larger context of the anti-profligacy campaign that targeted nonmarital sexuality, particularly of the lower classes. In this respect, the events in Munich corroborate Beate Schuster's thesis that the history of the brothel was but a subplot in an overarching German story of increasing intolerance toward the vagrant poor in general and toward women living on their own in particular.[29]

Munich's court and civic authorities deployed an array of legislative and disciplinary measures in order to purge the urban community of the profligate poor, vagrants, and beggars in the closing decades of the sixteenth century. The post-Trent politics of exclusion gradually recast poverty and vagrancy, which had provided reasons and even plausible excuses for promiscuous behavior, as signifiers of unacceptable profligacy. In contrast to a paternalistic understanding proffered to the impoverished in medieval Munich, a harsh view of poverty and sin came to prevail in the capital.[30]

The discriminatory politics had special measures in store for single women. Munich's magistrate, in line with city fathers all over Germany, for the first time passed laws against so-called masterless women, forbidding them to take up residence behind city walls. According to a council decision of 1596, vagrant women who were caught in the city for the first time had to take an oath that they were prepared to leave voluntarily. Second-time violators were subject to involuntary expulsion. Should these single women be caught inside the walls for the third time, they were to be put on display in the pillory before the executioner led them outside the city's gates. Subsequent entries in the council minutes indicate the seriousness of the magistrate in enforcing these measures.[31]

While steps against single women and female-headed households were initially aimed at outsiders, the city council soon put the right to "have their own smoke" and "earn their own bread" off limits for the daughters of citizens too.[32] Economic circumstances exacerbated the negative impact of the magistrate's legal measures against female-headed households, since the early modern labor market grew much more hostile to women's participation than its medieval variant.[33] Life without a man carried not only the danger of stigmatization but of destitution. Both in 1619 and in 1651 widows accounted for 51 percent of the poorest taxpayers in the Bavarian capital, single women for 14.0 percent and 14.9 percent respectively: approximately 65 percent of Munich's most impoverished burghers were "women alone."[34]

The institutional history of common houses of women was simultaneously part of these larger discriminatory trends and a formative force in their unfolding. If already some medieval stereotypes had confounded the sexual activity of single women, especially poor women, with venality, the rise and fall of urban brothels cemented this conflation, obliterating alternative, more flexible understandings in the process. The "sexualization" of the brothel in the early sixteenth century made prostitutes an identifiable group in the first place, as it turned the *Frauenhaus* into the only tolerable and tolerated site of nonmarital sex. The brothel closing of the late sixteenth century, by contrast, implied that prostitutes could in theory now be everywhere, while any form of nonmarital sex became akin to prostitution.[35] The institution, even in its final gasp, thus did significant definitional and discriminatory work, amplifying the already growing distrust in single women, who stood outside the system of householders.

Although these developments vicariously had an impact on all women, most of all they affected lower-class women who engaged in sexual relationships with men. The poor woman, who could not afford a sedentary existence and bargained her sexual honor in the hope of settling as a married woman, began to run the risk of being labeled a harlot. The blurry boundary between prostitution and permissible promiscuity leading up to marriage was disappearing, and with it the moral leeway it accorded lower-class women.

By the early seventeenth century, Munich's civic dowry foundation recorded a revealing change in its stated purpose. Initially set up to help poor women avoid a fall into prostitution, the foundation now made support of normative life choices its overriding concern, rather than the applicants' financial dire straits. The funds were designated for "virgins when they wanted to get married or otherwise enter the religious estate."[36] Clearly, the Tridentine's dictum for women—*aut murus, aut maritus*—had made its mark on Munich's institutional apparatus, and so had the Counter-Reformation's elevation of female virginity. The dark side of this trend was an intensifying discrimination against single women, whose way of life ran counter to the Trent-inspired norm. Together with the economic disadvantages of being a "woman alone" and the pressure of anti-profligacy measures to abstain from sexual relations, this discrimination was a mainstay of the state's attempt to build a society of propertied householders, whose privileges entailed the privilege of state-sanctioned sexual activity.

Religious Houses of Women: Open Doors and Social Services in the Middle Ages

The history of Munich's so-called Ridler and Pütrich communities provides a revealing foil to the history of the common house of women. The
two religious houses of women came into existence when the term *Frauenhaus* still had its neutral connotation. As open communities whose members lived lives of self-directed piety and interaction with the urban community, these houses of laywomen were on the fringes of organized piety.
Over the span of centuries and through repeated reforms, however, their
female inhabitants were forced to find their way into the Franciscan fold
as tertiaries and then to become cloistered nuns under the wing of the Tridentine church. The evolution of these institutions therefore exemplifies
key issues surrounding religious houses of women from the Middle Ages
through the Counter-Reformation; women, it reveals, were a primary
object of ecclesiastical boundary-drawing between the sacred and the profane. In addition, the history of these communities shows that the history
of religious houses of women, like the history of secular houses of women,
was tightly connected to changing attitudes toward marriage and sexuality
and also to shifting conceptions of public order and the place of single
women in society.

Wedged between the ducal court and the houses of burghers, the two
women's communities together with the adjacent convent of the Minor
Brethren formed the Franciscan quarter in medieval Munich.[37] This complex of Franciscan houses had its origins in the late Middle Ages, when the
young city was growing by leaps and bounds and the urban landscape of
religious institutions was taking on contours. A cloister of Augustinian
Eremites and a convent of Poor Clares, which were located further in the
outskirts, represented the other two dominant fixtures on the city's map of
religious establishments. Strewn in between the preeminent cloistered
areas were a dozen dwellings with chapels owned by nonlocal cloisters or
the bishop of Freising. A number of small female lay congregations—so-
called soul-houses (*Seelhäuser*)—completed the picture of religious houses
in pre-Trent Munich.[38]

The architectural triangle of court, burgher homes, and male convent
that demarcated the physical boundaries of the Ridler and Pütrich community also signified the field of forces shaping the history of these
women's congregations. During the early days, patrician patronage featured prominently, since powerful families founded the two soul-houses
that were the institutional forerunners of the Ridler and Pütrich convents.[39] The exclusively female residents of these houses met crucial needs
in the city. They devoted their time to the care of the sick and dying,

attending to their fellows' needs within their community and also in private homes. The general care of the soul, which earned the sisters the title "soul-nuns" (*Seelnonnen*), extended beyond the deathbed. The women accompanied bodies to their place of last rest, where they performed dirges and vigils. As civic mourners, they finally took care of annual commemorative prayers for the dead.[40]

While soul-sisters met urban needs in general, the physical and spiritual needs of sponsoring families enjoyed priority treatment. It is difficult to assess precisely to what degree the soul-houses served those particular families as residential homes for their unmarried women. Ridler family members equipped the communal house with glass windows.[41] A luxurious item, rarely found at the time, these windows clearly served purposes of representation worthy of a patrician residence. The mixed composition of the communities—including widows, older female servants, and women without a husband or without work—further supports the assumption that patrician sponsors treated these houses as a possible retreat for or even an extension of their *familia*.[42] It also shows that these houses, while tied to wealthier social strata, nonetheless made room for women of lower station and lesser means.

There was no firm rule to govern the community, nor did an impermeable wall shield the women from the world. Rather, activist forms of piety, transitory residential arrangements, and close affiliation with families intertwined to create a flexible way of life. The women's tasks, by their very nature, necessitated frequent forays into the larger urban environment. Beyond these temporary absences, the possibility of leaving the community for good remained open to the female inhabitants.

While this lack of regulation was compatible with the interests of the communities' residents and many of Munich's burghers, initiatives for more control came from other quarters. Guilds repeatedly strove to limit the existence of open religious houses of women. The economic vagaries of unlocked female religious communities had their inmates resort to textile work in times of need, which the guilds considered an infringement on the markets they claimed as theirs alone and sought to protect against female workers in particular.[43]

More crucially, the Bavarian princes took an interest in the two women's communities shortly after the court first took up residence in Munich. Their interference in the convents' affairs was part of a larger undertaking to place their rule on a religious foundation by cultivating close ties with the Franciscan order and to stake out a claim to the regulation of public order in the city. Ludwig the Strict (1253–94) initiated the building of a new Franciscan convent in close proximity to the court. The year the Friars moved, the court provided a generous endowment to transform their old convent into a nunnery of Poor Clares, the so-called Angerkloster, named after its location on a pasture in Munich's outskirts. The convent fulfilled tasks for the ducal family that were analogous to those the soul-houses fulfilled for patrician families. The sisters, for instance, were required to recite prayers on behalf of the souls of the duke, his brother, and their descendants.[44]

Simultaneously, the court began to extend its grasp to some patrician soul-houses and to utilize the spiritual and social services of their inhabitants for its own purposes. Ludwig the Strict thus ordered the incorporation of the Pütrich convent in the Franciscan order and the imposition of the tertiary rule upon the community. The Friars, whom Ludwig had set up near his court and relied on for spiritual guidance, were charged with the supervision of the sisters in order to counter "all kinds of nuisance" associated with uncloistered women.[45]

Yet the new regime apparently made little difference at first. Open doors and also an open attitude toward some worldly pleasures remained distinctive characteristics of these female religious houses. A Franciscan visitor named Vinzenz Ridler learned this much when faced with the task of updating the rules for the Ridler and Pütrich sisters more than a century later.[46] His book of revised regulations conveys the picture of a community where private property, including jewelry, money, and fur coats, had been the norm and the presence of outsiders a matter of course.[47]

Not only clerics paid regular visits to the women's communities but also secular men. Some male guests seem to have persuaded sisters to choose matrimony over the religious life. Several women in the Ridler tertiary house "married out of it and took husbands," and the trend prompted the issuance of a papal breviary in 1396. Interestingly, the breviary threatened not only the female offenders with excommunication. It held the same measure in store for any man brazen enough to look for a wife in the soul-house.[48] Like their less reputed secular counterparts, these religious houses of women apparently offered possibilities for gatherings with and courtship of women who donned noble accessories.[49]

It was in the late fifteenth century, around the time that the term *Frauenhaus* lost its purely descriptive character and connoted instead the social danger of disorderly women, that Munich's female religious houses finally experienced the winds of change. The collective memory of the Ridler and Pütrich sisters later identified this event as the convents' "first great reformation," which only the second, Tridentine reformation would supersede.

Again, the impetus for reform came from the Bavarian court, which was rebuilding its alliance with the Franciscan brethren. Duke Albrecht IV intervened in the contemporary Franciscan controversy over apostolic poverty to side with the Observants whose uncompromising refusal of property appealed to him, since it legitimated the state's appropriation of ecclesiastical resources. Albrecht drove their opponents, the more lenient Conventuals, out of his city in 1480. He entrusted the Observants with the renewal of religious discipline in the local Franciscan houses, paying particular attention to issues of property and propriety.[50]

One result of Albrecht's efforts was a first, rather short-lived reorganization of affairs in the convent of Poor Clares. It culminated in the (failed) attempt of the abbess and several sisters to escape from the nunnery and rescue valuables from the reformers' disdain for property. The brethren subsequently removed the most defiant women and replaced them with docile nuns from Nuremberg, ensuring the permanent triumph of the new disciplinary regime.[51] During the stormy times of the Reformation and Counter-Reformation, this female convent indeed became a spiritual stronghold of Catholicism in Munich.[52]

Reform wore a somewhat different face in the Ridler and Pütrich tertiary communities. There the goal consisted of raising the two congregations to the status of a true religious order with its attendant privileges, such as exemptions from civic taxes,[53] and also its obligations, such as stricter monastic discipline. In 1483, the Observant Visitor to the Ridler convent, Johannes Alphart, thus interdicted the custom of "roaming around the city hither and thither" to attend sermons and go to confession wherever the sisters felt like.[54] He assigned a special confessor and decreed a stiffer version of the rules of 1369, which bound the women more closely to the confines of their house and prohibited the possession of private property. Over one-third of the Ridler sisters decided to abandon the community rather than their old ways.[55]

Reforms took an even greater toll among the women in the Pütrich convent. With a single exception, the sisters left the community in 1484 "because they did not want to renounce property" and did not want to take permanent vows.[56] They stripped the soul-house of their possessions and moved into a new dwelling in the city of Freising, where Munich's bishop resided. The bishop personally selected lodgings for the sisters, in which they continued to carry out their mission of attending to the sick.[57]

Spaces for this kind of less structured community obviously still existed in Bavaria, and so did the possibility of simply leaving a female convent community. In Munich, too, patrician families founded uncloistered soul-houses as late as 1487 and 1495.[58] Within the immediate orbit of Munich's court, however, there was no longer room for a religious community that served the larger public and accordingly enjoyed a degree of openness. The Wittelsbachs had discovered the importance of the spiritual resources these women represented—a discovery that was to shape their dealings with the convents during the confessional age.

Sexualizing Nuns, Spiritualizing Convents: Protestant and Catholic Reforms

The "wanton nun" and the "lewd monk" were stock characters in the rhetorical and iconographic armory of Protestant reformers, stirring up powerful waves of anticlericalism among Germany's people. As reformers made the case that sexuality was a human need and hence natural and inescapable, the allegedly amoral state of Catholic religious houses served as empirical evidence for their theological assertions. Monastics became embodiments of contested doctrines, held up by Protestant preachers and pamphleteers as living proof of the falsity of Catholic claims.

Although both monks and nuns suffered accusations of sexual misconduct, this type of charge was more likely to stick to convents. The institutional resemblances and parallels in way of life between religious houses of women and common houses of women proved particularly consequential in this respect. Nuns and prostitutes wore special clothes, eschewed matrimony, and inhabited separate institutional spaces. The two groups of unmarried women enjoyed a certain amount of power and independence, yet they were simultaneously deemed servants of the common good and the larger community on behalf of which they carried out their respective tasks.[59]

Once the Reformation had thrust existing understandings of marriage and sexuality into flux, the numerous structural and symbolic parallels between nuns and prostitutes quickly turned the behavior of religious women, and not the conduct of religious men, into the primary measurement for gauging the theological credibility of Catholics and Protestants. The specter of the convent as a brothel in disguise featured as centrally in the later Catholic counterdiscourse on convent reform as it did from the start in the Protestant discourse on the dissolution of female monastic houses. In both instances, the openness of female religious houses and their accessibility to men were read in sexual terms.

In the well-documented debate over the dissolution of Nuremberg's house of Poor Clares, the nuns played on precisely this fear of convents as brothels, when they cautioned city fathers against opening the convent doors to Lutheran preachers. The preachers had their minds set on "all kinds of liberty and carnality," the women argued, hence it can "be predicted that soon our locked cloister will be an open house, everybody will run in and out whenever he wants to."[60] Magistrates and kin were clearly susceptible to these arguments. Willibald Pirkheimer, brother of abbess Caritas and father of sister Katharina, threatened "to pull them out by their hair before he would let them remain in an open cloister."[61]

After a Lutheran preacher and several of his friends entered the convent and proposed marriage to several nuns, an angry faction formed in the council and pushed for a policy of closed doors. Their reasoning further illuminates the pivotal place of the convent-turned-brothel in the Protestant-inspired discourse on female religious houses.

> Dear men, with what do you want to be indicted that you bring upon yourselves such a disgrace? You have your blood and flesh, your children and daughters, your sisters, your aunts and nieces, and many of them in the cloisters; is it going to be granted to any lad to go in and out? . . . they will be open, common houses rather than cloisters.[62]

The language of honor and kinship, linking as it does the nuns' proper sexual conduct to the moral standing of their male relatives, also bespeaks the centrality of class issues in the discourse on nuns and whores. Even Protestant polities, which negated the spiritual value of convents, could not ignore their social function. Female religious houses traditionally served the upper classes as sites of patrimonial strategizing and a depository for unmarried daughters regardless of the women's specific spiritual disposition. It was simply not feasible to abolish the convents and marry all former nuns, many of them old, according to their families' station. Unlike monks, who could become preachers or scholars, religious women had no alternative vocations available to them.

With the abolition of the brothels, the fate of unmarried former nuns ironically took on even greater urgency and heightened the need for an honorable refuge. After the brothel closed its doors and the common women were set free, one could encounter prostitutes possibly anywhere. Convents therefore represented an institutional means of maintaining the difference between the unrestrained lower-class prostitute and the upper-class unmarried woman.

The unresolved issue of placing unmarriageable women helps explain why Protestant rulers on occasion abandoned any theological scruples for the comfort of keeping their upper-class women in an honorable setting. In a number of instances in which abolition proved particularly tricky, Protestants thus acquiesced to the mere conversion of the convents, leaving us with a historical contradiction in terms: a Protestant nunnery.[63] Nominally Lutheran, these female religious houses presented families with an institutional safeguard of their daughters' virginity.

In addition, such institutions offered a range of other services. The surviving female religious communities in Strasbourg, for example, instructed the city's girls not only in Protestant doctrine but, equally crucially, taught them domestic skills and proper behavior.[64] Carrying out a multiplicity of social functions, these women's communities were able to secure the approval of the magistrate and the local elite, including some of the most avowed Protestant families. They adopted the institutional label *Zuchthäuser,* houses of discipline and decorum, to indicate their new mission as educational institutions and advertise their ongoing utility.[65]

It is telling that the only Strasbourg convent to suffer dissolution at the hands of the magistrate later in the sixteenth century fell prey to the charge of operating as an undercover brothel.[66] City fathers were apparently quite willing to compromise theological positions, as long as convents offered useful social services. In stripping the female religious houses of their traditional spiritual function by outlawing Catholic worship and ritual, magistrates tried to maintain the convents' traditional social function and use them as places of honorable retreat for women of the upper classes. Yet once the stigma of sexual misconduct, in particular the dreaded image of the convent as brothel, attached itself to a female religious house, it instantaneously made the institution useless from the viewpoint of magistrates and elite families.

The attempt to reduce convents to their social function and use them as reputable way stations for women who had not yet reached, or could not reach, their true destination, matrimony, produced its own contradictions, for it implied safeguarding the women's reproductive capacities and bodily integrity. Preserving the virginity of convent inmates, the same "unnatural condition" cited to justify the dissolution of female convents, thus turned into the prime rationale for maintaining these institutions. By focusing on the nun's body as an instrument of sexual and social reproduction, Protestants paradoxically created at once a rationale for both abolishing and keeping female convents as they sexualized their female inmates.

While radically different doctrinal considerations motivated the treatment of convents in Catholic Bavaria in the wake of the Reformation, with authorities focusing on the spiritual rather than the social function of female religious houses, the reforms nonetheless resembled Protestant measures in their new emphasis on nuns as sexual beings. For centuries, the virginal religious life had accorded women the possibility of transcending the limits of their sex and achieving equality with men.[67] The convent reforms decreed at the Council of Trent, however, drew a definite line between nuns and monks, gendering the religious, who could represent a kind of "third gender" during the Middle Ages, unequivocally as women and men. On the one hand, the council fathers stood in a long tradition of clerical attempts to cloister religious women, and they explicitly invoked Boniface VIII's bull Periculoso of 1298, the first papal elaboration of the enclosure norm. Yet the Tridentine application of Periculoso and the larger sociopolitical context in which it took place turned nuns into "women." Discourses that promoted the sexualization and gendering of virginity were thus already available in the late Middle Ages, but the altered circumstances of the Reformation and Counter-Reformation era made these discourses more compelling and more effective institutionally.

The council fathers took a number of measures to reinvigorate the moral and spiritual life of monastics and to address the anticlerical grievances so successfully exploited by Protestants. Monastic spaces were conceptualized as sacred spaces within the world but not of it. A general prohibition on private property among members of a religious order was key to the desired avoidance of worldly contamination.[68] The council further announced that it was no longer permissible for a convent to accept any material goods from parents, kin, or curators of a novice before the person had taken their vows. Financial obligations toward a family should not impede the expulsion of an unsuitable applicant.[69]

Along the same lines, the taking of vows itself was to mark a real rite of passage from the secular to the spiritual sphere. After Trent, monastics fell into two groups: those already initiated and those truly aspiring to initiation. Hence the minimum age for profession was raised to sixteen.[70] Novices had to either take their vows or leave the community altogether immediately after the probationary period had passed.[71]

Significantly, however, the council decreed more regulations for nuns than monks, and it put a premium on reining in female religious conduct.[72] Although this unequal treatment was in line with a long tradition of clerical misgivings about women's moral capabilities, it also reflected a new, post-Reformation ambivalence about the chaste life, which attached itself to the bodies of the female religious. The council fathers indeed debated the merits of virginity in the context of marital reforms, a clear indication of the heightened importance of matrimony and marital sexuality within Counter-Reformation Catholicism.[73] They put off the discussion of convent reform until the very last session of the council, as if hesitant to touch this hot iron.

The increased valorization of marriage and marital intimacy among the Counter-Reformers also expressed itself in a radical reversal of the official Church position on prostitution. The council fathers abandoned centuries of grudging acceptance of prostitution as a "lesser evil," a theory Thomas Aquinas had formulated on the basis of Aristotle. Instead, the Council of Trent took a stance akin to the Protestant position on the subject. Any type of nonmarital sexuality, including the activities of formerly sanctioned public brothels, was treated as an offense to the divinely ordained state of matrimony. In so doing, they authorized the closure of urban brothels in Catholic polities.[74]

At the same time that the Council of Trent authorized the abolition of common houses of women, it opted for strict enclosure and male supervision of religious houses of women as the two central measures of convent reform. The Council of Trent thus recognized convents as an integral part of Catholic society, but it also saw in them a disconcerting memento of the dangers associated with women living on their own. Mandating strict cloister and male control, the Council of Trent laid the doctrinal groundwork for re-creating nunneries in the image of male-headed households with the added component of confinement. The latter would clearly differentiate female religious houses from the open and now unequivocally offensive common house of women and other morally suspect secular houses of women. The former targeted women's religious communities as spaces of all-female governance whose autonomy and power Church authorities were eager to curtail.

After Trent, female communities could not form congregational affiliations with one another. Rather, they were inevitably subject to male supervision by either a bishop or a member of a male order. These restrictions on female religious communities stood in stark contrast to Tridentine male monastic reform, which rested precisely on the formation of congregations and centralization.[75] In advancing a uniform yet gender-specific institutional norm for monastic houses, the ecclesiastical reforms paralleled the secular trend toward a society composed of male-headed households. They too show modernization at work, since they are predicated on the same attempt to homogenize institutions and improve governmental efficiency. Moreover, like their secular counterparts, these ecclesiastical efforts to impose a single institutional norm reflect the centrality of gender to political centralization in the early modern period.[76]

Mandatory enclosure, the second main feature of Tridentine convent reform, further restricted women's ability to exert authority over their communities and in the larger social realm (besides facilitating their differentiation from less reputable open houses of women). Aside from a brief prohibition on unapproved absences of male regulars from their convents, all clauses on cloistering pertained to the female religious.[77] The council ordered women's cloisters in unpopulated areas to move within city walls. Civic fortifications became the outer circle of walls for female convents, while cloister walls constituted an inner barrier. Nuns from urban convents could no longer leave the cloister confines, "not even for a short time" and "under whatever pretext." Conversely, no outsider had permission to intrude in the cloistered area regardless of "his origin or station, sexus or age."[78]

The new directive imposed restoration and even a tightening of discipline in already cloistered communities, while it called for the imposition of sequestration on previously open religious houses. So adamant were the council fathers in advancing this agenda that they had few misgivings about recruiting the help of secular authorities whose influence in ecclesiastical matters they otherwise usually sought to limit. Reminding Christian princes of their duty to support the Church, the council threatened them with excommunication if they refused aid.[79]

By 1566, the Church even extended its requirement of strict enclosure to uncloistered female tertiaries, overriding retroactively the more liberal conditions under which current members had entered.[80] The liminal status of women's tertiary communities, which placed them betwixt and between laity and ecclesiastics, ceased to be acceptable. When viewed in this light, the cloistering of women expresses the Tridentine church's sharper boundary drawings between the sacred and the profane and the ways in which the Church designated women as threats to as well as guardians of boundaries. Male tertiary communities faced no such restrictions of their openness. So it is the larger context of changed clerical attitudes toward religious women and their specific resonance with new trends in secular society that accounts for the enclosure campaign.

The council fathers resorted to Boniface VIII's bull Periculoso of 1298 whose initially ambiguous meaning subsequent commentators had slanted in significant ways in the centuries leading up to the Reformation and Counter-Reformation. Periculoso drew on two incongruous understandings of the female religious life within the Christian tradition. An emphasis on the spiritual equality of monks and nuns was at variance with a stress on the vulnerability of the female sex and hence the need for women's guidance by men. In the centuries following its issuance, commentators on the bull singled out the second strand and spun it further, expatiating on the difference, rather than the equality, between monks and nuns. This difference was anchored, they argued, in the nun's special duty and role as a bride of Christ; it was anchored in her very body whose intactness she was called to preserve. Chastity, in this discourse, became the nun's defining feature and her primary task, whereas vagrancy imperiled its accomplishment. Later commentators accordingly treated the enclosure of women religious as a particularly efficacious means, if not "an end in itself," and concentrated their efforts on the logistical difficulties of imposing complete sequestration.[81]

When the Council of Trent reiterated Periculoso, it not only backed up Periculoso's prescription with specific penalties, but it did so against the backdrop of developments in church and society that would amplify the enclosure norm's gender-specific effects. On the discursive plane, the Protestant debates about marriage and sexuality had advanced an understanding of the nun's body as female and sexual; they had underscored a distrust of unmarried women, especially if they were vagrant. Counter-Reformation Catholicism accorded greater import to matrimony and sexual intimacy, shaping understandings of spiritual matrimony in the process. Even spiritual marriage carried a more decidedly sexual resonance, and the bride of Christ became more fully a woman. To put it differently: the spiral of Protestant discourse and Catholic counterdiscourse resulted in the sexualization of virginity and the gendering of the nun as female.

On the level of social practice, these theological discourses converged with powerful secular trends, such as laws against "masterless women" or the intensifying campaign against any form of nonmarital sexuality. After the abolition of secular brothels—itself an outcome of the convergence of theology and secular legal developments—female religious houses in Germany's Catholic territories would be the only all-female institutions. Their singular status led to an increase in moral expectations for their inmates. It made enclosure an appealing option because it promised a clear differentiation from the disgraceful houses of women that had effectively been defined out of an honorable social and sexual existence by legal and theological means.

But Catholic convent reform, too, had its paradoxes and ironies. While mandatory enclosure certainly safeguarded the chastity and reputation of nuns, it foreclosed the possibility of the active, self-directed spiritual mission the Council of Trent otherwise sought to encourage among the religious.[82] Even before Trent, female orders were pushed toward the pursuit of the contemplative life. Holy virgins, above all consecrated nuns, represented a precious public resource. Endowed with the spiritual powers of the chaste, they served as intercessors for their communities in times of warfare, plague, or other social ills. Secular and ecclesiastical authorities on occasion called for stricter cloistering of these valuable brides of Christ. Yet, in the days before Trent, comings and goings in female religious houses remained the norm, and cloistering a high religious ideal rather than a social dictate. Moreover, it was also possible for an active apostolate to flourish within some female religious communities, such as beguinages or tertiary houses like Munich's Ridler and Pütrich communities.[83]

Tridentine monastic reform legitimated the convents' function as depositories of virginal intercessors between the divine and human society, while it obstructed alternate spiritual paths for religious women. In the wake of Trent, discipline was renewed and rigidified within female contemplative houses. Socially active religious communities, on the other hand, were required to become cloistered communities and to embrace the spiritual labor suitable to life behind closed doors. Tridentine enclosure, however, urged these communities to turn outward at the same time that it restricted them to cloister confines. A life of complete sequestration and contemplation was a costly affair so that Trent's reforms in effect pushed these female houses toward a greater dependence on high dowry payments and financial dependence on wealthy secular patrons. Differently put, the Tridentine prototype of the nun was a virginal, contemplative, and upper-class woman.

Religious Houses of Women: Between Church and State

The story of Munich's Ridler and Pütrich communities highlights the practical difficulties and institutional destiny of Tridentine convent reform. Taken to their logical extreme, the new regulations could replace the permeability of convent walls characteristic of the period before Trent with a regime of sequestration that would certainly purge convents of the dreaded worldly contamination. But this regime would inevitably seal nunneries off from their social environment, on which all of them were more or less dependent and from which many were loath to part. Tridentine enclosure was therefore not necessarily attractive to female convents and their local networks of kin and patrons that had their own vested interests in the status quo. Active resistance on the part of nuns and their local supporters quickly combined with the tenacity of tradition to derail, or at least delay, the cloistering efforts of the Tridentine church in various parts of Europe.[84]

In the case at hand, convent reform meant extricating Munich's two tertiary communities further from their urban matrix and fostering an even closer connection to the Bavarian court. This trend was well under way before the council fathers even concluded their deliberations at Trent. It dated back to medieval reform initiatives under Wittelsbach aegis and accelerated following the "first great reformation" in the fifteenth century.

By the early sixteenth century, the sisters, who were once civic mourners and nurses of Munich's sick, shared intimately the grief of the Wittelsbach dynasty and cared for the physical and spiritual well-being of its descendants, living and dead. When the youngest daughter of Duchess Kunigunde passed away unexpectedly, the Wittelsbach woman turned to the Pütrich convent for help. Kunigunde had cultivated something akin to a friendship with Mother Clara for some time, exchanging letters and visiting one another. During the funerary rites for Kunigunde's daughter

Susanna, Clara carried the body of the child to the grave in her bare arms while Pütrich sisters accompanied her in solemn procession.[85] The duchess bestowed frequent favors on the religious women, and upon her husband's death in 1508, she resolved to spend the remaining days of her life among the sisters. After her death in the Pütrich convent in 1521, the community inherited her furniture, jewelry, a significant amount of money, and several precious objects of devotion, such as, relics, two Christ dolls, and a cradle with Kunigunde's heraldic code.[86]

Wilhelm IV, Kunigunde's son, continued the tradition of exchanging spiritual labor for economic support. He made a generous endowment to the Pütrich and Ridler community in return for the nuns' pledge to perform weekly vigils and requiems in the Franciscan church. Wilhelm, his wife Jacobe, their descendants, and both ducal houses of Bavaria and Baden were the beneficiaries of their spiritual efforts.[87] More elaborate rites took place every three months, when an actual deathbed was set up, surrounded with forty burning candles. While the musicians performed the requiem for the souls of the deceased Wittelsbachs, the two mothers of the Pütrich and Ridler convents twice sacrificed bread in an act that overtly paralleled the priestly celebration of the eucharist.[88]

The sisters' care for the Wittelsbach family finally encompassed the physical needs of the living. Several rooms in the Ridler convent served as sickrooms, where the duchesses or other female members of the court sought rest and care. A generous Wittelsbach endowment freed the religious women from other obligations so that they could make themselves available and wait on the courtly ladies as needed.[89]

The sisters could not have averted the first onslaught of the Tridentine reform movement in the 1570s and 1580s had it not been for the help of the court, which at this point had a greater stake in keeping the two communities open rather than enclosing them. In 1574, Johann Nas, General Comissarius of the Franciscan order and friend of Munich's tertiaries, dispatched a letter of admonition to the Pütrich sisters. Apparently Nas had been entrusted with conducting a visitation in the convent in the near future and securing compliance with Tridentine dictates, a mission that he much rather would have passed on to somebody else. Bound by his orders, however, he could do no more than give the sisters an advance warning and thereby an opportunity to take preemptive measures before his arrival. Among other things, Nas made it very clear that the frequent hosting of people from the court and other secular folk was problematic. So was the close contact with the Friars Minor, whom the sisters invited over for meals and whom they visited in their monastery. These interactions and the permeability of convent walls that they presupposed were "completely adverse to the planned claustration."[90]

The sisters sought and found support at Bavaria's political center of power. Duke Albrecht V approached Cardinal Morone, the man who had concluded the Council of Trent as its president to serve later on as Apostolic Legate in Germany.[91] The duke made the case for maintaining the uncloistered status quo of the Ridler and Pütrich communities.[92] In so doing, Albrecht also defended the unrestricted access of courtly ladies to the two religious houses. He actually cited the long-standing tradition of the convents' openness in their defense; after all, they were commonly called "not monasteries but houses."[93] Yet since the accessibility of a house filled with unmarried women quickly raised the specter of the common house, Albrecht added two important modifications to this argument. First, the sisters stemmed from distinguished families, and second, their visitors were honorable matrons and girls. The fortifications of class supposedly stood in for the fortifications of cloister walls. Indeed, the visits of girls to these communities, Albrecht argued, had proven to be especially propitious. "Captivated by love for this kind of life," these young women subsequently "embrace the institution."[94] The rhetoric of love drove home the point that the tertiary houses, far from endangering women's morality, channeled the explosive emotions of young unmarried females into a safe haven and protected their honor and that of their families.

Albrecht's intervention halted the reform of the two convents for the time being. Upon his death in 1579, however, Felicianus Ninguarda, bishop of Scala and papal nuncio in charge of implementing Tridentine regulations in the diocese of Freising, took up matters again with Albrecht's son and successor, Wilhelm V. Precisely because his father had spared the Ridler and Pütrich communities from Tridentine enclosure, the question turned into a litmus test for the new duke's commitment to Tridentine reform.[95]

A fortnight before the nuncio articulated his wishes, Ninguarda gained a firsthand impression of the openness of the Ridler and Pütrich houses. During the funeral ceremony for Albrecht V, a cortege of honorable mourners gathered in Munich's cathedral. It featured a contingent of duchesses and princesses, as well as sisters from the Ridler and Pütrich convents.[96] The sisters' appearance and place in the procession was indicative of their public presence in the larger community and their close affiliation with the court and its interests.

Ninguarda's official inquiries soon confirmed his personal impression. Convent reform went against the grain of convent customs, the desires of the sisters and their families, and those of the court. Even more basic, the two religious houses lacked the necessary architectural preconditions for cloistering. There was no separate parlatorium or chamber for conversation adjacent to the cloistered area, in which one could receive outsiders. The communities' chapels and churches were accessible from various directions.[97] After inspecting the environs, Ninguarda arrived at the conclusion that instant enclosure was not feasible.

> Because we found in our inquiries into the places that there is no real opportunity for the mentioned enclosure . . . because you can neither hear mass nor do other kinds of pious services unless you go out or the priests come in . . . we have postponed the ordered claustration.[98]

By 1583, two years after his first visit, the nuncio resigned himself to preparatory reforms to lay the groundwork for real enclosure in the future. Recognizing the sisters' obligations toward their benefactors, he gave them leeway in visiting civic churches for the performance of commemorative prayers.[99] Ninguarda's endorsement stemmed from the recognition of important patronage bonds and the revenues attached. The same awareness led Ninguarda to make concessions in another contested arena: the presence of secular women in the convents and the sale of handmade textiles. Already in June 1581 Ninguarda permitted the Pütrich sisters to invite "consanguineous kin, or other . . . male or female persons with whom you have to conduct business" into a chamber adjoining the gate "but no further."[100] The sisters soon complained that the assigned room was so uncomfortable as to cause a decline in alms and sales of their handcrafted goods. If they did not wish to end up impoverished, they badly needed the occasional assistance of "kin, and also other pious and honorable women."[101]

While it is virtually impossible to verify whether the nuns' rhetoric was based on economic realities or motivated by the desire to maintain social contact with the world, this line of reasoning swayed the nuncio to keep the cloister gates open to benefactors. In a letter dated March 16, 1583, Ninguarda concurred that economic affairs would suffer if the community were deprived of the helping hands of devout matrons. Economic difficulties would delay the architectural remodeling of the convents even further, so Ninguarda found it preferable to let in kin as well as "other honorable and pious matrons or women who either customarily pick up the work you did, or hand over alms to you."[102]

Ninguarda, however, made it clear that these allowances were provisional, pending the installation of a true parlatorium next to a truly cloistered sphere. Only kin and benefactors of the female sex had his permission to enter, and he limited their visits to four per person each year. Festivities during these visits were no longer permitted.[103] In short, the nuncio had resigned himself to a binomial strategy of convent reform, displaying respect for already existing ties while launching their dissolution over time.

The same principle can be seen in other areas of reform as well. Even though Ninguarda sanctioned the sisters' attendance of masses in the nearby Franciscan church, where the vigils and requiems for the ducal house took place, he sought to make sure that the daily outings were the sisters' only excursions and became occasions for inculcating a new discipline. The women had to walk in small groups and in a procession, preferably in the early morning hours when encounters with others were most unlikely.[104] They had to display honor and discipline in their deportment and were forbidden to linger after church and engage in conversations.[105] During the religious services, they were confined to a separate area, set apart from the community of ordinary believers. In other words, the uncloistered nuns were forced to carry cloister walls with them.

Ninguarda also blended ad hoc compromises with long-term changes that affected the sickrooms in the Ridler convent. He cordoned them off from the cloistered area as much as possible and hired secular nurses to bring medicine and food into the rooms via a stairway leading into the city.[106] The nuns could not attend to patients while secular acquaintances were visiting.[107] Trying to turn a liability into an asset, Ninguarda then designated the sickrooms as future guestrooms for all female guests, even those who enjoyed a papal dispensation to enter the cloistered area itself, such as the Wittelsbach duchesses.[108]

Finally, the nuncio initiated the metamorphosis of these open communities of religious women into cloisters of virgins by stipulating new rules for admission. Prior to the reforms, the convents provided widows with a place of retirement, some of whom even enjoyed a reputation for sanctity, such as Magdalena of the Ridler convent, venerated among court members for her ecstasies and ability to levitate.[109] Women in trouble apparently also found temporary shelter there. By contrast, the nuncio decreed that the sisters "should no longer take in their care any old woman but rather only virgins about whom there is hope that they may wish to enter your claustrated cloister."[110]

Because the nuncio viewed these arrangements merely as steps toward the goal of Tridentine claustration, he called on the secular arm to supervise and promote the completion of the task after his departure. He negotiated with the court and obtained Duke Wilhelm's promise not to disrupt the flow of ducal donations to the Ridler convent, once cloistered life put an end to the economic benefits of the sisters' health-care services. In addition, the duke offered "to give a hand" with the remodeling of convent space, particularly with the construction of a closed-off passageway and a separate house of prayer in the Franciscan church.[111]

In this manner, many specifics of future enclosure came into ducal hands. Far from diminishing outside influence on the religious community, the nuncio ended up inviting interference by Bavaria's rulers. The following four decades did not yet bring the fundamental changes for which Ninguarda had sought to pave the way. Apparently content with the status quo, neither the duke nor local Franciscan superiors pushed for the sisters' quick sequestration.

Enclosure came during the reign of Maximilian I, when fears of open houses of women were once again on the rise and the eradication of nonmarital sexuality moved to the forefront of state concerns. Aegidius Albertinus, Maximilian's secretary and a widely read moralist, offered his reflections on the topic of women's cloister while extolling the importance of the virginal estate for a functioning Catholic commonwealth. His comments are symptomatic of the altered post-Reformation stance on female virginity among Catholics. Like the Protestant convent critics a century earlier, this popular and influential Bavarian advocate of a Catholic order displayed distrust in the religious virgins of his time, questioning their ability and willingness to abstain from sexual relations.

His section "On the great fortitude with which numerous virgins remained firm in their virginal intention" thus went to great lengths to praise the heroism of women who fended for their virginity during the days of antiquity, often under threat of death. Such lists of exemplary virtuous women had been a familiar device of women's advocates in the *Querelle des Femmes,* the Europe-wide scholarly debate over women's capabilities and worth, since Boccaccio used it in his *De mulieribus claris.* Yet Albertinus added an interesting twist. He concluded by proclaiming his faith in the virtue of "pagan women," not by lauding the women of his own day and age. Instead he used the examples as a foil to express his concerns about the lack of morality among Christian nuns, who did not even have to fear for their lives.

> For years ago, people used violence to force holy virgins to enter the unchaste common house of women. But these days they [holy virgins] are kept behind walls and locks, with violence as it were, to keep them safe from ravishers. Note the difference in times and customs. Then they were forbidden to live a chaste life according to their desire. Now our [virgins] are not permitted to commit some unchaste act according to their desire.[112]

These pronouncements on female cloisters resembled the writings of Protestant convent critics in other respects as well. Albertinus, too, viewed the common house of women and religious houses of women as part of the same institutional family, and he deployed the familiar trope of the convent as brothel. The openness of religious houses also signifies sexual openness and pollution in his discourse. As a Catholic, however, Albertinus saw the solution to the problem in complete enclosure of all brides of Christ.

> Oh what great horror/oh what great vanity/oh what great shame/that a virgin who was consecrated and sanctified with such glorious solemnities and mysteries of religion/turns into a dirty sack and toilet and puddle of impurity. And how necessary it was to cover and lock you with high walls, since unfortunately we see that in many places holy cloisters have been turned around and changed into houses of ill repute due to the negligence of their shepherds.[113]

This chapter has shown that the conflation of nuns and whores and mounting concerns over open houses of women preceded the sixteenth-century debates among Germany's Catholic and Protestants about the fate of convents and brothels. The Reformation merely exacerbated the medieval trend of stigmatizing houses of women since it promoted patriarchal marriage as "God's first order" and dispensed with medieval ideals of chaste living. In replacing celibacy as the highest ideal of religious life, marriage became the primary locus of purity in Protestant polities, and the social site of sacrality shifted from continent ecclesiastics to the procreative patriarchal family.

Houses of women—be they female religious communities, urban brothels, or female-headed households—suffered from the disappearance of virginity as a feasible permanent life choice; women were still expected to remain chaste until they reached their destiny of marriage and motherhood. Unmarried women in turn were sexualized beings, in constant danger of succumbing to their innate desire, and female-headed households were defined out of a respectable existence. Protestants initiated the abolition of houses of prostitution and of female convents, which they viewed as brothels in disguise, in the Protestant areas.

In the Catholic context, houses of women and unmarried women also felt the repercussions of the Protestant rupture of traditional linkages between sacredness, sexuality, and the body social since Catholics reasserted and redefined their doctrinal stances in reference to women's bodies. Although the dissolution of urban houses of prostitution was initially a Protestant cause, the Council of Trent put the fight against organized prostitution on the Catholic agenda. The ill repute that had descended upon female-headed households also cast a shadow of suspicion on female religious communities, especially if these houses of women had a tradition of self-government and unregulated access to urban life, such as tertiary communities.

The Trent-inspired reform of female monastic life and the drive toward the enclosure of all women religious is best understood as an attempt to differentiate women's religious communities from morally dubious houses of women and to safeguard the sexual purity of convent inhabitants. Women religious came to embody the contested doctrine of the superiority of the virginal to the married life more fully than monks or clerics, and they did so as women who required special protective measures, such as cloister walls. Tridentine enclosure was thus part of the gendering of ecclesiastics, producing the body of the nun as an unequivocally female and sexualized body.

Notably, the polities of Counter-Reformation Italy did not abolish houses of prostitution. Italian Catholics embarked upon the foundation of a range of institutions to serve as way stations for women who were former prostitutes, were in danger of falling into prostitution, or suffered from marital problems. Although these institutions worked in ways that recapitulated the predominant gender order, and even though they served the needs of the state and patriarchal families, the greater flexibility of Italian conceptions of marriage and sexuality is evident in the institutions' very existence.[114]

The absence of these establishments and the disappearance of brothels from Bavaria's institutional landscape mirror the much sharper boundary drawings of German Catholicism. State authorities erected a sharp divide between the state of marriage and the state of chastity, as exemplified by the monastic life. They increased the moral pressure on both states of being and made women the main bearers of new moral obligations and also the involuntary guardians of new social and sexual boundaries.

When it came to marriage, the state strove to confine sexual activity to officially approved, patriarchal marriages and to the wealthier social strata. Denouncing any nonmarital sex as profligate "whoredom," state authorities shut down urban brothels, which in effect left the specter of prostitution everywhere. As a result, single women, in particular poor women—who could ill afford to turn relationships into publicly sanctioned unions—faced greater risks of being suspected of prostitution.

While state authorities, to the particular detriment of lower-class women, put economic obstacles in the way of those who wished to join the respectable circle of married citizens, they did little to create alternatives to marriage. Rather, they pushed the life of the cloister as the only honorable alternative and initiated its transformation into a more socially exclusive institution that no longer offered social services or temporary refuge to women in need. Unlike in the Low Countries, where a great variety of both contemplative and active institutions existed before and after Trent, there was a deliberate move toward greater uniformity among women religious in the Bavarian capital.[115]

The case of Munich suggests that rivalries among Protestants and Catholics in the German context resulted in unique developments. The principle *cuius regio, eius religio* (he who governs the land, determines the religion) that underwrote the Peace of Augsburg of 1555 contained outright violent confessional conflict on the imperial level by redirecting it to another terrain, the battlefield of competitive moral politics and social disciplining among individual territories. As the German princes obtained permission to pursue ambitious agendas of internal reform, this settlement invited each of them to strive for external differentiation from one another by producing a particularly pure body politic. It resulted in a spiral of reactive legal and institutional initiatives, whisking Germany's Protestant and Catholic polities down parallel paths of sociopolitical change.

The question of purity in Christian body politics—its definition, locus, and guardians—thus remained a contested issue in Germany throughout the confessional age. Even though the Protestant Reformation altered the framework of marriage, sexuality, and gender, the truly innovative force of the Reformation derived not necessarily from the radical nature of Protestant ideas themselves. Rather, the catalyst appears to have been the competitive dynamic between Catholics and Protestants that the Reformation set in motion.[116] Not surprisingly, then, it was not until the Thirty Years' War that the legal, discursive, and institutional trends discussed in the first two chapters released their transformative power.

Part II

Engendering the Catholic Polity: The Thirty Years' War and Its Aftermath

CHAPTER 3

Pregnant Bodies, Personal Purity, and Public Goods

In the year 1593 the widow Felicitas Kainninger sued Hans Ellinger, a journeyman in Munich, before the civic court in the Bavarian capital. She explained to the city's highest judge (*Stadtoberrichter*) how she and Ellinger had met in an inn near Salzburg where she had worked as a domestic servant after her husband's death. Ellinger had pursued her and finally had "promised her marriage, (and) made her a big belly." With her lawsuit, Kainninger "desired that he offer restitution on account of the child and her lost honor."[1]

In Hans Ellinger's view of his relationship with Felicitas Kainninger, there was never any talk of marriage. He characterized the plaintiff as a seductress who wanted nothing but sex. While "it was true that he had been involved with her," Kainninger "had entered his chamber of her own accord." For Ellinger, the key issue was indeed one of male rather than of female honor. Confronted with a woman's desire, the defendant explained in court, he considered it a matter of masculine prowess to meet the challenge and sleep with her:

> He was a single journeyman at the time and it was proper to his honor, especially so since he paid her every time just like a common whore.

Ellinger's notion of male honor thus encompassed single men's exploration of the realm of sexuality. The woman who enabled this initiation to satisfy her own desires—his defense implied—deserved payment but certainly no more. The judge disagreed. He counted Kainninger among the reputable women whose honor the civic court was called to restore and sentenced Ellinger to make a payment of twenty-seven Gulden to the plaintiff.

By 1642, a different discourse about sexuality, gender, and honor became audible in the civic courtroom. When Kunigunde Pfaller sued the journeyman Hans Haid for breach of marriage promise, defloration, and impregnation, she made a point of emphasizing the "strong pressure" that Haid had used to persuade her to surrender her virginity. The accused, however, stressed that he owed nothing to her. At most, he would take care of the child—if it turned out to be his. This was not self-evident in his view, since Pfaller was no longer a virgin when they got involved, but rather an experienced "profligate woman" (*leichtfertige weibspersohn*). Far from admitting that he instigated their involvement with a marriage promise, Haid proceeded to accuse Pfaller.

> She had given occasion to this act and the profligacy [*Leichtfertigkeit*] that took place . . . hence hopefully he owed nothing to her . . . rather he, as a young journeymen, had lost his discipline and honor to the plaintiff.[2]

This mid-seventeenth-century statement provides a striking contrast to Hans Ellinger's defense of the late sixteenth century. Ellinger's statement of 1592 denoted skepticism about the honorability of sexually active unmarried women. Yet in his words we still caught a glimpse of the acceptability, indeed potential honorability, of sexual experiences outside of marriage for a single journeyman. Even though Ellinger denied his accuser any claims to restoration of honor through marriage, he did not deny that he owed her a payment of sorts for their sexual involvement. More important, the court's decision to award financial compensation to the plaintiff settled the question of honorability in the woman's favor.

Haid's remarks of 1642, on the other hand, hint at an escalating stigmatization of so-called profligate women (*leichtfertige weibspersohnen*) as solely responsible for nonmarital sexual encounters. If anything, his words imply, these women owed men for taking their honor. Here sexuality outside of marriage unequivocally connoted dishonor and—in terminology resonating with sexual as well as socioeconomic meaning—a loss of "discipline." Discipline is lost to the "profligate woman," who literally embodies moral pollution in the new order of things.

This chapter explains this shift and its gender-specific implications. The legal and institutional groundwork were already laid in the second half of the sixteenth century, when the ecclesiastical regulations of Trent started to converge with state profligacy laws. It would be misleading, however, to envision the implementation of this post-Trent morality as a linear development along an axis from tolerance to repression. Rather the implementation of new standards was subject to the fluctuating pressures exerted by state and municipal authorities on the city's judicial system. The first flickers of intolerance in the courtroom around the turn of the seventeenth century were followed by a period of renewed leniency, as strong cultural undercurrents of tolerance toward nonmarital sexual experiences reasserted themselves. During the socioeconomic crisis of the 1620s, however, secular understandings of marriage as a privilege of the propertied began to outweigh the ecclesiastical concept of matrimony as an a priori sacramental right. State authorities made the eradication of profligate marriages, or unions contracted between partners of low economic standing without official approval, their political priority.

This development had distinct implications for men and women due to their asymmetrical positions and dissimilar stakes in courtship and marriage. Lower-class women, more than their male counterparts, bore the brunt of the state's regulatory efforts. While lower-class men could invoke the more restrictive attitudes and laws to avoid obligations toward women, lower-class women faced increasing risk if they engaged in nonmarital sex. State legislation in effect demanded that these women uphold the boundaries of the new social and sexual order by avoiding sexual relations altogether: life in a perpetual state of virginity became their moral obligation. Although the state could never completely prevent sexual unions among the lower classes, and the demographic recovery after the Thirty Years' War even made such prevention seem less urgent for a while, the state's anti-profligacy measures resulted in long-term reinterpretations of certain sexual behaviors and new gender-specific norms of respectability.

Weakened Virgins and Profligate Women: Female Plaintiffs before the Civic Court, 1592–1618

Civic court records from the Bavarian capital offer a detailed picture of the gender-specific impact of post-Trent orderings of marriage and sexuality. The nature of court records has been commented on extensively, and so has the question of their usefulness as historical sources. Rather than opening a window on sexual practices, relations between men and women, or the workings of desire, judicial sources allow us to investigate how the law frames and co-constructs gender and sexuality by forcing subjects to explain their behavior, emotions, and identities from a set of speaking positions.[3] In this light, the Munich records reveal that significant shifts in legally tenable and culturally plausible narratives took place between the late sixteenth and mid–seventeenth centuries.

While the state's anti-profligacy measures dated back to the sixteenth century, they unleashed their full force only in the 1620s, when the question of access to the city and its resources took on unprecedented urgency, and confessional rivalry reinvigorated official interest in the eradication of sexual vice. The law gradually dealt lower-class women the lion's share of responsibility for nonmarital sexuality. One could measure this process in terms of the respective penalties for men and women, as some have done, and point to the progressively harsher punishments for women and their comparatively more severe socioeconomic and cultural consequences.[4] While the question of inequitable punishment is an important dimension of sexual regulation, the focus of the following discussion rests on changes in legal paradigms and the ways in which these changes circumscribed female sexual behavior more narrowly than male sexual behavior.

Munich's highest judge (*Stadtoberrichter*) regularly adjudicated cases of broken marriage promises, defloration, and nonmarital pregnancies. Between 1592 and 1651 a total of 191 women sued their former lovers before the civic court. Although the secular court could not make any decisions about the validity of a marriage promise, since questions about the sacramentally binding nature of private promises fell in the purview of the ecclesiastical court located in Freising, the jurisdictional prerogatives of the civic courts encompassed disputes over marriage and sexuality. Thus the secular judge was in charge of settling conflicts that pertained to the financial aspects of sexual relations and had a bearing on sociopolitical ordering in the community.

Court records classify cases of broken promises and nonmarital impregnation under two rubrics: either "matters of rumor and injury" or "matters of debt." In other words, these lawsuits touched on two types of economic systems whose running was crucial to the functioning of public order in early modern polities: the symbolic economy of honor and the material and financial transactions accompanying courtship and marriage. Both types of exchanges valued female virginity as a currency.

The entry under two rubrics and the fact that the plaintiffs in these cases were female reflect women's greater vulnerability in matters of sexuality and marriage formation.[5] Women's honor, more centrally than men's, was predicated on sexual behavior such that sexuality inevitably put female honor at risk.[6] During the exchange of words, objects, and gestures that accompanied the formation of a marital union, women often gave their female honor as a kind of advance and had intercourse with their lovers in the expectation of a return—marriage and economic stability. Such risk-taking was part and parcel of traditional marriage formation, based as it was on private consent and physical consummation.[7]

If men failed to uphold their end of the bargain, early modern society offered women various mechanisms of redress.[8] On the institutional level, ecclesiastical courts represented an important ally in enforcing marriage promises or securing financial compensation for female plaintiffs. In the late Middle Ages, women initiated the majority of lawsuits in cases of broken promises, and judges regularly sided with the plaintiffs.[9] It is significant that courts arrived at these decisions on the sole basis of female testimony and that they generally weighed women's words even more heavily if the alleged marriage promise had resulted in intercourse: sexual activity counted as evidence of high stakes rather than of female dishonor.[10]

Honorable and dishonorable conduct obviously represented matters of gradation rather than criteria marking an absolute difference. This blurry boundary between honor and dishonor corresponded to the blurry boundary between the state of marriage and the state of courtship that had evolved out of the medieval doctrine of private consent. While these ill-defined boundaries frustrated attempts of state and church authorities to regulate marriage formation, they also gave moral leeway to those men and women who did not turn their relationships immediately into permanent, officially sanctioned partnerships.

Such room for maneuver was of crucial importance to lower-class women. In their world of limited resources, sexuality was an even more important bargaining chip in forming relations with men. These women might take monetary gifts from their lovers because the distinction between signs of affection and much-needed economic support was something they could not afford. These were the women who were most directly affected by the new twin requirement of a public marriage ceremony and of proof of property in confessional Munich. Interestingly, these were also the women who turned to the civic court for help both before and after these requirements transformed judicial practice.

Like Felicitas Kainninger and Kunigunde Pfaller, whose stories opened this chapter, the majority of plaintiffs came from places other than Munich.[11] Most of them had come to the city from surrounding villages, often to earn a living as domestic servants in the Bavarian capital. Insofar as we can trace their socioeconomic background, the plaintiffs belonged to the lower classes, the very group whose sexuality was targeted by profligacy legislation.[12] Cut loose from their social networks and without sufficient economic backing, these women turned to the institution of the civic court for help in their conflicts with the opposite sex.[13]

There is evidence that some female plaintiffs chose the civic court above the ecclesiastical court, even though the secular judge could not rule on the validity of a marriage promise.[14] Among other things, the secular judge's impressive repertoire of means of enforcement must have been appealing to women bent on forcing their lovers to meet obligations. As the highest police officers in the city, the *Stadtoberrichter* could deprive men of their right to work, strip them of their guild honor, and ask respectable burghers to stand surety for a defendant's solvency—or even imprison a male culprit until he provided such guarantors or otherwise reached a settlement with the plaintiff.

Just like the ecclesiastical court, however, the civic court also altered its workings under the influence of the Counter-Reformation. Fueled by Trent's condemnation of nonmarital sexuality, the statewide fight against profligacy engendered novel norms for honorable sexual relations. As state profligacy legislation was making inroads into the urban environment, cases of broken promises and nonmarital pregnancies began to pose a dilemma for the civic judge. State police ordinances took priority over conflicting urban regulations; this contrasted with all other legal arenas where civic law invariably overrode state law.[15] Yet state law after Trent both underpinned and eroded the judge's traditional role as protector of female honor.

On the one hand, state Ordinances of Good Police explicitly called upon local authorities to take steps against the so-called weakening of virgins (*Jungfernschwechen*) and secure compensation for every wronged woman who "had been brought to her fall and deprived of her virginal honor by seduction, match-making, gifts, pledges, intoxicating potions or false marriage promises [*sic*]."[16] On the other hand, state initiatives against profligacy pushed the judge into the conflicting role of a prosecutor of profligate women. In 1597, Maximilian I charged the city's highest official with the ex officio prosecution of "profligate marriages" and nonmarital pregnancies.[17]

Thereafter female plaintiffs who sued their former lovers for defloration, a broken promise, or a nonmarital impregnation automatically directed judicial attention to an act of profligate sex between two people: their indictments of men by necessity implied self-indictments. Given the judge's dual mandate, his policing power was a double-edged sword that he could either put at a woman's disposal if he found her honorable or turn against her should he find her to be profligate.

Immediately following the judge's new appointment, several female plaintiffs lost their cases on the basis of profligacy and whoredom. Ursula Wolschlager was one of them. She cited Sebastian Kühn before the *Stadt-oberrichter* in a case of defloration and impregnation. Kühn admitted to the sexual relationship but mentioned in his defense that Wolschlager "gave him more than plenty of reason; besides, he had not found her a virgin, had given her a bunch of cash, as much as was due . . . to a whore." Although Wolschlager tried to explain the transfer of money as payment for a meal she had provided for Kühn, the judge gave credence to Kühn 's characterization of the transaction. He absolved Kühn from any financial obligations toward the woman, concluding that "she lay with him for a whore's salary."[18]

In an analogous case from the same year, Ursula Zenz claimed that she had received money for soup instead of sex, even though the defendant Bastl Hülmayer claimed he had given her cash for sexual service. According to the defendant, Zenz had "in an unsolicited and profligate manner lain down next to him, hence he paid her 4 Kreuzer like a common whore." Again, the court believed the male defendant, denying the female plaintiff financial compensation "since as a common woman she took the pay."[19]

The exchange of money clearly made these cases tricky for the women, particularly since Munich's civic brothel was shut down the same year, and prostitutes in theory were now on the loose. Among the lower classes, even small financial donations had economic implications, creating a firm link between signs of affection and much-needed material support. In light of post-Trent legislation on profligacy and prostitution, however, the meaning of economic exchanges within a relationship between unmarried people quickly became subject to contestation in the courtroom. Was money given toward marriage or was it given for sexual favors? Or was it simply given in return for other services?

The existence of the morning gift (*Morgengabe*) in law and practice added yet another layer of complexity to the redefinition of traditional exchanges. Bavarian women could and did expect payment for giving their virginity in the context of marriage formation. As the societal legitimation of a marriage promise became more and more difficult after Trent and most of all for the lower social strata, private virginity payments were in danger of losing the traditional interpretive context and becoming suggestive of a whore's salary. While an honorable virgin deserved marriage and the morning gift (or at least proper compensation equivalent to a dowry), a common or profligate woman could be paid off with a paltry sum.

In recounting their sexual relations with women, men began to invoke the polarity that secular law constructed between deserving honorable women and profligate harlots. Because most women plaintiffs stemmed from society's lower strata, their economic standing already situated them in the category of potentially profligate women. Men's imputations against women plaintiffs' moral standing aimed at unequivocally labeling them "profligate." Men cited payments for services in their defense, and they portrayed women as active seductresses. For example, Jörg Inning, charged in 1606 by Maria Mitzenberger with breach of promise, defloration, and impregnation, told the judge that "the plaintiff had provided much opportunity and occasion to engage in fornication with her, even gave the key to her chamber, and the first time she left three doors open."[20] Concepts of female passivity and purity provided the implicit foil for men's disparaging stories about women. As these concepts were gaining in importance, the stories of men were gaining in plausibility.

Male honor had a different basis and a different significance in the exchanges in the *Stadtgericht*. Basically, men found additional rhetorical ammunition in cultural constructions of masculinity that associated a man's honor with sexual achievement. Wolf Schad portrayed his sexual involvement with Katharina Spitzer as the proper response to the woman's provocative behavior. Spitzer, he told the judge, "lay down in bed next to him, announcing that a man must be a fool and a thief if he did nothing when a person [*mensch*] lay down next to him."[21] Schad was not alone in characterizing such an advance as a challenge to male sexual prowess and as a threat to male honor whose only redress lay in engaging in sexual relations with the challenger. Hans Abel, too, felt called to the defense of his masculinity, when Elisabeth Gehnab first pursued and then questioned his courage. Speculating that Abel "did not have enough gall to be allowed to sleep with a woman," Gehnab pushed the issue: "did he think she was going to be his fool if he did not give her money?" In the end, Abel accepted the dare and "whenever he lay with her, he always paid her like a whore."[22]

When the authorities cracked down hard upon *Dirnen* in and outside the brothel around the time of the closing of Munich's *Frauenhaus,* several male defendants in the *Stadtgericht* took advantage of this opportune moment and refuted their accusers' charges by reframing them in terms of female promiscuity. Male defendants certainly still sought to extricate themselves from women's claims by tapping into the legal drift toward outlawing profligacy and prostitution. However, the sexual disciplining from above did not instantaneously create new categories for evaluating women's sexual behavior, even while it provided the legal tools for such reevaluation.

Prior to 1618, records bespeak judicial tolerance toward nonmarital sexuality in general and flexible understandings of female honor in particular. The judge did frequently fine the two parties for the "fornication" (*Unzucht*) involved, but the penalty did not interfere with what, in modern parlance, would be called a civil lawsuit. If a male defendant was found guilty, he was ordered to cover the fine for the woman as well.

Plaintiffs were astonishingly frank and unashamed about prior sexual experiences. Elisabeth Gehnab, who willingly admitted having carried a child by another man in the past, did not think her prior pregnancy had any bearing on the legitimacy of her current claims against Hans Abel: "As far as her previous child was concerned, that happened 12 years ago. Because of it, the authorities at Wolffertzhausen punished her. Once again she desired to have him imprisoned."[23]

Standards for female honor in the civic court were indeed flexible enough so that even a confession of clerical concubinage did not automatically preclude the possibility of financial compensation. Anna Maria

Freischer, in the course of her 1617 breach-of-promise suit against Kaspar Schwaiger, acknowledged her prior involvement with a priest and the pregnancy resulting from it. Nonetheless, the judge deemed her worthy of financial compensation.[24]

Women at times even volunteered information about their sexual past to the judge. Jacobe Schmitt, suing Mattias Schmidten in 1599, stated that "she did not sue him for her virginal honor because she had been involved previously with their doctor Pirckmayer"—Schmitt's and Schmidten's employer. In spite of the unsolicited revelation on the part of Schmitt, the court did not agree with the defendant's portrayal of her as a woman who had led "a whore's life."[25]

Interestingly, not a single woman brought charges for loss of virginity alone—in spite of the legislation on the "weakening of virgins" that invited such charges. Rather, several female plaintiffs rejected payment for their virginal honor outright. Rosina Laidnis made explicit her rationale for turning down financial compensation. Suing Kaspar Scherer for breach of promise in the year 1600, Laidnis had her mind set on forcing the journeyman, who had deflowered and impregnated her, into matrimony. She considered restitution for her virginity inappropriate "for she was the child of people who were as honorable as his."[26] On one level, Laidnis's statement can be interpreted as a rejection of Scherer's ready avoidance of responsibility by paying her off like a common woman. Laidnis placed herself squarely in the category of women who deserved marriage and morning gift rather than pay for sexual services. On another level, her reasoning points to the various factors figuring into the cultural assessment of a woman's honor: physical purity was only one factor; the standing of her family or the size of her dowry constituted others. Differently put, understandings of female honor were malleable and the loss of physical purity did not automatically imply the loss of honor.

Just as judicial knowledge of a woman's prior sexual experiences did not necessarily work to her detriment, the absence of a marriage promise did not significantly decrease the chances of winning a case in the civic court. Women could and did sue successfully for a range of legal claims. Whereas eighty women sought restitution for impregnation and/or loss of virginity, child alimony payments, or custody, only fifty-nine female plaintiffs leveled charges at men in conjunction with a marriage promise. Regardless of the exact nature of their claims, close to 94 percent of the plaintiffs won their cases, that is, they received what they asked for (at the very least, that the father take the child into his custody) and had their fine covered by the defendant. Women who mentioned a marriage promise stood the same chance of winning their lawsuit as did women who did not place their sexual activities in the context of marriage formation.

In a telltale choice of words, the judicial record characterizes cases from the earlier decades as pertaining to "a fall from honor," a temporary lapse from an ideal condition to which the plaintiff hoped to return by way of her lawsuit. By comparison, the term *Leichtfertigkeit* (profligacy) appears rarely; rather the sexual acts are usually characterized as a form of *Unzucht* (fornication).[27] Nonmarital sexuality and impregnation, no doubt, did do damage to female honor. But this damage could be reversed and honor restored with the assistance of the civic judge.

On occasion, a female plaintiff might even leave the civic courtroom with the prospect of marrying the male defendant. The secular court's prerogative did not include validity disputes over marriage promises, and the judge in fact frequently referred plaintiffs to the proper ecclesiastical forum in Freising—an indication that the two courts worked in tandem in an attempt to supersede noninstitutional mechanisms of conflict resolution. Yet precisely because the secular judge represented civic concerns with marriage's nonsacramental aspects, economics and honor, he could respect medieval traditions of consensualism and a process-oriented understanding of marriage in a manner the ecclesiastical judge no longer could. In some instances, this judicial leeway enabled the civic judge to facilitate a marriage between two litigants.

The lawsuit of Christina Zeller against Augustin Perkhoven provides an interesting case in point and further underscores the malleable conceptions of sexuality that initially characterized proceedings in the secular court. Zeller sued Perkhoven for loss of virginity and child support in 1596, admitting that "he actually did not once promise marriage to her." In the midst of judicial proceedings, however, Perkhoven suddenly suggested matrimony "if she were able to recognize him in her conscience as the true father, and if she were to be patient for another two years, and wanted to wait, and no less [wanted] to go into service in the meantime . . . and behave piously [*frumb verhalten*], he would want to take her into matrimony after this time."[28]

Perkhoven's bid illustrates further to what degree marriage—in spite of Trent—remained the result of intricate emotional and economic exchanges unfolding over time. His marriage proposal was based on two preconditions: sufficient economic means and honorable conduct. He needed both the time to acquire the necessary means of subsistence and also Zeller's economic contribution before he could set up a household with her. His additional request for "pious behavior" reveals lasting post-Trent confusion around illicit premarital and licit marital sex.[29] "Behaving piously" or "being pious" (*frumb*) was the religiously inflected language litigants used to describe virgins. As long as Zeller remained faithful to him, Perkhoven considered their sexual involvement and the actual use of physical purity to be a morally acceptable part of forming a marital bond—even if the process of becoming husband and wife took years. The civic judge, uninhibited as he was by considerations of canon law, gave his fiat to the couple's marriage plans and facilitated their fulfillment by making both parties swear that they would comply with the agreement.[30] This marriage arrangement did not preclude a later church wedding, but neither did it require this ecclesiastical ritual of legitimation.

Practices and people's perceptions of love, courtship, and marriage apparently changed slowly. What did change over time was the legal meaning assigned to sexual relations and the range of judicially sanctioned stories about love relationships between men and women. As they tried to manipulate the civic court system to their own ends, men and women used different narrative strategies and invoked gender-specific norms of honorable behavior. The exculpation of defendants and the justification of the demands of plaintiffs depended on the plausibility and acceptability of the stories that these two parties told. It was during the third decade of the seventeenth century that the cataclysmic changes of the Thirty Years' War reshaped judicial practice and altered the stories men and women could tell in the civic court.

"Many Single Women with Pregnant Bodies": Profligacy Becomes a Political Priority

As a major force in European politics, Counter-Reformation Bavaria was reaching the apex of its power during the Thirty Years' War. Maximilian I led the Catholic League to the first series of victories and gained for his duchy the much-coveted status of an electoral principality in 1623. At the same time, and in connection with the expansive foreign policy, internal affairs in Bavaria were plummeting to new depths. Rural and urban population alike suffered from a severe shortage of food supplies, combined with soaring prices for the few items available. The monetary demands of warfare exacerbated the situation by necessitating the extensive production of low-value currency that drove inflation to ever higher extremes.[31]

The crisis hit especially hard in the Bavarian capital, where the socioeconomic situation was precarious to begin with. In the second half of the sixteenth century, Munich's urban population had already doubled, and the number of new immigrants began to outstrip the number of taxpayers. Civic income declined steadily, and so did the value of currency.[32] Because the urban population received its income in the form of salaries, Munich's residents felt the sharp sting of inflation.

The result was an atmosphere at once grim and explosive that would last for decades to come. Maurus Friesenegger, abbot of the Andechs monastery, includes chilling descriptions of the hunger, disease, chaos, and fear in the Bavarian capital in his diary of the Thirty Years' War. The community, Friesenegger's account illustrates, countered the crisis with a politics of exclusion:

> I followed the path to Weilheim and Polling, and on my way I saw things that were hardly bearable. I saw children, each one of them crying under a parcel, mothers carrying several children, two on their backs and one in their arms, men who had loaded their wheelbarrows with clothes, food, sick people, and children, pulling them with difficulty or driving one or more cattle in front . . . And this is what it apparently looked like on all roads. And perhaps it was still more miserable on the way to Munich where so many country folk piled up that the city did not hold them any more. Some were driven out of the gates with blows, others, which was even more despicable, had to pay their way into the city with money.[33]

Mounting hostility toward outsiders characterized Munich's local politics from the 1620s onward. It became a rallying point for three forces, each of them heavily invested (albeit for distinct reasons) in guarding the city and its resources against outsiders and socially or economically disempowered groups: the court, the magistrate, and the guilds.

Bavaria's guilds had pursued a policy of reducing admissions since the late sixteenth century. They were troubled by increasing competition and a widening social gap among their members.[34] It was only in the 1620s, however, that several guilds in the capital succeeded in implementing such restrictive policies. They owed their success to the support of Maximilian I, who propped up the interests of guildmasters and other propertied heads of households more forcefully than Bavaria's princes had done in the past.

While paternalistic government rhetoric had preceded his reign, Maximilian's rule forged a much tighter connection between the language and the politics of paternalism. His political vision mandated that God the Father exercise authority over humanity, he as the *Landesvater* (father of the land) exercise authority over his subjects, and the *Hausväter* (male heads of households) exercise authority over their dependents, including the women in their charge. The Bavarian state adopted the Roman concept of *patria potestas* in the sixteenth century, endowing at least some fathers with far-reaching power over their offspring and infusing the definition of fatherhood with economic meaning since patriarchal governance hinged on financial clout. Patriarchal rule was also a religious duty. Aegidius Albertinus, Maximilian's official and his literary mouthpiece, urged every husband to serve as "regent" and "prince" of his wife: her sal-

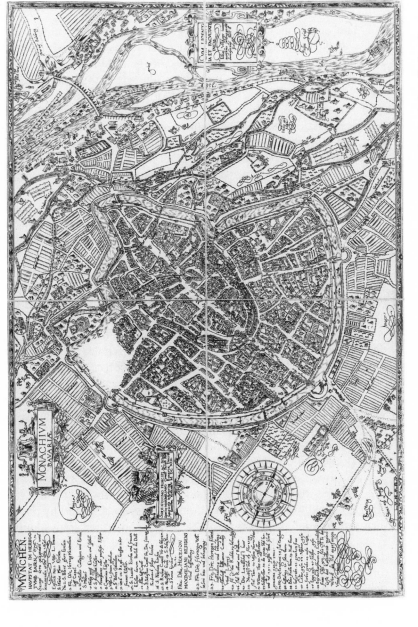

Fig. 3. Map of Munich in 1613. During the Thirty Years' War more people sought refuge behind the city's walls than the ruling elite was willing to tolerate. (Original in Bildarchiv, Bayerische Staatsbibliothek, Munich.)

vation depended on his ability to protect her against her own weak nature.[35]

The emphasis on patriarchal governance brought unprecedented rights as well as unprecedented duties for heads of households. Under Maximilian, state authorities made use of the legal instruments that had already been forged in the second half of the sixteenth century. They held men publicly accountable for the behavior of the members of their households, treating those whose dependents engaged in criminal behavior like delinquent state officials. The Munich apothecary Schmid learned about state expectations in 1614, when Maximilian commanded that the magistrate punish him harshly in order to deter other *Hausväter* from comparable actions. Schmid's crime was failure to show "due fatherly inspection." If Schmid was incapable of controlling the behavior of his lewd daughters, at least, he ought to have brought them to the attention of civic officials.[36]

The state made no secret of its intention to foist upon fathers full responsibility for controlling their dependents' behavior. A mandate of 1630 addressed Munich's male heads of households and stipulated that *Hausväter* prohibit "their children, namely sons and daughters, as well as male and female servants from roaming around during night time. Also, their beds ought to be in locked and sheltered chambers, and [*Hausväter* must] check frequently in this case too."[37]

If necessary, the Bavarian state was prepared to back up its demands on *Hausväter* with legal force. Heads of households in rural Bavaria received punishment in 50 percent of all fornication cases because they did not report the transgression to secular authorities.[38] The law also called upon fathers to assume responsibility for the actions of their grown-up sons in cases of nonmarital impregnations. In 1612, for example, Wolfgang Stauffer made payments in the civic courtroom on behalf of his son to the plaintiff Christina Eder so that "she would no longer insist on any claim because of the child either towards him or his son."[39]

In spite of its disciplinary dimension, the new paternalism primarily strengthened the position of *Hausväter* by endowing them with the officially sanctioned authority to dominate dependants and by protecting their property interests both inside their households and against outsiders. When Maximilian and his counselors interpreted the economic crisis of the early seventeenth century as due to three threats—competition by (often foreign) peddlers, an excess of guild members, and profligate marriages among the propertyless—they voiced their support for the same values of social exclusion, preservation of the material status quo, and political conservatism that propertied householders held dear. At least some Munich citizens must have welcomed Maximilian's active interference with the regulation of new admissions to the urban community. As of

1618, the Elector, convinced that only those who did not imperil the local economy through their behavior or lack of means should gain access to the capital city, forced the magistrate to report to the court on every new applicant instead of making an independent decision on admissions.[40]

Not surprisingly, the magistrate's response to the intensification of regulatory initiatives by the *Landesvater* was ambivalent. The city fathers supported his agenda in some respects but resented the inherent erosion of civic sovereignty, and they struggled with their own inability to resist centralization. Maximilian justified his infringements on civic privileges, which grew more numerous during the Thirty Years' War, in terms of his paternal obligations. Like a loving father who ruled his dependents with a strong but loving hand, the prince considered himself called by God to restore public order in every corner of his lands, first and foremost in his capital city. Overt resistance by the magistrate met with stern disapproval and warnings by the Elector, such as the threat of outright removal of the city's judicial sovereignty in 1622.[41]

Yet shared anxiety about the local economy and public order also united the *Landesvater* and city fathers. Afraid that an escalating economic crisis might trigger uprisings in the Bavarian capital,[42] magistrate and court moved on the same ground in their advocacy of regulatory and disciplinary measures to protect economic resources and social hierarchies. Profligate relations—which violated class-appropriate behavior, turned servants against their masters, and drained community chests— ranked high among the targets of such measures.

From the viewpoint of Bavaria's ruling elite, profligate behavior represented religious sin as well as social disorder; it undermined at one time human morality, the guarantor of divine benevolence, and economic stability, the guarantor of public order. An electoral decree of 1626, in an attempt to make sense of the socially and economically explosive situation in the capital city, pointed to "the evil of profligacy and (nonmarital) impregnations, which has highly incensed the almighty God."[43] In 1628, Maximilian cast "lewd marriages among country folk and other common people who have no means whatsoever" as the "main cause of dire poverty (*Bettl*)."[44] In order to "preserve and sustain the land and the people entrusted to us by God in flourishing prosperity," the court advocated control of guild admissions "so that one does not deprive the other of the means to make a living," and it outlawed marriages among "the wanton young people who have . . . neither a penny of dowry nor means of their own."[45]

Although the fight against profligacy targeted both men and women, the prosecution of female offenders quickly moved to the center. Nonmarital pregnancies, public and incontrovertible evidence of sexual transgression, provided such a convenient means of detecting profligate relations that the anti-profligacy campaign could easily turn into a campaign against nonmarital pregnancy.[46] This also helps explain why women represented more than 50 percent of delinquents in sex crimes in early-seventeenth-century Bavaria, but constituted a mere 30 percent of delinquents in overall crime.[47]

In addition, the experience of war mobilized powerful images of femininity and masculinity among the rulers as well as the ruled, with distinct implications for men's and women's behavior. Male citizenship pivoted more and more on wealth, female citizenship on sexual purity.

During the Thirty Years' War, feminine representations of cities proliferated in the German lands. The city as virgin symbolized a community's intactness, innocence, and determination to fend off enemies. Correspondingly, the city as raped woman stood for conquest, violation, and debasement. Actual women felt the power of these vitalized images. While they authorized female acts of military bravery in some instances, the representations more often underwrote sterner legal action against "wanton women" or "wenches": their sexual transgressions purportedly polluted communities and endangered collective survival.[48] To give up one's virginity willingly outside of marriage symbolized surrender of the city's incorruptibility. Proper sexual conduct hence distinguished the good female citizen from the woman traitor.

Sexuality by contrast was only a secondary feature of the good male citizen. He contributed to communal welfare during warfare either through active military defense or through his wealth. The amount of property men held determined the size of the provisions they had to make, according to a procedure that dated back to the Middle Ages. Significantly, during medieval times, Munich's women also fulfilled their obligations as female citizens by providing soldiers and weapons. Their share of provisions, just like the men's share, was then determined according to the property they possessed. Insofar as citizenship was based on the performance of military obligations, women and men were therefore on a par.

The early seventeenth century, however, witnessed a reinterpretation of citizenship for which gender difference was key. Women's alleged inability to carry arms became an argument for barring them from different forms of participation in public life, weakening their claim to citizenship. Concomitantly, the rising significance of marriage and belonging to a male-headed household pushed a derivative definition of female citizenship as tied to a husband and a family. Many polities limited women's ability to acquire citizenship independently from men and abolished women's traditional right to pass on citizenship to noncitizens upon marriage.[49]

The presence of growing numbers of billetted soldiers in urban communities added yet another dimension to these renegotiations around citizenship and public order. It had distinct ramifications for men and women. For male citizens, the move toward standing armies and a professional caste of soldiers implied that their contributions to the community's defense were increasingly financial in kind. Wealth made the burgher. For women, the large numbers of unmarried soldiers forged an ever tighter link between good female citizenship and good female sexual conduct.

Soldiers were generally forbidden to marry, yet sexual conquest of women was integral to the image and often also to the habitus of these warriors.[50] Women were exposed to more or less aggressive sexual pursuit by soldiers and systematic rape attempts by enemy troops. Such power dynamics notwithstanding, early modern culture and society tended to hold women responsible for sexual relations with soldiers. Contemporary depictions of war regularly portray women, including rape victims, as lusty and loose objects of male desire if not outright prostitutes (*Dirnen*).[51] Cities dealt harshly with women whom soldiers impregnated, expelling them from the urban community, together with other unmarried mothers.[52]

In Munich, too, the politics of expulsion and sexual discipline began to focus on unmarried sexually active women during the Thirty Years' War. The electoral court dispatched a mandate to the magistrate in 1626, requesting reports on the pregnancies of servants and unmarried daughters of burghers. The city council immediately scanned its minutes, compiled a list of culprits and enlisted the assistance of the midwives and the civic judge to obtain more names. After the judge submitted the midwives' report to the magistrate, the city fathers compared the record with their own and forwarded both listings to the Elector.[53]

As in other confessional communities, the ruling elite enlisted Munich's civic midwives to serve as informants about nonmarital pregnancies. The magistrate passed a new midwife ordinance in 1625, in which it required the city's midwives to report single mothers.[54] We can presume that its detailed stipulations resembled those outlined in the midwives' oath of office later in the century:

When you are called by unmarried persons (*menschen*) and see and detect there something suspicious and dubious, you should notify at this hour the just and knowing council, or the mayor, but above all the *Stadtoberrichter,* and every time you find some [women], who do not have husbands, you must not keep silent and report it to the mayor and the city council as soon as possible.[55]

The official perception that profligacy was on the rise in the 1620s and that the pregnancies of unmarried women were indicative of this social problem prompted the appointment of a special commission in Munich in 1629. Denouncing profligacy and nonmarital pregnancy as a "lack of respect toward God and his Most Honorable Highness," the electoral court entrusted a select group of court and urban officials with inquiry and exemplary punishment. The following justification was given for these extraordinary steps.

> The greatly prohibited vice of profligacy . . . runs rampant in this city, getting more ubiquitous and out of hand more and more day after day, so much so that the city is virtually filled with such profligate people [and] one dishonorable birth after another is taking place, one child after another is abandoned and found hither and thither, one can also see many single women with pregnant bodies running around. . . . one can never know what will happen to the fruit of the body and whether it will not be killed secretly and covered up.[56]

With the appointment of a special commission in 1629 Munich became the test site for the development of the statewide landmark mandate against profligacy to be issued in 1635.[57] The pressure from the electoral court rumbled in the city's bureaucratic apparatus, since the magistrate reacted by putting pressure on civic officials. The *Stadtoberrichter* experienced this pressure in the form of an order to take an even harsher stance on cases of extramarital pregnancy. Given the problem of "increasing fornication" in the city, the city fathers decided "to oblige the *Stadtoberrichter* to report each future case of pregnancy to the council."[58]

The development from the 1620s onward reshaped judicial decision making and brought about a harsh moral climate, as the urban community experienced warfare's devastating and destabilizing effects into the late 1640s. The virginal female body, emblem of the city's intactness and incorruptibility as well as its Catholic faith, gained in symbolic significance in Munich. After 1638, when Maximilian I had the pillar of the Virgin Mary erected in the midst of his capital city, the community's affairs, including the adjudication of cases of nonmarital sexuality in the civic court, literally took place under her watchful eye.

From the "Fall from Honor" to the "Fall of Profligacy": Female Plaintiffs before the Civic Court, 1618–49

The female plaintiffs who brought cases of nonmarital sexuality to the civic courtroom felt the repercussions of the political changes during the

Thirty Years' War. They were among the "many single women with pregnant bodies" whose sight so incensed secular authorities and spurred prosecution. Against this backdrop, Melchior Maier, defendant in a defloration and impregnation suit of 1627, encountered little difficulty in stereotyping the plaintiff Elisabeth Ettl as a profligate pregnant woman. Like male plaintiffs from the turn of the seventeenth century, Maier pushed for an unequivocally negative interpretation of the exchanges of money that had taken place between Ettl and him. Ettl admitted that she received a coin from Maier, but contended he gave it to her because "she had responded to his query about how she was doing, [by revealing] she had nothing to chew on, nor to eat." Maier presented a different picture of the transaction and of Ettl: "About three weeks before Candlemas of this year they fornicated several times, for which he gave her one *reichsdaler;* and besides, before him, another man . . . had lain with her." The judge believed Maier and freed him, absolved on all charges.[59] His role as prosecutor of profligate women was gaining the upper hand over his role as protector of honorable women.

The days when women could proudly own up to prior sexual relations or even pregnancies (as long as they had received due punishment for the acts) had come to a close. When Ursula Holftzapfl brought charges against Georg Schwefel for impregnation and child support in 1628, she admitted to a prior pregnancy, just as female plaintiffs had done in the past. Yet the judge denied Holftzapfl's claim and imposed a fine on her "because she became pregnant a second time."[60]

After a string of losses in comparable cases in the 1620s, women seemed to have learned their lesson. The general volume of lawsuits dwindled from forty-eight in the 1620s to twenty-two in the 1630s, the very moment when the criminalization and prosecution of sexual acts outside of marriage peaked in Bavaria.[61] More significant, certain kinds of cases disappeared from the civic court altogether. Suits for nonmarital pregnancy without charges of defloration or breach of promise—the most dubious cases in terms of official morality—dropped from twenty-four in the 1620s to nine in the 1630s to zero in the 1640s.

The counterpart of this disappearance was a sharp increase in the category of the most defensible cases, namely, those involving a marriage promise. These types of lawsuits reached a peak of twelve in the 1640s (after dropping from ten in the 1620s to six in the 1630s). The context of marriage formation gained in importance for making claims in the civic court. The plaintiff Anna Ridt made a telling remark in this respect when she argued her case against Wolf Humpel in a breach-of-promise suit in 1635. Humpel, she contended, "had engaged in profligacy with her, and to that end promised her marriage." His refusal to follow through on his promise had far-reaching implications for Ridt. "She had always behaved honorably and well, just once was she deprived of her honor by the defendant, and thus made into a whore."[62]

If we are to follow Ridt's reasoning, one sexual act sufficed to turn a woman into a whore before the law, so closely had female honor become tied to physical purity and marriage. Profligacy and marriage had become polarized terms that reflected a more dichotomous judicial approach to matters of female sexuality. Only within the frame of marriage, or, more specifically, courtship leading to marriage, could women relinquish their virginal honor without risking that the label *profligate* would stick in court.

Ridt's line of argument tapped into powerful legal currents. In 1635, Maximilian I passed his statewide mandate against profligacy, a landmark in the history of legislation on this issue. The state for the first time stipulated public shaming as a form of punishment in addition to fines and imprisonment. Furthermore, unlike men's prior sexual experience, women's experiences, their physical purity or impurity, had an immediate bearing on the question of punishment. The mandate drew a distinction between, on the one hand, "a single woman brought to her fall [by] seduction, matchmaking, gifts, pledges, intoxicating potions or false marriage promises" and, on the other, "common . . . women (*weibspersonen*) . . . who prostitute themselves with everyone." While the latter were considered guilty of "common and virtually public prostitution (*Hurerei*)," the first group was labeled "profligate."[63] According to this distinction, every woman who entered a sexual relationship with an unmarried man outside of matrimony was guilty of at least the crime of profligacy, if not of the crime of outright prostitution.[64]

Interestingly, the mandate resorted to the same legal language of fateful "gifts and promises" that one finds in the ordinances against the weakening of virgins (*Jungfernschwechen*). But in contrast to the legal discourse on the weakening of virgins, the legal construction of profligacy centered not on male seduction but female nonmarital sexuality. Rather than the protection of women against unwanted or consequential sexual advances, their punishment for sexual transgression provided the focal point. To the extent that the new discourse of profligacy criminalized all nonmarital sexuality, the figure of the weakened virgin faded into the background, whereas the figure of the woman as a source of profligacy moved to the center. The figure of the male seducer, in turn, became strikingly marginal.

These larger shifts help explain why female plaintiffs after 1635 seem driven by the need to convince the judge of their moral credibility and their initial physical purity. Their rhetoric marked a conspicuous departure from the uninhibited sexual confessions of female plaintiffs in the past. First of all, women harped on their physical purity prior to seduction, and the novel emphasis on virginity found judicial expression in women's request to be allowed to take an oath as a means to prove their purity.[65] Requests for oath taking started in the late 1610s and early 1620s, but they remained very rare. After 1635, oaths were in high demand.

Second, in their stories about sexual relations with men, women cast themselves as victims of cunning seduction. Ursula Höger told the judge in 1636 how Leonhard Reichart "brought her to profligacy with all kinds of means" whereas Margaret Werner spoke of "serious and unrelenting pressure" in 1642.[66] The promise of marriage, female plaintiffs asserted, was what swayed them to surrender their virginal honor. Eva Michel recounted in 1646 how her lover persuaded her "with all kinds of loving words, for he wanted to pressure her into profligacy, and finally explicitly he . . . promised her marriage, and repeated the marriage promise not just once but many times."[67]

Female plaintiffs, in a revealing change of judicial rhetoric, began to sue men for a "fall of profligacy"[68] instead of a "fall from honor." The change in terminology reflects that parameters for women's sexual honor were narrowing and thus also the basis on which women could make legal claims. Not just a temporary lapse, profligacy—the negation of lawful marriage and sanctioned sexuality—constituted a morally and economically despicable condition that was very difficult to reverse.

The new rhetoric of female plaintiffs indicates that the court no longer assumed female sexual innocence and that women correspondingly had to work harder to convince the judge of their purity and credibility. Within the legal paradigm of profligacy, female sexual transgression was indeed of greater concern than male seduction. At the same time, women's greater emphasis on how men had swayed them can be read as more than mere accommodation. It can also be regarded as a form of resistance: women persistently tried to reroute judicial attention away from their own sexual activities and back to male seduction, as if to remind the judge of his traditional legal duty to protect wronged women. This reading might account for the fact that women, albeit in declining numbers, still did bring lawsuits before the civic court.[69]

The changed moral climate was overtly inimical to women's claims and could be advantageous for some men. Let us not forget, as we emphasize the renegotiations of femininity through law and judicial procedure, that the civic court also functioned as a site of competing constructions of masculinity. It legitimated certain narratives about male desire and its objects, thus encouraging particular expressions of that desire and particular ways of being a man.

In this light, it is notable that male defendants did act more aggressively and argue more brazenly in court in the 1630s and 1640s. Compared to the statements of their predecessors, the discourse of later male defendants struck several familiar chords but took on a more daring tone. When Katharina Sedlmaier sued the servant Georg Stöckl to obtain financial compensation for breach of promise, defloration, and impregnation in 1635 "because she was no longer capable of working as a servant until the delivery," Stöckl turned the relationship between plaintiff and accused on its head. He admitted to having committed "profligacy" with her on a number of occasions, but he categorically denied the marriage promise. He had paid her for the sex every time and claimed that the child was most certainly by another man for she "had long been a whore." When Sedlmaier insisted on her version of events, Stöckl demanded angrily that the judge, on account of her steadfast refusal "to confess," throw her into the dungeon.[70]

Men's more vicious tone and aggressive stance vis-à-vis female plaintiffs could go hand in hand with a new, demonstrative submissiveness vis-à-vis the court. On the one hand, Christian Kerpamer made the unparalleled request to be admitted to the oath in order to prove "that he did not promise her [Maria Arnold] marriage." On the other hand, he told the judge "that he would submit to the decision of the authorities . . . with obedience."[71]

Male defendants of the 1630s and 1640s furthermore were able to present two new arguments for their behavior toward women. First, several men cited economic excuses for their refusal to marry women whom they admittedly had deflowered and/or impregnated.[72] Such economic reasoning fused very well with the legal perception that marriages without economic backing were by definition profligate and illegal. It appealed directly to the authorities' interest in economic stability and public order. Within this normative frame of reference, lack of financial means was a legitimate reason to break off a relationship, and honorable male behavior and good citizenship were compatible with reneging on promises one should not keep. When these men said no to women, they thus also said yes to the state.

Second, male defendants cited women's consent to sex as evidence of their loose morals and a reason for rejecting the legitimacy of women's legal claims. The domestic Mathias Gais refuted Katharina Fischer's charges of broken promises and defloration in 1643 on these grounds. Even though he had had carnal relations with her and confessed the "profligacy," he pointed out to the judge that "the act happened with both their consent, without force and without pressure."[73] Consensual sex, a powerful element of proof for the mutually binding character of a sexual relationship in the days before Trent, became transformed into an argument against mutual obligations within the post-Trent discourse of profligacy. If we follow the logic of this male argument, women had to show resistance to sex if they wanted compensation later on.

Work on breach-of-promise cases adjudicated in other regions suggests that this might have been a long-term and possibly Europe-wide trend. In Catholic Piedmont, for instance, the overall number of cases based on sexual intercourse declined dramatically between 1600 and 1800, and women began to speak of rape more and more frequently. While intercourse at first could be cited in support of a woman's claim in court, later on evidence of a physical relationship easily worked to the detriment of the female plaintiff, forcing women to emphasize that the act had taken place against their will.[74]

There were comparable developments in Protestant territories as well. Conceptions of female virginity were initially malleable in sixteenth-century Basel, but these flexible understandings ultimately gave way to a definition of virginity based on physical purity alone.[75] In conjunction with this trend, marriage court judges shifted the judicial focus from arbitration of conflict to punishment of nonnormative sexual acts and enforcement of a new morality. Women's chances for a favorable ruling in cases of broken promises declined dramatically as a consequence of this new overriding interest in persecuting nonmarital sexuality. If female plaintiffs wanted to avoid charges of seduction and loss of legal claims to compensation, they had to make strategic use of tales of violence.[76]

Protestants also displayed an aversion to lower-class sexuality, in particular the sexuality of *Dirnen,* that echoed the moralist tirades of Munich's Catholic rulers against the evils of profligacy. Thus the magistrate of Schwäbisch Hall blamed the "profligate and defiant behavior of servants" for the debilitating effects of the Thirty Years' War. By the second half of the seventeenth century, disobedient and lewd maids attracted even more scorn and scrutiny than their male counterparts. Dishonoring punishments for sexual misconduct were dealt out mostly to women, decreasing significantly their chances for marriage later on. Also, antifornication laws took account of women's sexual history in assessing the severity of a violation, while men's sexual history was exempted from judicial examination.[77]

The regulation of marriage and sexuality following the Reformation, then, led to a worsening of already existing inequities between men and women in Protestant and Catholic polities. What distinguishes the case of Munich from the case of Protestant Basel, however, is the overt and pronounced class bias of moral and social disciplining. To require proof of property for the validity of a marriage was unheard of in Basel.[78] Paradoxically, the Protestant city fathers kept marriage untainted by the worldly considerations of economics, whereas Munich's Catholic magistrate, who in theory subscribed to the Tridentine understanding of marriage as sacrament, ran an institution, the bureau of marriage, explicitly set up to secure worldly matrimonial concerns' pride of place above spiritual ones.

There was also the abiding religious ideal of chastity that created a distinct set of circumstances in Catholic places like Munich. But what was its institutional relevance for women of the lower classes who could not afford (and perhaps had little desire) to join religious communities? The decline of alternatives to married life made this an even more pressing question. At a minimum, though, this ideal seemed to suggest the possibility of abstinence (something the Protestant view of a natural sex drive denied single women), and in so doing it perhaps helped women create collectively shared religious meaning out of an involuntary personal choice.

Then again, the ideological pull of the virginal life could translate into pressure on lower-class women to guard lines of sexual and social purity, an interpretation supported by the court records. Munich's civic judge and the law he represented increasingly treated an economically stable marriage as the sole rightful site of sexual activity. Subsequently, lack of financial means, or rather the specter of profligacy, could serve as an excuse for lower-class men. They could invoke the more restrictive attitudes and laws to avoid obligations toward women. We might even say that citizenship required men to say no—a no that significantly was directed mainly at the consequences of sex rather than sex itself, creating a subterfuge for male desires. Men might still desire and even sleep with women, but they might only feel the need to meet certain obligations vis-à-vis some women.

Lower-class women, by comparison, confronted greater risks in the wake of profligacy laws if they engaged in nonmarital sex. Virginity was most safely given in the context of marriage, while access to this institution was predicated on economic standing. The Tridentine concept of marriage as a sacrament for all Christians remained utopian for poor women. Trent's importance to their lives lay elsewhere: the distinction between nonmarital sex and marital intimate relations (a differentiation that became possible with the Tridentine publicity requirement) caught up with these women in the guise of new forms of female respectability. It was increasingly tricky for them to meet the novel sexual norms—short of abstaining from sexual relations altogether and embracing chastity instead.

To the extent to which issues of population control drove the antiprofligacy campaign, the economic and demographic recovery after the Thirty Years' War led to a temporary relaxation of measures. The Bavarian state indeed mandated more lenient punishments in 1651 for cases of nonmarital sex if offenders agreed to marry one another.[79] But in the 1680s Munich's authorities once again sharpened punishments for profligacy and reiterated prohibitions against marriages among the poor.[80] A state ordinance of 1722 introduced even harsher forms of humiliation for fornicators, making special provisions for the poor. While these punishments were seldom meted out, it was women who suffered from them most of the time.[81]

More important still, surface adjustments, such as temporary reductions of punishments, did not reverse the subterranean shifts in constructions of gender and sexuality that had taken place. The discourse of profligacy attached new meanings to particular sexual practices, and those meanings stuck. In the city of Munich, the state's view of matrimony (and of sexuality) as an estate privilege had become firmly established. A letter of 1723 by Munich's bishop (who resided in Freising) to one of the local clerics brings this long-term development into sharp focus. He granted the clergyman permission to solemnize a marriage between two people from small villages outside of Munich, yet he could not help but add a cautionary note: "Also you should indicate to them [the spouses] in case they should not be wanted in this territory as nonresidents [*unansessige*], they cannot get help from here [i.e., the bishop]."[82] A religious wedding, in other words, pulled little weight in the civic environment where marriage was restricted to those who could establish themselves as economically viable members of the civic community before the bureau of marriage. This is indeed how Munich's city fathers read the letter. They kept a copy and glossed it as follows: "Marriages might very well be granted by Freising, but it is up to the secular authorities to tolerate those people or drive them out."[83]

The post-Trent transition from marriage as a private contract to marriage as a public performance entailed a profound redefinition of the body politic because it enabled differentiation between proper and improper forms of sexuality. Urban authorities fitted the publicity requirement to a political agenda of creating a community of economically reliable married Catholic burghers. The *Hochzeitsamt* combined attempts at *sexual* with attempts at *social* purification, inevitably criminalizing lower-class sexuality in the process. The regulatory efforts were mapped in a gender-specific manner on to male and female bodies. Above all, the discourse of profligacy led to a labeling of lower-class women as a source of moral pollution and therefore grave social danger. Hence, they were relegated to a state of virginity.

"The Most Cruel Mother": Who Cares about Children?

Amidst the stories of men and women, which the civic court coauthored, and the constructions of masculinity and femininity, which it underpinned in its judicial practice, one can also find tales about children and changing conceptions of parenthood under profligacy law. Most pertinent is a reinterpretation of motherhood that privileged the maternal over the paternal tie in cases of illegitimate offspring. This further exacerbated the detrimental consequences of profligacy legislation for lower-class women and amplified the pressure on them to remain chaste.

Paternal obligations determined the traditional judicial approach to nonmarital pregnancies. If court records apply the term "natural" to characterize the bond of obligation uniting child and parent, they do so only in reference to the fatherly tie and never to the mother's connection to the offspring. The discursive counterpoint to the "real natural father"[84] is the "faithful mother."[85] The former's rights and duties are absolute, the latter's merely contingent. The plaintiff Ursula Steigperger put it in pithy language to make her case for compensation before the civic judge: "it is not disputable that every father takes his child in accordance with the rights of nature [*natierliche rechte*] from the time of birth until the time when [children] can earn their own bread."[86]

Fathers who surrendered this right to control over children to the child's mother still had the duty to make financial provisions for the offspring: payments, clothing, and, later on, a dowry or marriage portion.[87] The law thus placed the primary burden of proof in nonmarital pregnancy suits on men who were accused of fathering children. Unless a defendant could supply sufficient evidence that a child was not his, his obligation to assume financial responsibility for the child remained unquestioned, even in cases where the court denied the female plaintiff all other claims.[88]

Over time, however, the anti-profligacy campaign accented the maternal rather than the paternal bond by moving the "woman pregnant outside of wedlock" into the limelight of state sexual regulation. There is a shift in the civic court records, subtle but noticeable, toward a closer discursive association between mothers and children in the context of illegitimacy. By the mid–seventeenth century, unmarried pregnant women, especially those who had carried a child before, received a less favorable hearing in the courtroom. Their prior sexual history mattered, while the issue of whether a man had previously fathered another child was of no interest to the judge.[89]

Along the same discriminatory lines, the law was more likely to push women toward avoidance of nonmarital sexual involvement or, at the very least, self-indictment and acceptance of punishment for profligacy if they became pregnant. Women eventually needed to report the pregnancy in order to secure their full legal rights. Ursula Steigperger, the woman who spoke so eloquently to the natural duties of fathers, had a very strong case for breach of promise involving witnesses, including a priest. Still, she left the courtroom with rather small gains. Although the judge ordered the defendant to take the child, he denied Steigperger any compensation for her nonmarital pregnancy, arguing that she "had hidden this affair irresponsibly from the authorities for such a long time."[90] In all likelihood, Steigperger had refrained from bringing suit because she held out hope that her lover would come through on his promise, but profligacy legislation had turned her reliance upon traditional courtship mechanisms into an offense that limited her rights.

By the 1680s, state law had created a virtually automatic association between concealment of a nonmarital pregnancy and what was arguably the crime of the century: infanticide. Even though infanticide—an offense confined to unmarried women—was a serious crime punishable by death, prior to the seventeenth century it was one among other severe criminal acts, and its prosecution occurred on criminal rather than moral terms. By the seventeenth century, infanticide connoted sexual immorality as well as criminal cruelty. The nonmarital sexual act now constituted a factor in assessing the severity of the punishment and in the intent behind its execution. The unmarried pregnant woman developed, in Isabell Hull's phrase, "into the state's legal nightmare."[91] When an alleged child-murderess was put to death in the city of Augsburg in 1687, authorities thus explained their actions as a measure "to deter other profligate women of this kind (*andern dergleichen leichtfertigen Weibs Persohnen zum schröcken*)."[92]

Bavaria passed its first statewide mandate against infanticide in 1684. It reflected official anxieties over what looked like an inescapable slippery slope from profligacy to infanticide:

> Because it happens that the women who are impregnated in dishonor, do not only hide and deny their pregnancy maliciously, but also give birth to their children secretly and in a dangerous manner in secret places, or drop them, and if afterwards they are asked and imprisoned because the child was found dead, they deny everything, just like they hid their pregnant body all the time before. . . . So we order and mandate . . . that if in the future some such women hide their pregnancy, deliberately give birth on their own, and finally leave the child in hidden places for disposal so that the same child dies of hunger or cold, or for any other reason loses life, that such women will be treated not any differently from the mother who kills her child willingly.[93]

Interestingly, it is in this context of illegitimate sexuality and infanticide that the legal discourse invoked the natural bond between mother and child. The mandate decreed that such "most cruel mother, who goes against nature and kills her own flesh and blood be brought from life to death by the sword—of this every woman should beware (*davor sich eine jede Weibspersohn zu hutten weis*)."[94] The natural duties of (unmarried) mothers, in this scheme of things, dictated that she publicly bear the child and in effect turn herself in to the authorities.

There is significant evidence that child abandonment and infanticide was on the rise in Bavaria. Electoral privy council minutes from the late seventeenth century register a sharp increase in cases that can hardly be explained as the result of a mere increase in persecutory state activity.[95] Admission registrars of Munich's Heilig-Geist foundling hospital document that the number of abandoned children soared from 22 (1670–1700) to 86 (1700–1730) to 190 (1730–60).[96] Barbara Gebhart, one of the plaintiffs in the civic court, also brought her son Kaspar to the foundling hospital in 1644 after the father, Georg Windthamer, had taken flight.[97] A servant by profession, Gebhart would have encountered great economic obstacles if she had kept the child. A note attached to one of the foundlings of the Heilig-Geist hospital speaks to the precarious situation in which unmarried lower-class mothers could find themselves. The mother, also an unmarried servant-maid, justified her decision as follows: "I have given to this point everything I have saved up during my time of service, spent everything on [the child], so that I don't know what else to do."[98]

The subsequent Enlightenment debate on infanticide was a specifically German phenomenon absent from public discourse in other European countries. This debate singled out avoidance of humiliating punishment as the prime motivation of child murderesses—an explanation that earlier literature on the topic took at face value. More recent research, however, has pinpointed economic rather than psychological factors behind infanticide.[99] While dread of shame probably played a greater role in the urban context where pollution fears led to a harsher attitude toward dishonored persons,[100] more flexible attitudes toward dishonor and the better integration of illegitimate children in the social structure of the countryside minimized the impact of public humiliation and thus anxieties about its consequences; instead, in rural society, progressive impoverishment appears to have driven lower-class women toward infanticide.[101]

For the state, profligacy constituted an economic as well as a moral offense. If we accept that both economics and shame were factors in child abandonment and infanticide, albeit factors of varying importance, anti-profligacy legislation contributed to these phenomena in two ways. First, it turned the nonmarital sexuality of lower-class women into a particularly dishonoring activity and decreased their chances for marriage. Second, it placed greater obstacles in the way of lower-class female litigants who sought economic restitution in cases of broken marriage promises and nonmarital impregnations in the courts. An altered judicial climate was likely to have negative effects on women's chances for out-of-court settlements as well. In the Altmarck, for instance, successful arbitrations outside of the courtroom declined immediately once word got out into the communities that judges had become less zealous in prosecuting men for nonmarital sexuality and more likely to hold women completely responsible.[102]

The Enlightenment debate on infanticide, by focusing exclusively on the issue of individual shame, masked the most pressing socioeconomic problems of lower-class women and also how state measures contributed to these problems, even while it professed concern for the women's point-of-view and a critical attitude toward state sexual policies. The Enlightenment's greater emphasis on the individual arguably reinforced rather than countered the effects of absolutist regulation and women's greater responsibilities in sexual matters. On the one hand, the Enlightenment opened the door for the removal of state-sponsored humiliation of female sex offenders and the decriminalization of all consensual sexual acts, replacing reliance on coercion with reliance on education and individual responsibility.[103] On the other hand, it concealed the mechanisms by which previous state activity had already shaped this individual responsibility along gender-specific lines and placed the main burden upon lower-class women. This chapter uncovered some of these mechanisms.

CHAPTER 4

Behind Closed Doors: The Public Dimensions of Private Acts

The regulatory forces unleashed by the Thirty Years' War also transformed the second institution alongside marriage that regulated women's lives and gender relations after Trent: the convent. Women's social location in marriage became defined more sharply in terms of subordination to a male head of a household who represented his dependents in the newly emerging public sphere. This legal, institutional, and discursive redefinition had a negative impact on women's experience of married life and their abilities to refuse matrimony altogether. It was most consequential for women who lacked the means to enter matrimony, presenting them with the meager options of either a life of nonmarital sexual relations or a life of sexual abstinence.

A close look at the dynamics of cloistering Munich's religious women during the Thirty Years' War reveals that analogous trends characterized developments in this social arena and that the reform of female religious convents amplified the gender and class biases of marital legislation. In design as well as in effect, the Trent-inspired reform of Munich's female convents mirrored the secular reform of marriage. By making men public representatives of the women in their charge, the Tridentine church's and the confessional state's strategies for reforming society came together. The convergence of these reform measures accentuated control over women as one of the hallmarks of masculinity, including that of celibate clerics. In this context, male ecclesiastics, whose renunciation of sexuality could position them as a "third sex" beyond gender dimorphism in the centuries leading up to the Reformation, were unequivocally gendered as men.

The Trent-inspired reforms of Munich's female religious houses had a range of effects on religious women and constructions of femininity. Enclosure channeled traditionally activist forms of piety into inward-looking, mystical venues, and it turned female communities into more exclusive as well as more hierarchical institutions. Institutions that once represented an alternative to marriage for women of varying social backgrounds began to serve an increasingly select group of wealthy women. One alternative to marriage was thus disappearing for lower-class women outside the cloister at the very moment in time when these women also suffered from restricted access to matrimony.

For the upper-class women inside the cloister, virginal purity acquired greater social and symbolic value. The virginal female body was deemed the most efficacious means for conferring God's grace upon a polity, and the female religious life came to be the only truly honorable estate aside from matrimony. Against the backdrop of mounting concerns over uncontrolled female sexuality in society at large, cloistering ensured the religious virgin's inviolate condition and her abiding potency. It also promoted a cultural image of the nun as first and foremost a bride of Christ, simultaneously gendering the nun as a woman and sexualizing her body as a female body that—like all female bodies—necessitated male supervision.

However, while some religious women embraced the new regime of confinement more or less willingly, many of them fought subordination to men and exclusion from public life in a surprisingly ingenious manner. Among the examples of their resistance discussed in this chapter we find the organization of intercessory prayers on behalf of the larger community and also the display of decorated holy bones for public veneration in cloister churches. Ironically, these practices were authorized by the same Council of Trent that otherwise decreed the sequestration of nuns. The paradoxical outcome points to the enduring emancipatory potential of the Catholic ideal of virginity, which could enable women to utilize the space of the convent and their virginal bodies for their own purposes in spite of and, at times, in fact because of Tridentine enclosure.

In theorizing the relationship between space and social practices, Michel de Certeau has drawn an intriguing distinction between strategy and tactics based on control over space. De Certeau uses this distinction to capture the essentially asymmetrical power relations between ruler and ruled without depriving the ruled of their agency. While the powerful can devise long-term strategies from their own "proper place," de Certeau suggests, the weak can at best resort to short-term tactics. Quasi exiles in the social territory of the powerful, they have to make creative use of the spaces assigned to them, seizing opportunities for the pursuit of their own interests as they arise and, if necessary, appropriating the norms of the powerful.[1]

De Certeau's reflections offer a useful tool for thinking about the space of the Munich convents after Trent-inspired enclosure. When the

space of the cloister became important to secular and ecclesiastical authorities who could operate from their own place, these men decreed enclosure,
and the religious women had little say in the matter. Yet even though
structural boundaries were effectively imposed upon nuns, the women
proved themselves to be resourceful tacticians who made the best of circumstances they did not choose and even devised clever ways of countering new controls. Closed doors may have locked women in, but they also
locked men out. After the abolition of urban brothels in the sixteenth century, nunneries were in fact the only all-female institution in early modern
Germany, leaving women to their own devices in an unparalleled space of
their own.

Cloistering, Confessional Conflict, and Centralization

> Anno 1620 on the third of May, the day of the Holy Cross, there came
> hither an Italian Franciscan and 10 others with him from Milan,
> Reformati in wooden shoes.[2]

With this laconic characterization, an anonymous Pütrich sister began her
account of the Trent-inspired reforms, which transformed her convent and
the Ridler community from open religious houses into cloistered nunneries in the third decade of the seventeenth century. To the anonymous nun
the most remarkable feature of the Franciscans coming from afar was
their footwear—a tangible image of their foreignness and their import of
things Italian into the world of Bavaria. While the women in the two convents had been able to fend off a first attempt by Italians to implement Tridentine reform in their convents in 1583, outright resistance to enclosure
was no longer an option by 1620. The men in the wooden shoes brought
with them reform measures that were meant to alter key features of female
monastic life.

During this first decade of the Thirty Years' War, state efforts to
regulate behavior and extirpate sin achieved new levels of intensity in
Munich. Maximilian inundated his capital with a wave of mandates and
ordinances, and he marshaled an army of secular officials in charge of
seeing to the moral purification of Munich.[3] These changes hit lower-
class laywomen particularly hard, foisting upon them the primary
responsibility for purging the community of the stain of nonmarital sexual regulation. During the 1620s, Bavaria's prince also initiated the
process by which the religious women in the Pütrich and Ridler convents
were to be put under lock and key. Inviting the ecclesiastical reformers
from Italy to implement the reforms that had been decreed at Trent more
than half a century earlier, Maximilian extended his regulatory efforts to

the city's female tertiary communities and enlisted their inmates for the purification of the community.

Holy virgins constituted an important public resource in early modern communities because their religious work, sanctified through their denunciation of the sexual life, was believed to confer spiritual protection upon the collectives that housed them;[4] they became an especially precious commodity in times of great need. The cloistering of these women at the center of Trent's project of drawing sharp boundaries between the sacred and the profane could accomplish two goals for the Bavarian prince. It could increase the religious women's spiritual efficacy by safeguarding permanently its foundation of virginal purity with a bulwark against worldly pollution. It could also create the preconditions for redeploying the spiritual resource that they embodied out of society and toward service for the state, by isolating these virgins from the larger urban community.

Not only the timing and context of Maximilian's collaboration with the Italian Reformati but its motivation and institutional articulation reveal the compatibility of the prince's designs for a centralized Catholic state and the monastic reform agenda of the Tridentine church. An unusually ascetic and conservative yet very popular group of Franciscans,[5] the Reformati belonged to the new and reformed religious orders that were among the most powerful forces behind Catholic renewal. Like the Jesuits and Capuchins, the Reformati promised to propagate the Catholic morals that Maximilian hoped to instill in his subjects.

Above and beyond their impeccable credentials as promoters of orthodoxy, the monks operated within a unique and portable organizational structure with the potential of advancing the institutional unity of the Bavarian state. Unlike other Franciscan branches, the Reformati could form their own provinces and did not have to work within already existing institutional frameworks, even though they were subject to and hence legitimated by the leadership of the Franciscan General.[6] This mode of organization made it possible for Maximilian to dislodge the Franciscan Observants whose province included Bavaria's Franciscan houses but spanned territories beyond his control. Because the Observants' province disrupted the institutional unity of his evolving state, the Bavarian prince entrusted the Reformati not only with the reform of the Observants' houses but also with the foundation of a new Franciscan province with contours that had to be identical with Bavaria's political borders. The monastic establishments in the Bavarian capital were designated as the starting point of the territory-wide reconfiguration and institutional centralization.[7]

The Reformati's program finally complemented Maximilian's social vision of an orderly commonwealth built on Catholic male-headed households, insofar as it included the Tridentine reform of female convents. Foregrounding male governance and female obedience, Trent's design for convent reform in essence promoted an ecclesiastical version of the male-household model for religious institutions. With the implementation of this program, the space of women's cloisters became a site where ecclesiastical authorities could prove their ability to rule and their masculinity, but also an arena where religious women resisted the society-wide trend toward male public governance.

Social Relations and Public Identifications after Enclosure

Shortly upon their arrival the Reformati, under the leadership of Antonio Galbiato, took over local Franciscan institutions. They deposed Munich's Franciscan Guardian and turned the convent of the Friars Minor into a base for orchestrating monastic reform. From there the Reformati conducted a string of visitations to the female houses, deposed mother superiors and confessors as they saw fit, and replaced them with officials more amenable to reform.[8] While Galbiato let nine male novices depart from the convent of the Friars Minor, he seems to have prohibited such departures in the women's communities.[9] The female Franciscan tertiaries whose convent life had begun under different rules had years of experiencing the effect of Galbiato's reform ahead of them: approximately two-thirds of the Pütrich sisters were in their twenties, thirties, and forties.[10] For Antonio Galbiato himself, the claustration of the two women's convents represented a first step on the ladder toward an impressive church career. By 1628—the year in which the first visitation without concomitant oustings of officials took place in the Pütrich convent—his reformatory zeal had earned the Franciscan monk the rank of General Commisarius of the newly founded transalpine Reformati provinces.[11]

Galbiato's ascent on the ecclesiastical career ladder left the Ridler and Pütrich convents fundamentally transformed. To begin with, the physical structure of the religious houses was altered and contact with secular people became severely restricted. After much architectural remodeling, living quarters and devotional spaces in the Pütrich convent formed a compact area of confinement to which the mother superior and the newly appointed gatekeeper alone held the key.[12] A bell at the gate announced visits by the confessor or the call by a doctor should a serious illness require his presence. The cloister interfaced with the larger world at two points. A chamber adjacent to the cloistered sphere, the parlatorium, served as an area for the reception of outsiders who could speak to the nuns through the barred windows separating the chamber from the cloister itself.[13] There was also a convent church where nuns fulfilled their liturgical duties in the choir while Munich's faithful gathered for prayers and masses in the nave.[14]

Not only did confinement bring greater isolation from the secular world, it also implied closer supervision by male Franciscans. It has been argued that enclosure reduced female networks and multiplied dependence on male clergy.[15] In the case of Munich's tertiaries, their religious networks of clergymen apparently shrank along with the women's secular networks, pushing them under the central authority of the Reformati. No longer able to choose spiritual guides of their own preference among Munich's religious, the women had to rely on the spiritual care of the Reformati only.[16] At the same historical moment when the post-Trent church promoted salvation through regular partaking of the eucharist and frequent confessions,[17] the women were barred from meeting their spiritual needs in the larger environment. Instead they became entirely dependent on the daily masses, which the Reformati conducted in the cloister, and the opportunities for confessions these Franciscan men provided. The central role of the Reformati in indoctrinating the women in the spirit of the Counter-Reformation is also evident in the examinations of female novices, which they began to conduct after the reforms and which also included testing the knowledge of the catechism.[18]

Doctrinal exams, mandatory masses, and regular confessions were but some of the means of exacting compliance with the new regime. An even more powerful technique of disciplining the bodies and minds of these women, who had been deprived of their freedom of movement and their choice of religious supervision, was the imposition of the Latin breviary upon the nuns.[19] Prior to cloistering, their spiritual labor entailed daily recitations of the Hours of Our Lady. A relatively short routine in the vernacular, this form of ritual prayer accommodated lengthy absences from the religious house. The Latin breviary, by its very design, served the opposite goal since it bound the nuns to the rhythms of monastic hours and thus more closely to the cloistered space. Again and again, it forced the women into the universe of a language other than their mother tongue, adding linguistic distance to the insurmountable physical distance between convent and larger community.

This realignment of pious practices and spatial movement was inseparable from the establishment of a two-tier system of convent members and the permanent inscription of social stratification upon the spiritual community. Galbiato established a whole new class of lay sisters whose primary purpose it was to free up the so-called choir-nuns for their liturgical and spiritual work by taking care of the manual labor in the communities. Although the lay sisters took vows like nuns, they were excluded from electing the convent's mother superior and were generally second-class citizens within the convent community. Their habit was plainer, the rituals surrounding their entry less elaborate,[20] and their work was the work of social inferiors in early modern society. In line with this set of social expectations, lay sisters were recruited from lower social strata, including the peasantry,[21] while the choir-nuns in charge of prestigious contemplative work had family backgrounds that ran the gamut from esteemed professions[22] to patrician origins all the way to the nobility.[23] This social differentiation simultaneously paralleled and reinforced the growing class differentiation among women in the world. Future choir-sisters, all of them upper-class women and none of them among the disenfranchised women barred from secular matrimony, were screened for their ability to read, write, and sing after enclosure.[24] They were even encouraged to bring their own musical instruments into the cloistered convents,[25] which developed a reputation for their impressive choral music in the decades following enclosure.[26]

The raising of walls transformed the nuns' collective identity and its public presentation. The meaning of religious life and the metaphorical, iconographic, and ritual means of expressing that meaning had always differed for men and women. Consecration rites for nuns focused on their commitment to permanent virginity at the same time that they defined nuns through the nuptial symbolism of bride of Christ. Both symbolic poles tied religious women first and foremost to their body and to the heavenly husband to whom they gave their virginity. While female religious identity thus pivoted on the metaphor of marriage, male religious identity drew on a military symbolism that was at its most pronounced in the Jesuit concept of the soldier of Christ.[27]

The case of Munich's nuns illustrates that physical segregation could foreground even further already existing nuptial understandings of women's monastic identity. When the Reformati, who themselves embodied rather well the masculine and militant spirit of the Counter-Reformation, cloistered the women in the tertiary communities, they transformed two rites of passage in ways that played up the marital theme of female religious life. With the installation of a permanent border between cloister and world, entrance into and exit from the community upon death became particularly charged rites of passage and forceful vehicles for the promotion of the matrimonial model of female monasticism.

Traditionally the day of entry into the communities was referred to as *Einkleidung,* the investiture with the garments of the religious woman. After claustration the ritual segment viewed at a public ceremony by the urban community was labeled "spiritual wedding" and came to bear greater resemblance to secular weddings. Novices began to send out invitations to kin, friends, and guests of honor, whose presence they desired at their wedding day.[28] Like secular brides, the women who were destined to marry God wore wreaths of varying sizes symbolizing chastity and social status and investing them with the identity of the virgin ready to receive her groom. Novices of lower strata, whose future station was that of lay sisters, wore small wreaths and loose braids,[29] whereas the upper-class women, who joined the ranks of the choir-sisters, adorned themselves with wreaths akin to crowns and kept their braids hidden underneath the headdress.[30]

What made the symbolic parallels with secular weddings particularly effective was the circumstance that after enclosure a nun's wedding day represented her first and last appearance on the public stage of the civic community. Before embracing the austerity of cloistered life and vanishing behind cloister walls, there was only one chance to display earthly wealth and claim the honor attached to choosing the heavenly spouse and cloister walls over a secular husband and life in a male-headed household. Because cloistering telescoped one's life choice into this moment of transition and self-dramatization, it fostered not just the identification of nuns as brides of Christ but rather an equation of nuns with brides. Novices indeed began to carry down the aisle a doll of the heavenly bridegroom whose lavish garb of precious stones bespoke their desire to commit to public memory an image of themselves as pious, reputable (i.e., virginal), and fortunate women.[31]

While the spiritual wedding turned into the sole possibility of self-presentation to Munich's urban community, its counterpart, the so-called heavenly wedding, or death of a nun, changed from a rite of community-controlled self-display to an externally staged reminder of the nuns' invisibility. Prior to enclosure the religious women themselves carried the corpse of a dead sister through Munich's streets to its final resting place in the convent of the Friars Minor, a conspicuous reminder of the sisters' control over their own bodies and their access to the larger urban environment. After they were locked in, the women were forced to hand over dead members to secular men, who assumed the role of carrying these female bodies to their grave. Displaying the bodies of dead sisters in the street, these men inevitably communicated a message about the living nuns behind walls: they no longer had a place in public, not even to bury and mourn their dead whose graves were located in the male monastery beyond the nuns' reach. The question that male superiors began to pose to every new applicant—"did she intend to go into the cloister, so that she may live and die there and not wish to get out of there until one will carry her dead [body] out?"[32]—not only evoked the indissolubility of marital vows that only death had the power to sever; it also placed the surrender of the body squarely at the heart of female cloistered life. During her lifetime the nun's body was dedicated to the contemplative service of a bride of Christ. After her death it became a quasi-public object handled and watched over by men.

Contesting the Meaning of Enclosure

In 1957, the leading (male) church historian of the two Munich convents reported that the nuns "approved of and accepted unanimously" Tridentine reforms in 1621, and that once the architectural alterations were completed

> the sisters in the Pütrich cloister could be truly locked in and claustrated on the eve of the first of December and the nuns in the Ridler cloister finally also on the third of December. Apparently strict claustration was implemented in both places without *any* resistance or friction.[33]

Narratives by individual sisters that have survived among the convents' archival holdings belie this twentieth-century portrayal of enclosure as a smooth, unproblematic event to which the sisters happily consented. These internal records conjure up a rather different, more disquieting image of Tridentine reform, in which the locking of convent doors marked only the beginning of decade-long struggles. Munich's female tertiaries had long resisted enclosure for the same reasons religious women sought to avoid it in other parts of Catholic Europe: it spelled a departure from centuries of close contact, facilitated by crannied walls and open doors, between nuns, their families, and urban communities.[34] Although they ultimately had to live with the imposition of cloistering in the 1620s, their varied responses, ranging from stubborn resistance to grudging acceptance to wholehearted embrace, show that their convents remained highly contested spaces in which conflicts were played out long after the actual reforms.

In the Pütrich convent a struggle ensued immediately over the adoption of the breviary and the acquisition of the Latin language it presupposed. Galbiato ousted a string of convent confessors who failed at the task of teaching the nuns Latin. Even the final confessor to hold the office had "a lot of trouble" with the sisters.[35] Over a third of the women, mainly of the older generation, some of them in poor health, completely refused to learn and pray the breviary, continuing to honor the old order of doing things through the breach of the new.[36] Noncompliance with convent prayer signaled refusal to participate in a communal life that was no longer one's own, a potent way of claiming agency in a situation of meager options. The same mechanisms that made the breviary an effective disciplinary tool, its everydayness, repetitiveness, and ritualistic quality, also made it a powerful tool of resistance. Like other "weapons of the weak,"[37] this weapon could only be wielded to signal dissent, not to change circumstance, but in the charged and repetitive context of convent ritual nuns could wield it forcefully again and again.

Some nuns also expressed resistance and perhaps resolved the psychological quagmires of involuntary enclosure through apparitions. While these visions took place in the theater of the individual self, their collective remembrance in convent records and oral traditions suggests the deep roots of these individual experiences in communal concerns. On the eve of cloistering in 1620, Sister Anna Prumer from the Ridler convent supposedly came face-to-face with the Franciscan Saint Bonaventure because the religious woman experienced feelings of great indignation at the prospect of a life in claustration. Faced with her obstinacy Bonaventure banged his fist on the table in her cell, leaving no room for debate about the wisdom of women's cloistering and commanding: "Thus it must be! [So muß es sein]." The story became part of convent memory. Long after sister Anna departed from this world, the table on which Bonaventure's fist imprinted a clear message about sequestration was displayed in the convent to prove the authenticity of Prumer's vision and, by implication, the inevitability of women's cloister.[38]

Over time, these Tridentine values appear to have become even more internalized. In a later apparition to a Ridler sister in 1689, Caecilia Reischl, mother superior of the Pütrich convent during her lifetime, took Saint Bonaventure's place as an advocate of the norms of enclosure and obedience toward male superiors. During her visitations to the younger nun, Caecilia allegedly specified a long list of prayers needed for the rescue of twenty-nine tormented suffering souls, including her own. Soon the convent confessor became aware of these requests and urged his spiritual advisee to find out why Caecilia was suffering in purgatory when next she visited: did she perhaps have any words of warning for his flock? Caecilia's answer, as related by the visionary Ridler nun, stressed two things: obedience and seclusion from secular life. Caecilia supposedly named unwillingness to obey and to punish her sisters for disobedience while she was in office as the reasons for her purgatorial pain, and she passed on the following message for the confessor:

He should admonish them [his female charges] to be obedient, for disobedience must be punished most severely; and he should admonish them that they may lay off all shame during confession, and that they confess all their sins, and that they do not have as much community with secular folk, for it is a destruction of the spirit.[39]

Caecilia's exhortations and the circumstance of their utterance reveal both the sisters' abiding desire for connection with the secular sphere and the taboo of enclosure that now effectively circumscribed the experience of that desire. On one level, Caecilia's alleged words of wisdom from the beyond suggest that nuns continued to insist on their own way of doing things and that, decades after the involuntary reform, obedience to the new rules was still not to be taken for granted. Claustration apparently could not squelch the thirst for contact with the world outside of the cloister. On another level, the wish for "community with secular folk" already seems to have become charged with fantasies of destruction and punishment and coded as the kind of shameful sin for which only the confessional and its male agent could offer spiritual remedies and psychological relief.

On the other end of the spectrum of conceivable responses to enclosure stood Sister Maximiliana from the Ridler convent. What most sisters accepted grudgingly, Sister Maximiliana desired with all her heart. According to her biographer the lack of enclosure had been "odious" to Maximiliana for years, and she had long worked for a stricter religious discipline.[40] Maximiliana's time came when the Reformati arrived in Munich in 1620. Her story bespeaks two other crucial aspects of Tridentine reform: the potential attractiveness of sequestration to religious women and the unease of male churchmen in the face of a woman who took their own dictates to extremes.

Formerly Maximiliana of Wartenberg, this religious woman was related to the ruling dynasty and spent her youth at the Bavarian court where she enjoyed a humanist education. Her privileged background combined with a powerful character to turn her into a driving force behind the cloistering of the two tertiary communities. Although convent rumor had it that opponents to enclosure among the Ridler and Pütrich nuns plotted her assassination, Maximiliana, undeterred by hatred and danger, collaborated with Galbiato, who found in her, at least initially, a most willing executor of his reform program.[41] With the backing of the Franciscan monks, Maximiliana began climbing the ladder of convent offices. By 1623 she was instructing the convent's novices with great energy, writing books of special teachings and rules for the new generation of nuns. When the sisters were struggling with the newly introduced breviary, she labored hard to pass on her knowledge of the Latin language, which she had acquired during her early years at the court.[42] By 1626 Maximiliana reached the highest level of the administrative hierarchy when Antonio

Galbiato, conducting another visitation in the Ridler convent, ousted the convent's mother superior and put Maximiliana in her place. By deposing the administrative assistant of the old mother superior and replacing her with a peasant woman,[43] he in effect maximized Maximiliana's power over the community. Up to this point, the cooperation between the Reformati and Maximiliana was unequivocally advantageous for both parties.

In 1627, however, Maximiliana had an encounter that changed her life. The General of the Reformed Carmelite Order, Dominicus a Jesu Maria, paid a visit to the Bavarian court and took the opportunity to converse with the mother superior of the Ridler cloister nearby. In the wake of this encounter, the nun chose St. Teresa of Avila, canonized five years earlier and already a role model for nuns all over Europe, to be her special patron. She embarked upon a rigorous course of incessant prayers and physical mortification, emaciating her body and letting her flesh suffer under the sharpened spikes of a chain. Between her spiritual practices, she took drastic measures against private property, having the sisters remove "everything from the cells, except for the little [that was] required for basic needs."[44] For the first time, the Reformati developed an interest in tempering her piety.[45]

Maximiliana's hopes for convent reform and for her own religious career were shattered not on cloister walls but rather on the resentment that her extreme zeal eventually aroused among the hierarchy and among other nuns. External events precipitated the turn of fortunes. When Gustavus Adolphus's Protestant troops occupied the Bavarian capital in 1632, Munich's nuns, with the exception of a few brave souls in charge of guarding convent possessions, took flight to Tyrolia. The loss of physical confinement revealed that not everyone had internalized the new regime. Dislocated from their cloister, some tertiaries obviously enjoyed the regained freedom of movement. They insisted on the openness of their exile community to the point where they began having arguments with the nuns from the traditionally more conservative Angerkloster of the Poor Clares.[46] Maximiliana did her best to re-create the world of a post-Trent cloister in exile,[47] reining in the movements of her flock and having them observe monastic silence and follow the rhythm of their usual prayers.[48] While she tried hard to maintain the spiritual discipline she had been inculcating in her community for years, the truncated Ridler convent back in Munich began to grow. Nuns from convents in Munich's ravaged outskirts were seeking shelter in the comparatively safer urban nunnery. When Maximiliana returned she would find the community she had shaped with great care for more than a decade suddenly outnumbered by a group of much less compliant strangers: twenty-five Ridler sisters faced forty nuns from other religious houses.[49]

The newcomers were not keen on Maximiliana's religious regime, choosing to stay in bed instead of rising for matins.[50] Matters turned from bad to worse when her male superiors began to subject Maximiliana's regime to close scrutiny. In part alerted by her malcontented nuns, in part prodded to such action by the higher ranks of the Franciscan hierarchy, the local Reformati subjected the convent to a visitation that sealed Maximiliana's fate. What pushed her Franciscan superiors over the edge was that she began transforming her own extremism into a basis for the critique of male ecclesiastics—a stratagem known to religious women for centuries.[51] In 1633, the Franciscan Superiors found themselves reprimanded for their rule of the Ridler convent by the General Chapter that met in Spain, St. Teresa's country, of all places.[52] Apparently, Maximiliana had launched a complaint against their rule of her convent before the General Chapter. In January 1634, the local Reformati and the vast majority of Ridler sisters, who were tired of the religious discipline exacted by Maximiliana, joined forces against the mother superior and had her ousted.[53] When push came to shove, spiritual perfection appears not to have been the central point of cloistering in spite of the Trent-inspired rhetoric to the contrary; gender norms quickly outweighed religious values. The Franciscan Visitor in charge of the proceedings against Maximiliana could not help but display his unabashed pleasure with himself for putting a woman with extreme religious aspirations in her place and asserting the superiority of his gender in matters religious. On the evening after the visitation, he bragged before his brethren in the refectory about how he had "won a victory over Maximiliana."[54]

Two practices in particular raised the hackles of Maximiliana's critics. Following St. Teresa's example, she introduced a regime of strict apostolic poverty and a daily spiritual meditation, for which the Franciscan Visitor found only derogatory words: "the Carmelite monkey game."[55] This meditation consisted of a special form of mental prayer that Teresa, borrowing from Ignatius of Loyola, had developed in reaction to the traditional practice in many nunneries where the religious busied themselves with the vocal recitation of intercessory prayers on behalf of aristocratic benefactors. The nuns in Teresa's first convent were praying for the aristocrat Bernardo Robles virtually around the clock, taking turns in a succession of one-hour shifts.[56] Mental prayer, as Teresa understood it, was intended to develop the spiritual powers of nuns instead of turning them into prayer wheels for others. Available to all souls in need of salvation and not just to wealthy benefactors, it was an exercise in concentration rather than vocal recitation and was aimed at fortifying nuns. This special form of prayer represented the most controversial aspect of Teresa's entire reform program.[57]

Maximiliana could easily apply Teresa's suggestions for prayer within the Ridler cloister. There too intercessory prayers for wealthy patrons, above all for the ruling dynasty, threatened to become the fulcrum of pious practice in ways that could jeopardize the spiritual life of the nuns through commodification. A life in monastic seclusion took its economic toll, and many female convents experienced grave economic difficulties upon enclosure because they were generally less well endowed than male monastic houses and already more limited in opportunities for generating revenue due to gender-specific expectations of what constituted appropriate work.[58] The greater contemplative orientation, which enclosure automatically effected, encouraged the nuns to capitalize on prayer and use the opus dei of the divine offices as a fund-raiser.[59] In the case of Munich's female tertiaries, sequestration put an end to many traditional means of accruing income, such as care for the sick and dying, the production and sale of textiles, and the performance of prayers in parish churches or private homes. The pecuniary troubles of the first decade of enclosure had the sisters collect very high dowry payments, a compensatory move that ultimately would reinforce the greater social exclusiveness of their communities. Moreover, what they experienced as a "difficult time"[60] and "great misery and poverty"[61] had them turn to the Bavarian prince for help. Because enclosure was bound to loosen patronage bonds with some benefactors, it made a tighter connection to the court desirable if not inescapable.

Maximilian I willingly seized on the opportunity to appropriate the religious labors of the nuns and harness their spiritual protection more firmly to the fortunes of the ruling dynasty. He endowed the two women's cloisters with an annual payment of 300 florin "in order for claustration to be suffered more easily."[62] In return for the funds, the sisters had to attend a daily mass read by a court chaplain in their convents and recite prayers for Maximilian's and his wife's salvation.[63] While they had been civic mourners in the days before Tridentine reform, the economic readjustments of enclosure pushed the religious virgins toward functioning as primary guardians of the spiritual well-being of the ruling dynasty. They not only suffered enclosure because of the state, but on its behalf as well. In economic terms, state power first increased the surplus value of the women's spiritual labor by surrounding their virginal bodies with the "additional hymen" of enclosure, then tried to monopolize the gains rather than distribute them among the larger community.[64]

Imagined Communities and Spiritual Places

Although Sister Maximiliana failed to counter this trend with Teresa's remedy of mental prayer, the sisters in the Ridler and Pütrich convents ultimately did not let themselves be reduced to spiritual delivery devices for the powerful. These religious women instead found in prayer a means both to cultivate ties beyond the cloister and to have an impact on public life. Differently put, the nuns availed themselves of their own virginal bodies, bodies that enclosure charged with renewed spiritual potency, to regain at least some of the ground they had lost because of their physical segregation.

With its doctrinal discourse on purgatory, the Council of Trent ironically provided the same nuns it otherwise ordered to live in enclosure with a potent vehicle for transcending cloister walls. In countering the Protestant attacks on intercessory prayers to Christian saints, the council fathers reaffirmed the existence of purgatory as a distinct place between heaven and earth, and listed the efforts of the faithful to deliver souls from purgatorial pain among the "works of piety."[65] Purgatory offered an imaginary terrain and site of escape where sequestered religious women could exercise good works and thereby create encounters with the larger world.

The Tridentine pronouncements had a powerful echo in Bavaria's popular culture, where the dead suffering in purgatory represented a forceful and tangible presence in everyday life. According to folktales, poor souls roamed the land in search of someone to perform good works on their behalf.[66] Munich's nuns simply needed to heed the dictates of local culture and of the Tridentine church to make the organization of prayers for suffering souls a vehicle for weaving networks among the city's female cloisters.

Consider the case of Sister Clara Hortulana, who lived in the cloistered convent of Poor Clares across town, but whose labors for the tortured souls in purgatory involved nuns from the Ridler and Pütrich houses. Frequented by apparitions of poor souls, Clara turned into a virtual prayer broker, assigning spiritual works to nuns in her own and other convents, with her confessor serving as a go-between. Clara supposedly rescued over a thousand souls from purgatory, among them thirty Pütrich sisters, whose delivery Clara effected by recruiting the help of living Pütrich nuns.[67] Clara's lengthy assignment for each Pütrich sister provided the cloistered women with a deeply meaningful routine and an occasion to bond with one another in a joint effort to improve the lot of dead members.[68] They could create a powerful imaginary community of religious women spanning the otherwise unbridgeable distance between this world and the next, between one female convent and another, and binding together the living and the dead in a "mutual economy of salvation."[69]

These intercessory prayers facilitated interactions between the religious women's communities but could also function as a conduit between the cloister and the families the nuns had left behind and were barred from.

Fig. 4. Community of believers, including laity and ecclesiastics as well as men and women, united in prayer for the delivery of souls from the fires of purgatory. (By Melchior Bocksberger. Original in Staatliche Graphische Sammlung, Munich.)

Among the souls who entreated Clara Hortulana to facilitate their rescue from the pangs of purgatory was Mathias Barbier, Munich's former mayor. During his lifetime Barbier had held office with Clara Hortulana's father, Joachim Empacher.[70] Barbier was also the brother of Barbara Barbier, then mother superior of the Pütrich community. Clara Hortulana allotted a considerable share of the prayers on Mathias Barbier's behalf to his sister's convent community. When Barbier appeared one last time to report the success of the intercessory efforts to Clara, he announced his determination "to intercede with God on behalf of all who helped him, especially on behalf of the Pütrich cloister."[71] In the reciprocal logic of salvation, Barbier now offered his services to the sisters, especially to those under the care of his biological sister. To complete the circle of exchanges, Barbara Barbier urged one of her nuns to compile a record of the intercessory accomplishments of Clara Hortulana after Clara's death.[72]

The nuns' pious works thus radiated beyond convent walls in waves, reverberating in other monastic houses and in kin households. Strengthening the appeal of their cloister church and attracting Munich's faithful, the sisters could expand their work on behalf of all suffering souls and extend their influence even further into the urban community. In the course of the seventeenth century the two tertiary communities acquired important indulgences for their churches that drew the Catholic faithful into the orbit of the female convents.[73] The women's cloisters came to stand tall in Counter-Reformation Munich as two prayer and purgation factories (to resort to a modern image) whose pious workers set souls free at assembly-line speed; their bustling activities were matched only by the combined spiritual labor of priests, confraternities, and the laity in the convent churches.[74] Parallel practices allied the nuns with uncloistered Catholics in a common project of reducing suffering in purgatory. A stairway modeled after Rome's Holy Stairs was installed inside the Ridler cloister for in-house pilgrimages. A plenary indulgence awaited the cloistered pilgrim after the completion of her journey in a spirit of penance. A twin stairway was available to penitents outside of the convent church; there ordinary believers undertook their attempt to climb to new heights of repentance and purity.[75]

Although the prayers of the sacred virgins behind walls were considered very potent, they could not equal the intercessory power of Catholicism's most efficacious conduit between heaven and earth: the saints. Not surprisingly, the cloistered nuns who, shortly after enclosure, engaged in the large-scale delivery of suffering souls also became involved in the cult of the saints. No longer part of the urban textile trade, the nuns in the Pütrich cloister used their expertise with cloth in outfitting the remains of Christian saints for public exhibition, thus transforming a medieval tradition of textile work into a pious practice suitable to a cloistered convent.[76]

In 1647 Dean Kaspar Heyfelder from Munich's Church of St. Peter commissioned the ornamentation of two skulls of followers of the martyr St. Ursula, "together with other unknown holy relics to be framed with pearls and other embroidery work and two beautifully decorated containers."[77] Eight years later the men from St. Peter unwittingly set an inspiring example for the cloistered nuns when they acquired the entire body of St. Honoratius from Rome and set it up for public veneration in their church.[78]

The recovery and sale of corpses of supposed martyrs from the Roman catacombs grew steadily in the seventeenth century after the accidental rediscovery of the subterranean tombs in 1578 and their subsequent exploration by archaeologists and clerics, who spread news of their finding "holy martyrs, in innumerable numbers."[79] Counter-Reformation Bavaria itself witnessed a revival of traditional pilgrimage sites, the foundation of numerous new ones, and the rapid proliferation of miracle stories in oral and literate culture. Ordinary people as well as clergy streamed to these local shrines in large numbers.[80] The Bavarian state was an especially enthusiastic supporter of these pious practices, sponsoring the compilation of martyrologies and promoting devotion at local shrines. The Wittelsbach dynasty deemed mass pilgrimages and reports of miracles to be powerful means of demonstrating the superiority of the old faith and also of the dynasty's power as a key defender of this faith.[81]

In this hospitable cultural context the cloistered women in the Pütrich convent decided to acquire the entire skeleton of a Christian martyr from Rome, decorate the body, and exhibit it for public veneration in their convent church, combining intercessory prayer and devotion to the holy. Bones and bodies of saints, the nuns were well aware, were endowed with a sacred power that could translate into social and cultural capital. It was a power that captivated the attention of the faithful and guided believers not only toward the veneration of saints but also toward respect and admiration for those who exhibited and housed them. Providing a place of final rest for a holy body was a means of attracting visitors.[82] The Council of Trent itself had thrown the weight of orthodoxy behind this practice by encouraging believers to make pilgrimages and venerate "the holy corpses of the holy martyrs" and other "relics of the saints."[83] In so doing, it unwittingly encouraged the nuns' development of yet another spiritual technology for transcending cloister confines.

Bones of Contention or Holy Corpses and the Constraints of Enclosure

An anonymous Pütrich sister left a handwritten narrative that further illustrates the gendered dimensions of convent reforms and the extent to

which the cloistered women managed to counter the constraints of enclosure over time.[84] From this narrative we learn that sometime in the summer of 1662 the sisters, under the leadership of Mother Superior Maria
Gerold, entered into negotiations with a Capuchin brother named Gregorius, who was a friend of Sister Caecilia Reischl. Like other members of his
order, Gregorius was known for his skillful trading in relics. Even though
they did not have their Franciscan superior's official permission, the cloistered women could not pass up an opportunity to exploit the Capuchin's
expertise and mobility. When a meeting of his order's General Chapter
took him to Rome, Caecilia asked Gregorius to pick up a precious relic for
the convent church during his sojourn, a service for which the nuns would
compensate him financially. Once in Rome, Gregorius chanced upon a
special treasure that he knew the sisters had coveted for a long time: the
entire corpse of an early Christian martyr from the catacombs. He immediately wrote the religious women in Munich to inform them of the possibility of purchasing the corpse of an early Christian virgin martyr named
Dorothea.

Delighted at the prospect, the sisters set the wheels in motion to move
the sacred virgin's corpse across Europe's map, never mind that they
themselves were stuck behind cloister walls. First of all, the nuns corresponded with Gregorius and made arrangements with him for the purchase and transportation of St. Dorothea from Rome to Munich via
Bologna, Venice, and Bozen. Letters, according to the convent statutes,
had to be approved by the mother superior, who had a vested interest herself in facilitating communication in this instance. It was arranged that the
corpse would travel the distance in a trunk, which also enclosed a carafe of
the martyr's thickened blood and Roman attestations identifying the body
as that of St. Dorothea. The Capuchin order's network of religious houses
criss-crossing Italy and Germany was to provide secure way stations for
the corpse. Gregorius's task also entailed keeping the sisters up to date on
the progress of the precious trunk. Finally, he had to make sure that the
body would not be put on a merchant carriage lest "the holy bones . . . will
be broken and will come out less than whole," which would reduce the
body's value as a sacred object in a culture whose spiritual taxonomy
ranked wholeness higher than fragmentation.

Cloister walls also did not prevent the nuns from using kin connections to organize payment for the shipment and for Gregorius's efforts in
Italy. In part because conversation within the parlatorium was possible,
enclosure could never sever completely the bonds between cloistered kin
and their families in the world, and strong attachments persisted. In the
same decade that they acquired their first holy corpse from Rome, the
female tertiaries were chastened for letting small children into the clois-

tered space.[85] The size of these secular intruders was probably a function of the limited possibilities accorded by the so-called *Winde,* the device used to pass objects from the outside into the cloister itself. To pay Gregorius, only money needed to traverse the boundary between cloister and world. Several nuns were from merchant families and were therefore familiar with long-distance trade. Given this family background, it was no accident that the convent settled on the bill of exchange, the means of payment used by many merchants. A local merchant named Gugler, a relative of a Pütrich nun, agreed to forward the bill directly to Gregorius in Italy.

Although the plan was simple, its execution proved to be difficult. Gregorius obtained the body of St. Dorothea, but due to an idle courier the corpse did not leave Rome for about a month. And worse was yet to come. Somewhere between Rome and Bologna, Gregorius lost track of the traveling martyr. Enclosure did not deter the frenzied correspondence that ensued between Gregorius and the convent, wherein the Capuchin assured the sisters that he was doing his best to find it. Nor did it deter the sisters from doing what they considered their share of the recovery mission: the convent immediately commenced an involved program of daily prayers and masses, appealing above all to St. Anthony of Padua, the celestial helper in cases of loss.

Just in time, St. Dorothea's body surfaced in Bologna. Anxieties over the corpse's whereabouts had been rising, and a faction of nuns had indeed begun to question the wisdom of the purchase as well as the good judgment of their mother superior. As soon as Gregorius's missive with the good news appeared, Mother Maria assembled her convent in the hope of soothing tempers of mutinous members. Undoubtedly with relief she read out loud the Capuchin's letter, which incidentally also contained a rather enticing reminder of the benefits of acquiring and housing a saint. Gregorius reported the recent Capuchin success in transferring three sacred bodies to Linz in Austria. His account stressed that a large crowd of people had come to watch the solemn procession through the city's street and later on to visit the saints in their final resting place. The success story went to the heart of the matter: Gregorius's account of the events in Linz aimed at reminding the Pütrich sisters of this potential for attracting crowds and thus of their reason for acquiring St. Dorothea in the first place.

But apparently not all the nuns were mollified, because somehow word spread to the male Franciscans about these occurrences in the Pütrich cloister. Provincial Modestus Reichart, head of Bavaria's Reformati and the man in charge of the Pütrich sisters, was incensed. A new provincial of the Reformati province, Reichart was just completing his initial round of visitation of Franciscan houses in Bavaria when he learned about the activities of his charges. Two things most horrified Reichart:

first, that it was a Capuchin, even worse a Capuchin lay brother, and not a Franciscan, who had obtained the body; second, Gregorius's account of the public spectacle around the holy bodies in Linz. From Reichart's point of view, these two acts violated the fundamental rules of Counter-Reformation nunneries: supervision through male superiors and the constraints of enclosure. What linked these two issues and gave them their particular sting was the notion of the public presence of nuns.

The term *Öffentlich*—public—reverberated through the subsequent debate between Reichart and the sisters. Yet, the meaning of this term was far from unequivocal. A closer look at the debate between the clergymen and the nuns reveals that their disagreement was part of a much larger contest over gender roles in early modern European society that pitted male state and church authorities, on the one hand, against secular and ecclesiastical women, on the other.

Reichart essentially relied on the male-headed household model when he scolded the nuns for conspiring with the Capuchins. He dreaded the idea of a public translation of Dorothea through Munich's streets mainly because it would reflect poorly on his ability to control the women in his care. As the chronicling nun summed it up:

> It was going to be to the disadvantage and disrespect of them [the male Franciscans] that we obtained a holy corpse in Rome through the Capuchins, namely, merely through a lay brother, and not through the Reformati, under whose obedience we live.

Like the honor of any other head of a household (*Hausvater*), Reichart's honor was at stake if his women misbehaved publicly. It was somewhat ironic, though entirely in line with the logic of a society organized around male-headed households, that Reichart threatened to turn the nuns over to the Capuchins altogether if they further refused to obey him. If the sisters continued to undercut his male authority, Reichart needed to protect himself as well as cultural conceptions of masculinity by forcing the women to surrender to other men.

The Pütrich sisters, in a shrewd application of the same logic, defended their decision to have a Capuchin mediator on the grounds that the order had a reputation for the successful and inexpensive procurement of relics. The Capuchins had proven this ability many times, the women stressed, and they reminded Reichart that a Capuchin lay brother had also organized the transfer of the body of St. Honoratius, which adorned the Church of St. Peter. In this context the chronicler could not help but note "that up to this point the patres Reformati of this province had not once brought a single body out of Rome." The implicit message was clear: gov-

ernance was predicated on competence. The inability of one male authority could legitimate the women resorting to another.

Reichart also accused the sisters of plotting a public translation with
the Capuchins. Underlying the accusation was more than rivalry with the
Capuchins. Rather, Reichart had a very strict understanding of female
cloister. To his mind, the boundaries of enclosure would be violated not
only if there was a translation of the saint's body through the city streets,
but also if St. Dorothea would be exhibited in the convent church. At
most, he was willing to let the nuns keep Dorothea inside the cloistered
area for personal veneration.

The Pütrich sisters, on the other hand, argued from a different understanding of their place in public. They contended that they had never even
considered a public procession, but they did feel entitled to exhibit "publicly" Dorothea's body in their convent church. They treated their church
as an extension of the cloister, while Reichart treated it as an extension of
the *Öffentlichkeit*—the public—that was barred to religious women.

Interestingly, the nuns' defense of their access to the cloister church
mirrors the rhetorical strategies secular women used in defending their
access to the newly emerging, male-coded public sphere. Women of all
ages and social strata knew what the sociopolitical changes in the age of
confessional conflict meant for them: being relegated to the sphere of the
household. When fighting the new restrictions, women often justified their
presence in the world of men by claiming a continuum from their households to urban life.[86]

Secular women, like the early modern state, regarded the household
as part of the public realm; but, in contrast to state authorities, they conceptualized their role in the household as public and therefore radiating
outward into other social domains. While the state considered the household's public status a justification for enclosing women inside patriarchal
household governance, women thus inferred a legitimate claim to a public
role from this status. Since they already had a recognized public role as
wives, women argued they could also speak on other matters of public
concern.[87] Similarly, the nuns understood their cloistered communities as
part of a larger public. As spiritual protectors of this public, they felt called
to make their beneficial presence felt in the larger body politic.

When Reichart failed to sway the nuns through debate and moral
pressure, he resorted to a different strategy. He backed off from his initial
order to have the corpse of Dorothea delivered directly to his convent.
Instead he told the sisters that although they "had begun this work without his knowledge and approval, he had resolved to help them see it
through." Reichart gave the sisters permission to receive St. Dorothea and
initiate the procedure for authenticating the relic, once the saint had

arrived in Munich. All the while, however, the Franciscan monk was plotting an insidious course. He proposed that he would open the sealed trunk himself, ostensibly to verify Dorothea's identity. According to the Council of Trent, any newly acquired relic had to be approved by the bishop prior to its public display and veneration by the Christian community.[88] The procedure entailed several steps, none of which was easily performed from within a cloister. Most relevant in this instance, the shipped martyr, for the sake of legitimacy, had to be unpacked with a license from the bishop, who resided in Freising, an eight-hour walk away from Munich; the unpacking, moreover, had to take place in the presence of witnesses and a notary. The strict observance of the regulations was especially important because the temporary disappearance of Dorothea's body was bound to raise doubts about the relic's authenticity. Reichart planned to open the trunk without an episcopal license, thus violating proper procedure for authentication and stripping the body of any claim to sanctity.

The strategy, however, did not pass unnoticed by the nuns, who had done some information gathering of their own. At this juncture, their tight connections to the Bavarian court, even though initially forced upon them by enclosure, proved to be fortuitous. The nuns consulted a knowledgeable secular friend, a court official named Höcken, about the exact nature of the ecclesiastical guidelines. When Reichart made his well-calculated offer to open the trunk and verify the identity of the saint, the nuns were aware of his subterfuge. They were also ready to approach an even more powerful ally at the center of power: Duchess Maria Anna, widow of Maximilian I, who had subjected the convent to enclosure to begin with.

The relationship between the religious women and the women of the ruling dynasty, which preceded enclosure, deepened in its wake. In the course of the seventeenth century, various Wittelsbach women set up exchanges of economic goods for spiritual services in the cloisters (similar to Maximilian's arrangement of 1621).[89] Taking advantage of their class and their gender, the court women quite frequently entered convent space, in spite of Tridentine enclosure. By 1704 they would receive official papal permission to have their own private gates installed in the Ridler cloister.[90]

In the conflict over Dorothea, Duchess Anna's political and physical presence was crucial. Whether she was fully aware of it or not, the duchess ultimately helped the sisters contest the confines of the cloister. After she learned about the purchase of St. Dorothea and the procedures for authenticating a relic, Anna put pressure on Reichart to observe the rules. The interference of the duchess bought the sisters time to develop a defense tactic. Thus when Reichart tried to stop by at the cloister to discuss matters with the nuns, he decided to turn around as soon as he learned that the duchess was over for lunch.

When Dorothea at last arrived in Munich in December 1662, the religious women were prepared. They sent Reichart Christmas greetings, told him about Dorothea's arrival, and gently reminded him to request the episcopal license if he had not already done so. Alarmed by the nuns' apparent cognizance of protocol, Reichart paid a visit to the cloister "that very same evening." Speaking to the mother superior and the convent's administrator through the barred windows of the parlatorium, the provincial requested the extradition of the corpse. He claimed to have received orders from the bishop to open the trunk right there in the absence of a notary or secular witnesses. The nuns knew better and simply kept the doors shut. Ironically, the same cloister walls Reichart designated as boundaries for the sisters' radius of action now stood in the way of the realization of his scheme. "It was too late," said the mother superior and administrator to excuse the nuns' refusal, and she proposed that Reichart come back the next day.

The night passed in turbulent debate over future action. So determined were most sisters to thwart Reichart's plan to strip the corpse of any claim to public veneration that they decided to return the locked trunk with the bones to the Capuchins if they themselves could not accord the relic due respect. They also contacted court official Höcken again for advice and informed Duchess Anna about the latest developments so that she would continue to pressure Reichart. Höcken assured the sisters that Reichart lacked the authority to open the trunk without an episcopal license. He also advised them to recruit a notary and witnesses, open the trunk but not the sealed body, take out the attestations, and hand those over to Reichart to keep him happy for the time being. The mother superior and convent administrator did not dare follow this bold plan. Later in the day, Maria Gerold, perhaps swayed by the unanimous resolution of her nuns that Reichart must be stopped from opening the trunk improperly, began mustering witnesses and a notary among their uncloistered kin. Unfortunately for the women, Reichart returned before they could round up a notary.

This time, the provincial, in the company of two other Franciscans, had his mind set on getting his way. He demanded that "the honorable mother should either open up enclosure or have the trunk with the holy body carried down into the parlatorium." The nuns did neither. Rather, what followed was a very well-timed, tactical embrace of Counter-Reformation ideals. Instead of letting Reichart in or bringing Dorothea out, the sisters rushed into the parlatorium. They fell on their knees and began pleading with Reichart to rethink his decision, each making their case individually "in their simplicity with good ardor." The gesture signaled submission while in fact it amounted to a refusal of obedience. The women then proceeded to invoke various norms in their favor, norms backed by the authority of Trent. First of all, the nuns pointed to the need of obtaining approval from ecclesiastical superiors, in this case clearly the bishop and not Reichart. Second, they appealed to the duty to venerate the saints in a proper manner. And finally, the nuns did not hesitate to use their trump card: cloistering. They insisted that Reichart really needed to get an episcopal order, and they communicated their resolve to hold on to St. Dorothea: "In the meantime we will keep the holy body locked in our cloister and venerate it." Even when Reichart threatened to report the sisters to the Roman General of the Franciscan order, the nuns did not back down. In the end, Reichart was forced to accept that neither the door nor the package was going to be opened that day. He left "with great indignation and a bitter temperament."

There is no record of the subsequent settlement, but the official approbation must have gone through because nine months later Dorothea was the center of a public procession in the Bavarian capital.[91] Next to the saint, however, Franciscan men were the focus of attention as they carried the holy body through Munich's streets and into the Pütrich cloister church before a crowd of onlookers. The cortege featured large pennants with memorable epigrams from the Song of Songs, most notably "Here I wish to reside until my beloved comes" and "I will lead my virgins to the wedding."[92] Upon reaching their destination, the Franciscan men walked down the aisle to place the remains of St. Dorothea on the altar, and they intoned the song "Veni, sponsa Christi" (Come, Bride of Christ), the same tune that accompanied each Pütrich nun's "spiritual wedding." Dorothea's remains took residence in the convent church until the day of the Last Judgment, similar to the permanently cloistered nuns who awaited the day of their "heavenly wedding."

Given the struggles attending and following Tridentine reform, the Franciscan-led procession appears a telltale expression of the only identity offered to nuns by the Counter-Reformation church: brides of Christ behind cloister walls. While the sisters had little say in the matter, Franciscan men represented the women to the onlooking public. These ecclesiastical understandings found an ideological enhancement in contemporary secular trends. The promotion of marriage as a normative life path for women and of male-headed households reinforced the growing importance of the matrimonial model for cloistered nuns and their greater dependency on male superiors.

All the sisters could do was to catch a glimpse of the festivities from up high in the choir, once the procession had entered the convent church. Yet what the nuns saw from above was the result of the labor of their own hands. Prior to the translation, the women had spent no less than seven months preparing the corpse of Dorothea, tailoring and embroidering a radiant garment for the saint; individual sisters provided the labor and raw materials, as well as donating precious stones and other valuable objects. Some gave the rings they had received upon entering the convent, while others sold pillows and beds from their cells to be able to afford a seemly contribution. In this manner, the women behind walls essentially had secured themselves some kind of presence in the public spectacle.

This procession was only one of several ways in which the holy bones became thresholds for nuns to the world beyond the cloister. St. Dorothea was the first of a number of holy corpses and other relics that the Pütrich nuns acquired, decorated, and displayed "for public veneration."[93] The Ridler community and the Poor Clares also accumulated treasures for display in their cloister churches.[94] The prominence of these sacred bones suggests a profound connection between the symbolic, the sacred, and the somatic, straddling the physical boundaries of the cloister.

First of all, the practice of handling and outfitting sacred bones enabled the sisters to draw lines of continuity between the cloistered present and the uncloistered past of textile production and care for the dying. Instead of taking care of Munich's dead, the sisters took care of the remains of Christian saints. Rather than producing for the local market, the nuns produced textiles for relics. In this way, the women pieced together a world of their own from old traditions, such as care of bodies and production of cloth, on the one hand, and more recent Counter-Reformation dictates, such as the veneration of saints through their relics, on the other.

Caring for the bodies of others was also a social role that was reserved for women in early modern society. At least on the symbolic plane, care for the bodies of dead saints therefore connected cloistered women to women in the secular world. Beyond the symbolic, the bones of St. Dorothea, and perhaps also other relics, offered opportunities of direct connection and exchange with those living in the world. Once exhibited in the church, St. Dorothea is reported to have worked a series of miracles whose beneficiaries were mainly women and their children, among them a number of the nuns' kin. Out of gratitude to the saint, these family members donated precious materials of the kind the sisters coveted and collected for the outfitting of martyrs.[95] The body of St. Dorothea thus became a medium of exchange of spiritual and material goods, as well as gifts of affection between the female saint, the cloistered women, and their secular female kin.

Sacred remains moreover were a forceful vehicle of representing oneself to Munich's pious public. The nuns could no longer be in public, but they could draw the public into their own home, as it were, all the while engaging in a pious practice sanctioned by the Counter-Reformation church. It was for good reasons that the convent published a pamphlet advertising the treasures in the cloister church and encouraging visitors to worship and see for themselves.[96] These holy bones, lovingly decorated, could signal to the visiting public both the virtues and riches of the Pütrich nuns, women who were bound by vows of poverty and enclosure. A few nuns even sacrificed the Jesus dolls that had accompanied them into the cloister on their wedding day to the decorative projects.[97] Signifying their virtues and carrying the nuns' intimate objects, these sacred remains became an extension of self, if not virtually prosthetic bodies, for women whose own bodies had been barred from public view.

There is yet another intriguing possibility for thinking about holy bones as a means of transcending the physical limits of the cloister. The Catholic cult of the saints deemed dead martyrs intermediaries between this world and the next, and it endowed their physical remains with potency analogous to the possibilities with which contemporary sorcery credited bodily parts.[98] Counter-Reformation Catholicism, in spite of its outspoken contempt for bodily urges, drew on another powerful undercurrent of spirituality that profoundly affirmed the body. Scholars like Caroline Bynum have traced this hidden face of Catholic spirituality with its advocacy of embracing physicality, humanity, and especially the suffering body.[99] Counter-Reformation Catholicism continued this largely invisible tradition by fostering an understanding of the corporeal as a gateway to the sacred. Physical sensations, above all pain, were occasions for encounters with the divine, connecting the sufferer with suffering souls in the beyond. Physical sensations could be abstracted from the body of one person to be experienced by the body of another.[100]

Nuns meditating on the sufferings of Christian saints aspired to feel the pain of martyrdom, which they could not suffer because of the walls that surrounded them. Whereas throngs of women populated the ranks of the Church's holy community in the Middle Ages, the number of female saints underwent a dramatic decline. The Counter-Reformation fostered ideals of holiness that privileged masculine pursuits—the preacher reconquering territories that had been lost to Protestantism, the missionary furthering the Catholic cause in foreign lands, the martyr to the Christian faith sacrificing his life in the religious wars—and cloistered women were barred from these trajectories. Excessive physical mortification, contingent neither on freedom of movement nor on the involvement of others, became a means of bypassing these restrictions, achieving oneness with the divine and even a reputation for sanctity. Sister Elisabetha of the Ridler community, "a living martyr," was said to have become "isomorphic with her suffering spouse . . . through abidingly loving patience" in the face of her numerous (self-inflicted) pains.[101] Sister Clara Hortulana, the prayer broker from Munich's convent of Poor Clares, also took the route of transforming her body into a sacred object through redemptive pain. Bemoaning the fact that claustration stood in the way of being martyred at the hands of men, she longed for martyrdom with such intensity that in the end God allegedly took pity on her and permitted the devil to fling her down from the choir to a bloody death.[102] The convent's mother superior collected some of Clara's blood in a carafe and attached the container to Clara's corpse in a manner comparable to the funerary preparations of martyrs like St. Dorothea,[103] completing Clara's transmutation into a holy corpse.

The vitae of cloistered nuns contain tales of relics being alive and of nuns having experiences of corporeal transcendence while around holy bones and meditating on the pain of their bearers. To us, bones signify death, and talk of out-of-body experiences has a ring of New Age philosophies that makes scholars uncomfortable. Academic instinct tells us to ascribe these tales to either psychological or hagiographic invention because they concern a realm with which scholarly discourse does not deal easily: the realm of the spirit. Unless studying spiritual experience as "exotic" (e.g., spirit possession in Asia or Africa),[104] scholars generally have difficulties suspending Western epistemologies and locating it inside "modernizing" Europe. But we should at least consider grounding these seventeenth-century European tales of spirituality in the anthropological context of post-Trent cloistering, with its belief in a holy relic's ability to transport the faithful to higher states. In so doing, we might begin to probe Counter-Reformation spirituality for one way it allowed cloistered women to move beyond convent walls and to counter exclusion from public life by entering into another world altogether. The invisibility of some means of female resistance should not blind us to their power.

These varied tactics illustrate the complexity of the relationship between women's subordination and their resistance to state power. While the majority of sisters would have originally preferred to escape enclosure, cloistering turned these religious women into powerful sacred figures for the larger community and permitted them to develop new sets of practices that in turn could be deployed against enclosure. Economic and spiritual fortunes declined in the short term because cloistering impeded the revenue-generating charitable acts that in the past lay at the center of the sisters' religious practice. Yet these same fortunes boomed in the medium run. Soon the women behind cloister walls were well known for feats of piety that could be accomplished behind walls—austere mortification of the flesh, potent visionary gifts, or the skillful decoration of sacred objects.

To the extent that enclosure achieved (symbolically, if not de facto) a

Fig. 5. Clara Hortulana depicted with her instrument for self-flagellation and the carafe filled with her blood. The inscription above the carafe reads: "Whose blood is still intact." (By Carl Gustav Amling. Original in Staatliche Graphische Sammlung, Munich.)

purification from the secular pollutants that church and state authorities dreaded, cloistering undergirded the claims of these holy virgins to be vehicles of divine grace. Their spiritual work could both radiate outward into the world beyond walls and draw patrons and admirers toward them. Nobility and patriciate soon competed for admittance of female family members to the sisters' honorable ranks.[105] The result was a steady influx of wealthy women, paralleled by an influx of high dowry payments and generous financial bequests by the sisters' kin. This increase in financial clout made it possible for the sisters to change their convent churches from modest houses of worship into ostentatious spaces of baroque piety whose abundance of precious decorated reliquaries and array of indulgences pulled the surrounding community into the orbit of the women's cloister. The nuns lost one form of prestige due to cloistering but eventually gained another one precisely because of enclosure. Their virginal bodies, hidden from scrutinizing view, could have a tangible sacred presence in an urban community increasingly conditioned to perceive the sexual in every visible female body.

CHAPTER 5

Public Services and Private Lives: Schooling Women for Society

What Ernst Bloch termed "gleichzeitige Ungleichzeitigkeiten"—the simultaneous occurrence of seemingly asynchronous events—bridges the distance between two diametrically opposed developments in the second decade of the seventeenth century. In the story of the Ridler and Pütrich communities, Elector Maximilian appeared as an ardent proponent of Tridentine reform, his mind set on excluding religious women from the urban public and utilizing their virginal bodies to augment state power. It is therefore startling to see how the Bavarian prince played the opposite role in a concurrent historical plotline. In the same decade during which Maximilian put the Franciscan tertiaries under lock and key, he voluntarily opened the doors of his capital to Mary Ward, foundress of the Institute of English Ladies, and her followers. Contrary to Tridentine norms, the English Ladies were neither married nor behind cloister walls, but they nonetheless claimed to champion the Counter-Reformation through their pedagogical work and found support for their enterprise among various ecclesiastical and social groups.

The contradictory nature of the simultaneous developments was not lost on contemporaries, including cloistered nuns themselves. According to a diatribe against Ward's institute in Vienna:

[The English Ladies] caused annoyance among the claustrated nuns who had just been given stricter rules, and besides they [the English Ladies] claimed to be better than these [nuns]. And when their Superior, during a visitation was presented with the Italian dictum ò muro ò marito she was said to have replied: one could very well serve God without a wall or a husband.[1]

This chapter explains how it was possible for the English Ladies to pave a third way beyond cloister and marriage. The English Ladies, it shows, owed their success to the support of the Bavarian state, which considered their work of educating the female part of the citizenry an invaluable service for the creation of public order. In order to gain and maintain secular patronage, the women had to give up many of their initial pedagogical and intellectual aspirations, most notably preparing women for participation in public life, as well as their goal of obtaining official recognition as a religious order. Co-opting Ward's vision, the state was able to slant the institute's pedagogical work toward preparing Bavaria's girls for domesticity; English Ladies trained Catholic young women in their private social roles as wives and nuns.

Yet the very existence of the English Ladies and the manner in which they were able to defy state norms ultimately broadened the spectrum of acceptable female choices beyond male-headed households. As unmarried virgins living together and working in the world, they embodied a new type of woman—the honorable single woman dedicated to social service. Their social backgrounds and their work for the ruling elite marked them as sufficiently different from lower-class women, whose bodies represented social and sexual threats, to sanction the English Ladies' presence in public life. Theirs was a body that could be associated with upper-class self-discipline. It was also a body that differentiated them from cloistered nuns, with whom they otherwise shared social distinction and sexual abstinence. Their educational work demanded a strong, fit, and cared-for body, unlike the spiritual labor and mystical feats of nuns that were predicated on a permeable corporeality produced through excessive mortification.

Serving God without a Wall and without a Husband:
Mary Ward's Institute of English Ladies

The English Catholic Mary Ward without doubt challenged the gender norms, clerical privileges, and political boundaries of her time. She could hardly have chosen a more provocative project than the one she embarked on: the foundation of a female order of Jesuits.[2] The Society's founder, Ignatius of Loyola, had negotiated the privilege of absolution from the burden of cura monialum with the papacy in 1547. As a result, the Jesuits were officially freed from the obligation to accommodate religious women within their order.[3]

No other corps within the Tridentine Church Militant breathed the Catholic spirit of reconquest and reform more fully than the troops of Ignatius of Loyola. It was a military spirit and a masculine spirit, combining religious reform with a forceful political presence. Ignatius and his followers, in imitating Christ, departed from the mystical path that St. Francis had trodden in order to strike out into the terrain of politics and indoctrination and redeploy Catholicism to nonmystical ends. Equipped with the weaponry of Catholic doctrine and the armor of moral impeccability, the Jesuits undertook the evangelization of territories lost to Protestantism. On the home front, the soldiers of Christ embarked on the orthodox education of the Catholic laity, aiming as broadly as possible but often veering toward the social elite, whom they served in the capacity of trusted confessors. Their advice to Catholic rulers—and they gave it amply—left an indelible mark on the course of confessional politics and religious wars in the sixteenth and seventeenth centuries.[4]

Ward's radical vision of imitating the Society of Jesus and gathering female soldiers of Christ around her took shape in the course of a lengthy religious quest. At age twenty-one, she left behind her life in England's Catholic underground and traveled to Flanders to join a conservative contemplative order. She was convinced at the time "that a religious person of the female gender cannot exercise good works on anyone's behalf except her own."[5] Subsequently, Ward tried very hard to fit herself into the existing mold of religious options for Catholic women and live the life of a contemplative nun behind cloister walls. But she could not achieve spiritual solace, and the practice of contemplation did not answer what she perceived to be her calling. At last, she decided to take a different approach and established an unenclosed religious community of English women in St. Omer for the primary purpose of educating England's female youth.

Ward still remained unclear about the exact direction this new path would lead her, yet she proceeded on it in spite of pressures by "many learned and ingenious men" to abandon the unregulated ways of her community and adopt the rule of a confirmed female order.[6] In 1611, she gained clarity about her destiny in a visionary insight: she believed herself called to found a female order that imitated the Society of Jesus "in substance as well as in manner."[7]

Although throngs of unenclosed female communities had sprung up in the shadow of Jesuit colleges all over Europe and looked to the Society for an institutional model, Ward's plan was unique. Her orientation transcended individual locales, and she sought papal confirmation of a female Jesuit order. In so doing, Ward mounted the most public and most explicit challenge to the Council of Trent's male-headed household model of women's religious life. Mirroring the administrative design of Loyola's Society of Jesus in conceiving of her Institute of English Ladies, she asked the papacy to approve of a female order whose structure aspired to the institutional model that the Council of Trent reserved for men alone.[8]

Differently put, Ward aspired to the religious identity that the

Counter-Reformation Church gendered as male by excluding women from its pursuit. Ward by contrast upheld the gender-transcending dimensions of the celibate life dedicated to serving God and on this basis laid claim to "male" roles. She addressed the ubiquitous prejudice that women were less capable of carrying out pious works in response to a clergyman's derogatory comment that her English Ladies were, after all, "but women":

> There is no such difference between men and women . . . It is not *veritas hominis,* verity of men, nor verity of women, but *veritas Domini,* and this verity women may have, as well as men. If we fail, it is for want of this verity, and not because we are women . . . fervour is not placed in feelings, but in a will to do well, which women may have as well as men.[9] . . . For what think you of this word, "but women?" but as if we were in all things inferior to some other creature which I suppose to be man! Which I dare to be bold to say is a lie; and with respect to the good Father may say it is an error.[10]

In this spirit, Ward challenged the institutional gendering devices put in place at Trent. The Tridentine church forbade female religious houses from forming of congregational affiliations with one another and insisted on male supervision of individual houses, yet it encouraged male orders to form congregations and centralize their government.[11] When Ward proposed that the various houses of her order were to be unified under the government of a mother general directly subordinate to the Pope, she asked for a degree of centralization and organizational independence that was both unprecedented and at odds with Tridentine norms for female religious houses.[12] According to Ward's plan, a chain of command was to run from individual communities to the mother general, dodging interference by local clergy, male monastics, or bishops and giving the members of her order great control over the shape of their pedagogical work.

The creation of this type of organization also collided with Trent's enclosure norm for female orders because it presupposed freedom of movement. After Trent, there existed a firm link for women between, on the one hand, solemn vows that permanently bound those who had taken them to a religious institution and implied their legal death in the world and, on the other, the condition of strict cloister.[13] Records indicate that Mary Ward, as the first mother general of her institute, actually accepted vows "in her own hands."[14] If Ward did so on behalf of the Church, she exercised a form of jurisdiction canonical law reserved for clergymen.[15] Ward also overlooked Trent's prescriptions for women religious and turned to the Jesuits for a model of organizational mobility. Neither cloister walls nor involved spiritual labor should be obstacles to the important educational work that her institute's members sought to carry out on behalf of the Counter-Reformation.[16]

Aimed at fostering women's self-development, autonomy, and impact on public life, Ward's institutional program was bound to clash with gender norms in the larger social arena as well. Her idea of professionally trained female teachers engaged in women's education posed a disruptive challenge on a number of fronts. Adamant advocates of women's education notwithstanding, the early modern period saw a growing educational gap between men and women on all levels.[17] Elementary schools for girls were few and far between in the early seventeenth century, and advanced education for women outside the convent or the humanist upper-class household was virtually unknown since the universities were closed to women.[18]

For the majority of people, many of them supportive of new educational opportunities for men, the idea of female education was charged with anxieties over undesirable social change. The contemporary commentary that "an eloquent woman is never chaste" bespeaks the era's profound suspicions of female learning as a detriment to a woman's morality and a seemingly automatic association of intellectual accomplishment and sexual promiscuity. A woman's knowledge, especially if displayed in public, could easily cast doubt upon her and her family's honor.[19]

In turn, the professional perspective for female teachers was bleak and confined to two career trajectories: schoolmistress or cloistered nun. Schoolmistresses, who instructed in their homes, were often impoverished since they stood in unequal competition with the officially licensed schoolmasters who were in charge of city and parish schools. Some cloistered nuns also carried out pedagogical work, but they did so in the restrictive context of a monastic existence. Not every woman with an interest in teaching had a religious vocation; nor did she necessarily desire teaching small and select groups of upper-class girls within the confines of a cloister.[20]

Unlike members of cloistered teaching orders, the members of Ward's institution were to be pedagogues in society at large, who instructed girls and young women of various stations in day schools and boarding schools. Ward even referred to her followers as "female scholastics."[21] The term reflects the high value she placed on intellectual pursuits and the profound influence on Ward of the Jesuits who called young members in training "scholastics." Like the Jesuits, Ward required that female members first receive a thorough training in academies (*collegia*) before the women could venture out and deal with students in the world.[22]

Ward's pedagogical agenda for women, which stressed the study of Latin, finally spelled encroachment on the male-coded conception of public life that was in the process of consolidating in Catholic polities. From the sixteenth century onward, access to public officeholding became more closely tied to the acquisition of particular forms of knowledge, and familiarity with Latin and the classical past functioned as primary markers of the governing elite. Advocates of a humanist education identified the very aim of studying classical Latin in the preparation for public service, and Latin-trained officials were a much-desired commodity among early modern rulers, who discovered tools for political centralization in Rome's institutional and legal traditions.

The methodical study and teaching of Latin advocated by Ward was a plucky project, for it implied preparing women for roles outside the parameters of propriety and squarely in the emerging political public. To speak in Walter Ong's terms, Latin was a "sex-linked" language whose acquisition by men amounted to an initiation rite into the European world of knowledge and power.[23] Uniting Europe's learned men across the divides of countries and vernacular languages, it was the gateway to careers in church and government. Women's exclusion from public office and political life, on the other hand, was the main reason why contemporaries deemed women's knowledge of Latin at least of questionable usefulness, if not outright detriment to their capabilities as wives and mothers.[24]

Given its scope and ambition, it is not surprising that many male ecclesiastics cast a suspicious eye on Ward's Institute of English Ladies. Some critics fought it actively on a local level. Others tried to put a stop to her order in Rome, once the papal curia began its deliberations on the confirmation in 1613. Ward proceeded with her plan, confident that resistance could be overcome and encouraged by the more tolerant papacies of Paul V and Gregory XV. She set up houses in several cities, such as Liège and Cologne, while final papal approval was pending. In December 1626, the foundress arrived with a small entourage in Munich. The English Ladies came with the intention of serving God with neither a wall nor a husband in the Bavarian capital.

The Foundation of the Munich Institute: Between Church and State, Phase I

While scholars have commented extensively on the contestation that surrounded Ward's Institute in Rome, we know rather little about the local dynamics that at times obstructed, at others promoted the expansion of Ward's Institute and the long-term survival of her vision of an educational institute for women. The case of the Munich branch is especially illuminating in this respect. The only house to escape the dissolution of the institute ordered in 1631, the community in the Bavarian capital turned into the single locus of institutional continuity between the days of Mary Ward and the revamped Institute of English Ladies that received confirmation from the papacy in the eighteenth century. The fluctuating fortunes of the Munich institute illustrate the centrality of state interest in securing the continuous existence of this female pedagogical enterprise.

Ward's plans clearly fell on fertile ground in Bavaria, where confessional politics dictated the education of subjects in the tenets of Catholic faith and the creation of political cohesion through religious conformity. Starting in the mid–sixteenth century, Bavaria's rulers turned their attention to education because so-called *Winkelschulen* (unlicensed schools in private homes) were often associated with Protestant teachings and the dangers of dissent. According to the Schooling Ordinance (*Schulordnung*) of 1548, religious instruction was the sine qua non of all human endeavors. The Ordinances of Good Police of 1553 and 1578 identified a tightly controlled school system as the best means of "establishing and maintaining an honorable, abiding, and good public order (*policey*)."[25]

Personifying the future of the state, every child in Bavaria was required to attend the catechistic instruction for the youngest (*Kinderlehre*). The teachers whom the state entrusted with the weighty task of forging good Catholic citizens were carefully scrutinized. Future pedagogues had to take a vow of allegiance to the Tridentine confession of faith before the state admitted them to the profession.[26]

In their endeavor to inculcate the populace with an unequivocally Catholic education, Bavaria's rulers relied heavily on the educational expertise of the Jesuits. Albrecht V, the first architect of a confessional state, arranged for the Society to send teachers to his capital in 1559. His son and successor, Wilhelm V, stepped up court patronage and created a lasting monument to the Society's prominent position in Bavarian cultural and political life through the construction of a church and a collegium. The structure's giant dimensions gouged the landscape of burgher homes in Munich, outsizing the city hall and even the court itself; upon its completion in 1597, the enormous complex housed no less than 900 male pupils.[27]

Wilhelm V also took an interest in the recently established community of English Ladies, whom he obviously linked with the Society of Jesus. He contacted the Jesuit General Aquaviva to inquire about the women and their pedagogical work. Aquaviva's comment that the Jesuits had no intention of ever providing spiritual guidance to Ward's followers[28] probably deterred Wilhelm from inviting the women to teach in his capital. However, the work of Ward's followers had come to the attention of the court, and by the time Maximilian I, Wilhelm's son, was in government the ruling house was among the active supporters of the English Ladies. In recognition of the usefulness of their work to the Catholic cause, Maximilian bestowed generous annual donations on the houses of the institute in Cologne and Liège, which lay in the domains of Maximilian's brother Ferdinand.[29]

Maximilian trod in the footsteps of his grandfather and father and further renovated Bavaria's educational system through new ordinances and guidelines.[30] Cognizant of the benefits of his own Jesuit education, he promoted Latin schools alongside traditional German schools. The arena of education was yet another central site of institutional activity in which Maximilian was able to claim that he represented the public interest, and he made this claim the basis for extending his government. Munich's magistrate could only welcome the state's initiative given its periodic lamenting of the damage lazy, undisciplined, and lewd youngsters did to parents and the public order in the city.[31]

As elsewhere in early modern Europe, educational opportunities for boys and girls in the Bavarian state capital bore the marks of inequality. By the 1620s, the Jesuits alone instructed over 1,400 young men in Munich, while schooling provisions for girls were very scarce.[32] Munich's German schoolmasters taught some girls together with boys for a fee.[33] Lack of female teachers could only exacerbate the problem. The foundation of a guild of city schoolmasters in the mid–sixteenth century pushed women out of the ranks of civic pedagogues. The only civic school mistresses, two widows of former schoolmasters, were under pressure from male colleagues to drop out of the profession. At least one of them counted girls among her students.[34]

In this context of pedagogical penury Maximilian's wife, Electress Elisabeth, who was fond of female teaching congregations, approached a community of French-speaking Ursulines from Pruntrut with the invitation to settle in Munich and teach girls. The Ursulines were still considering this offer when Mary Ward's small group arrived at the Wittelsbach court.[35] Elisabeth immediately extended an invitation to Ward and her English Ladies to take charge of female education in the city. Within the span of a few months, she and Maximilian provided the religious women with a dwelling and the necessary financial support for the establishment of a day school and a boarding school. Maximilian lent Ward horses and carriages so that she could transport more teachers from Cologne to Munich.[36] In April 1627, Mary Ward and her followers received the revocable and annually renewable right to live in the so-called Paradeiserhaus. The sizeable dwelling with its court and adjacent yard was named after its previous owner; it included rental space for eight craftmen's workshops.[37]

Situated equidistant from the Wittelsbach court and the Jesuit Collegium, the Paradeiserhaus had a geographical location that mirrored the precarious political position of the English Ladies between the city's two centers of secular and religious power.[38] The ruling dynasty treasured the women's pedagogical work for the exact same reason that many Jesuits despised it—because of its resemblance to the efforts of the Society of Jesus. From Maximilian's perspective, Mary Ward's Ladies were on a par with the male members of the Society of Jesus. His decretal of April 1627 referred to the women as "ten mothers and sisters di Jesu," and the women each received a pension of 200 Gulden, the exact amount of salary that Maximilian gave to Munich's Jesuits.[39] The equality in payment bespoke equality in expectations: the English Ladies were supposed to offer to girls what the Jesuits offered to boys.[40]

The Society of Jesus, on the other hand, had an interest in keeping its distance from the English Ladies precisely because of the striking similarities between the two religious groups. Munich's soldiers of Christ were, by and large, no different in this respect from many Jesuits in other European cities. Most followers of Ignatius neither approved of Ward's plan nor wished to be associated with the "Jesuitesses" in practice and public opinion.[41] Accordingly, it did not sit well with Munich's members of the Society of Jesus that the English Ladies received the same wages as they did, called their dwelling a *collegium,* and, even worse, were known among Munich's people as "Mothers and Sisters of Jesus."

High-ranking Jesuit officials gathered forces against the English Ladies from the minute the women arrived at the Bavarian court.[42] Most notably, there was Adam Contzen, Maximilian's confessor and counselor, a powerful Jesuit figure who shaped the course of European politics. Contzen prodded the Bavarian prince to take greater risks in the Thirty Years' War abroad and to launch large-scale witch-hunts against the alleged enemies of God, church, and state at home.[43] His skepticism toward Ward's institute, combined with that of Ludovico, Elisabeth's confessor, and of Rektor Manhart, head of Munich's collegium, was bound to have some negative effect on the relations between the Wittelsbachs and the English Ladies.

A first conflict erupted as early as April 1627 when the English Ladies began their pedagogical work in the Paradeiserhaus. Ward petitioned the Electress to obtain permission from the Society for the English Ladies to use the chapel in the Jesuit church for private masses. Rektor Manhart, however, was taken aback by the request and flat out refused the favor. The gesture sent a strong message to the court and the institute: the Society did not wish to be burdened with the spiritual care of the English Ladies in any way.

Support for the English Ladies came from Rome. Vitelleschi, the Society's general, dispatched letters to Munich, in which he chided Manhart for his decision and urged him to reconsider.[44] Still, the head of Munich's Collegium did not give in to the wishes of the English Ladies and the Electress, but instead obtained the Elector's endorsement of his course of action. Obviously, competitiveness for court favors and gendered patterns of patronage played a role in the conflict's unfolding. All Vitelleschi could do was to advise the English Ladies to avoid intervention by the court and contact the Society directly in the future.[45]

Against this backdrop, it is not surprising that Jesuits were among the strong supporters of the Electress's plan to bring the Ursulines from Pruntrut to Munich. Considerably more modest in their claims than the English Ladies, the Ursulines were content with an organizational structure firmly anchored to the moorings of episcopal control and in line with the Tridentine household model. The women's houses were independent from each other, and they individually submitted to the jurisdiction of their respective bishops. The Ursulines of Pruntrut thus accepted the leadership of the Basel Bishop, in stark contrast to Ward, who never even contacted the bishop in Freising to ask for his approval of her plan to establish a community in Munich.[46]

Presumably for reasons of greater control over the unenclosed, unsupervised religious women in the Bavarian capital, leading Jesuits advocated a merger between the Ursulines and the English Ladies. In June 1627, negotiations between Ward and the Abbess Anne Alteriét commenced with the goal of setting up a joint community in the Bavarian capital. The unification, however, was doomed from the start since no party was willing to compromise its organizational modus operandi. Alteriét, who anticipated sending 300 Ursulines to Munich, assumed the less numerous English Ladies would simply transfer to her order. Ward, on the other hand, demanded that the Ursulines redo their novitiate at her institute. She was most adamant in defending her community's organizational independence, accepting no authority other than papal supervision. Negotiations between the Ursulines and the English Ladies broke down over these issues.[47]

Ward's persistent refusal to succumb to the Tridentine model of female religious life also became her institute's downfall in Rome. During the late 1620s, Ward's enemies at the Holy See gained the upper hand. In March 1628, the papacy issued a first decree ordering the suppression of "Jesuitesses." Other measures against the English Ladies quickly ensued, and the communities in St. Omer, Liège, Cologne, and Trier had to be closed by 1630.[48]

The crackdown put the relations between the English Ladies and the Bavarian state to a serious test. Cardinal Francesco Barberini admonished Maximilian to pay heed to papal wishes and to withdraw his backing from the "Jesuitesses" in Munich. Maximilian sent a stinging reply to the Cardinal. The prince's appreciation of the English Ladies stood on its own firm ground, so much so that he was not easily going to sacrifice their services to his state for the sake of the Pope. His response stressed the useful work and laudable life of the English Ladies in his capital. Besides, the Elector concluded, he did not need to be reminded by anyone to pay attention to the Pope in those matters that belonged in the Pope's purview.[49] In other words, the matter of the English Ladies did not unequivocally belong there. It was at least as much in the interests of secular rule, where Maximilian followed no dictates except raison d'état. Soon this political position would become the sole place from which Munich's English Ladies could rebuild Ward's institute.

The Bull of Suppression: Between Church and State, Phase II

On January 13, 1631, Urban VIII sealed the fate of Ward's Institute of English Ladies in his bull of suppression.[50] Condemning her institute as an erroneous undertaking, the Pope ordered the immediate disbanding of her communities. The "Jesuitesses" were pronounced guilty of usurping forms of pious life that "men of knowledge in the Holy Scripture" undertook only "with difficulty, if not with circumspection."[51] The women's disregard of church law was compounded by their purported neglect of female decorum. A woman's virginal body belonged either in a male-headed household or an enclosed convent but not in public.

> Under the pretext of promoting the salvation of souls, [the English Ladies] carried out many works that were the least suitable to their sex, its mental weakness as well as womanly modesty, but [were unsuitable] in particular to the honor of virgins.[52]

Ward's knowledge of the events that began to unfold in Rome in the late 1620s was somewhat skewed. While the news about the problems of individual houses reached her in Munich, she was unaware of the Roman decrees aimed at her institute at large. Thus her own arrest "as a hereticke, schismatike and rebell to the Holy Church" in February 1631 took Ward by surprise.[53]

Dean Golla, the head of Munich's cathedral, appeared at the Paradeiserhaus on the seventh of the month to apprehend Ward in the name of the Roman Inquisition and deliver her to the designated prison, Munich's cloister of Poor Clares, the Angerkloster. Golla planned the arrest carefully, plotting to transport his prisoner in a carriage during nighttime for fear of unrest among the populace. Except for preparatory consultations with the Elector and the Poor Clares, Golla kept his mandate to himself for a fortnight.[54] It was necessary for him to inform the nuns because Ward's placement in the cloister entailed overriding the rules of claustration.[55] The sisters had to make arrangements to keep Ward locked up in a remote sick-room in their convent and assign four reliable nuns to watch the prisoner around the clock. Golla enlisted the help of the Reformati, the local agents of Tridentine convent reform, for the transport of the English woman, who had defied Trent's norms for female religious life.[56]

Judging from Golla's precautions, the general mood in the city appears to have been in Ward's favor. Once word got out about her imprisonment, however, feelings of doubt and disapproval began to fer-ment. When Ward fell ill in prison, there were rumors that she was dying because of her sins as a heretic.[57]

Ward spent more than two difficult months in the Angerkloster before she was cleared of all charges and released in April 1631.[58] In spite of illness and hardship, Ward found a way to keep in touch with the forty members of the Munich institute during her imprisonment. Ward and the women in the Paradeiserhaus used daily deliveries of food, wrapped in sundry pieces of paper, as the occasion for a secret correspondence.[59] Aside from informing her followers and friends about the conditions of her imprisonment or the status of her health, Ward wrote letters on behalf of herself and her institution. She forwarded memorials to the Pope and the Holy Office of the Inquisition in Rome and gave instructions to the women in the Paradeiserhaus on how to conduct themselves in their inter-actions with the Wittelsbachs.[60] The court revoked its annual payments to the women for the time being, but continued to give financial support to the community in the form of personal donations.[61]

In the face of decisive papal disapproval, Ward also started the ardu-ous yet necessary process of envisioning the direction in which she could and would want to take her institute once she regained personal freedom. "In a secular estate," she wrote to the women in the Paradeiserhaus," you may doubtlessly serve God much, and without your own or others' molestation."[62] Ward did not wish to suffer the fate of the Ursulines and turn her institute into an enclosed teaching order, nor could she hold out hope for confirmation of her unenclosed female order any longer.[63] By the third decade of the seventeenth century, the institutional structure of the Tridentine church, which was inhospitable for an active female apostolate to begin with, had rigidified to such an extent that there seemed to be only one way out: complete abandonment of the religious estate. Ward departed from Munich in 1632 and found a secular venue of activity. She pursued educational work first in Rome and then in England, where she died in 1645.[64]

This was also the venue that the Bavarian state sanctioned for those English Ladies who decided to remain in Munich. Although Maximilian,

pressured by his Jesuit confessor Adam Contzen, refrained from petition-
ing Rome on Ward's personal behalf during her imprisonment, he procured a papal exemption from the bull of suppression for the Munich community.[65] This move spared the English Ladies in the Bavarian capital
from the fate of destitution that Ward's followers suffered elsewhere.

The bull of suppression forced numerous women to leave their communities, pushing them into sudden homelessness and into dire economic
straits since it justified the confiscation of their property. Members of the
abolished institute were blocked from laying hands on the dowry payments they had made upon joining. Incapable of returning to their families
or entering another religious house, English Ladies ended up begging for
their livelihood and suffering scornful attacks because of it.[66]

By comparison, the situation in the Paradeiserhaus was stable and
comfortable.[67] The women had to divest themselves of the insignia of a
religious order and cease their teaching activities for the time being, but
they had a safe haven fittingly nicknamed "Paradise." Soon English
Ladies from the closed community in Vienna sought refuge and joined the
Munich community.[68] During the time of the Swedish occupation of the
Bavarian capital in 1632, when members of religious orders fled the city in
large numbers, English Ladies stayed behind for fear of losing the
Paradeiserhaus and the institutional future it symbolized.[69]

That future began four years later, when the English Ladies officially
reopened their school under the auspices of the state. In 1635, Winefried
Bedingfield, Ward's successor in Munich, made a successful plea to resume
the work in the Paradeiserhaus. Bedingfield played the right cards at the
right time and approached Maximilian with an irresistible proposition:

> That is my only regret, that we are idle without serving Your High-
> ness by doing well the small things we, by the grace of God, are capa-
> ble of doing for the education of the young, as young people for the
> benefit of the city and the public good, without violating the dictates
> of His Holiness.[70]

The offer of serving secular society and public order trumped any
doubts the Bavarian prince might still have harbored about sponsoring the
English Ladies after the outlawing of the institute. In response to Bedingfield's suggestion, Maximilian gave the women permission "to instruct
and direct young persons of the female sex in those things that are fitting
and in the manner customary among secular people in this land and thus
[they can] earn their sustenance."[71] In other words, he sanctioned their
pedagogical activity if they inculcated normative femininity in their pupils.
The shift in the English Ladies' official standing from a religious to a sec-

ular institution registered in the Elector's suggestion that the women should make a living through teaching girls in subjects appropriate to their gender. No longer an exercise in good works, their pedagogical efforts amounted to a useful social service that warranted payment from the point of view of state authorities.

The arrangement between the Bavarian state and Ward's followers marked the beginning of a gender-segregated development of the public school system in Bavaria.[72] Ecclesiastical resistance whittled down Mary Ward's initial vision of an unenclosed female order dedicated to teaching. The support of the Bavarian state, however, prevented the Church from stopping the forceful current of women's education that Ward unleashed.

After the reopening of the Paradeiserhaus, the English Ladies instructed girls in the context of an institute for wealthy boarders and a free day school for Munich's poorer inhabitants. Aside from religious subjects, they taught reading, writing, arithmetic, and domestic skills on the elementary level. Girls attending the advanced classes received instruction in Latin, Italian, English, and French, an advanced course of study that was open to the boarders as well as to external students.

Besides state sanction, civic endorsement was also essential in securing the survival of Ward's Munich institute in its secularized form. There was little difficulty in winning over the citizenry, which had been quite enthusiastic about Ward's all-female academy from the very beginning, especially because of its offer of free instruction to girls from less wealthy homes.[73] In 1636, the external school recommenced its work, and around the same time Anna Rörl, a German member of the institute, was put in charge of opening up a home for orphans and other needy girls, of whom there were many after the disasters of the early 1630s. This so-called Armemädchenhaus met a pressing social need in a city where burghers had been collecting money for the establishment of just such an institution since 1605.[74] Burghers and magistrate, like the Wittelsbachs, expressed their appreciation for the pedagogical services through financial support. The donations by benefactors and the dowries of members enabled the English Ladies to make ends meet without charging tuition.[75]

It did not take long for the community in Munich's Paradeiserhaus to prosper given the backing of the social and political elite. By 1662, the women had accumulated enough money to supply 8,000 florins as start-up capital for the foundation of a school of English Ladies in Augsburg.[76] The institute branched out into various parts of Bavaria in the course of the next century. Like the community in Augsburg, the foundations in Burghausen (1683), Mindelheim (1701), Bamberg (1717), Altötting (1721), Aschaffenburg (1748), and Günzburg (1758) involved monetary aid and help with personnel from Munich.[77] These new communities submitted annual reports to the Paradeiserhaus, now the seat of the revamped institute's mother general.[78]

With a headquarters and a well-frequented school, Munich's community of English Ladies inevitably began to overtax the spatial capacities in the Paradeiserhaus during the second half of the seventeenth century. Three hundred pupils in the external school, fifty boarders, forty teachers, twelve novices, and their occasional guests sought accommodation.[79] In 1691, local benefactors rallied to the support of an ambitious remodeling project for the dwelling. The various contributions provide tangible evidence for the firm place the English Ladies had staked out for themselves on the city's institutional map. Elector Max Emanuel transformed his predecessor's loan of the Paradeiserhaus into a permanent gift to them and added another present of 40,000 florins for the reconstruction and enlargement of the dwelling. Munich's magistrate made a donation of 20,000 stones to the building project in recognition of the invaluable educational services that the English Ladies provided for the city's youth.[80] Even the Jesuits came to terms with the presence of the women's community in its secularized reincarnation and added 14,000 stones of their own to the pile.[81]

Learned Women: The Educational Enterprise and Its Beneficiaries

Because the survival of the English Ladies hinged on secular support, the women experienced pressure toward accommodating the interests of authorities and families. In the course of time, several facets of the institute's work began to fall short of Ward's initial ambitions. Using the Jesuits as her yardstick, Ward's concept of women's education included advanced studies and scholarly standards that were without historical precedent. The pedagogy of "Jesuitesses" put the capabilities of girls on equal footing with those of boys, never voicing concerns over women's intellectual or moral disposition for the acquisition of knowledge.[82] The English Ladies taught an advanced course of study that included thorough training in foreign languages and familiarity with important authors. Pupils were expected to read, speak, and write in Italian, French, English, and Latin.[83] Although the study of Latin was a magnet of criticism because it was at odds with societal expectations for women, Ward remained convinced of its importance. In a letter to Winfried Bedingfield regarding two particularly proficient girls from Munich, Ward remarked that "no talent is to be so much regarded . . . as the Latin tongue."[84] Even during times of downright prohibition by the authorities, Bavaria's English Ladies upheld the instruction of Latin and other foreign languages, in some communities throughout the seventeenth century and into the eighteenth century.[85]

If the study of Latin is an indicator for Ward's faith in women's capabilities, its gradual disappearance from the institute curricula can serve as a gauge for long-term changes in the English Ladies' approach. In the early eighteenth century, French, the language most en vogue among Europe's upper classes, replaced Latin, the language of scholars, officialdom, and international communication. The linguistic shift went hand in hand with a shift from methodical study to speaking ability. Instead of plowing through the grammatical intricacies of the classical language, eighteenth-century pupils concentrated on the ability to converse in French.[86] The English Ladies no longer taught Latin with an eye toward participation in public life, as Ward envisioned, they taught French in an effort to prepare women for their private roles.

The emphasis on fluency in French was an expression of the overall refocusing of the advanced curriculum. The upper course of studies in essence became tailored to girls from the nobility and the rising bourgeoisie; it aimed at preparing the young women of the ruling classes for their social role. The ideal of the well-educated woman adorning the upper-class household loomed large by the eighteenth century.[87] The ability to converse in French was part of an entire repertoire of courtly skills, including dancing, playing musical instruments, and simply providing pleasant company.[88]

Increasing emphasis on women's social role and on class distinctions were the two main developments in the institute's educational orientation, and they occurred in response to pressures by state and church authorities as well as elite families. Already Maximilian I placed a premium on the education of upper-class girls, as reflected in his request of 1635 that the English Ladies charge tuition. Under his successors, it became customary for the Wittelsbach dynasty to pay tuition for the daughters of select noble families or award such payments to the daughters of loyal state servants.[89]

·Although the institute never resorted to tuition as the primary means of generating its income, it still depended heavily not only on the state but also on benefactors from Bavaria's upper social strata. This dependence was bound to shape the content of education over time. The impetus for new foundations often came from the nobility, and the English Ladies accumulated the majority of their funds by investing the dowry payments of wealthy institute members.[90] Not surprisingly, the English Ladies catered to the educational interests of the rich in promoting their schools. A typical advertisement included offerings of "good manners and whatever advances true virtue; in addition, reading, writing, sewing, needlework, cooking, domestic skills, [and] furthermore the French language."[91]

English Ladies also held theater performances and organized card games at their institutes in order—among other things—to recruit future pupils and members from the nobility.[92]

Clergymen reinforced class stratification as much as they could. Some even cited the English Ladies' noble background in defense of the institute's lack of claustration. Class was what distinguished these women from the single, unmarried poor and allegedly promiscuous women whom the confessional state targeted in its legislation on marriage and sexuality. If needed, class could in fact stand in for the cloister walls that these women had rejected. An ecclesiastical report from the late seventeenth century went so far as to praise the women's unenclosed status because it maximized their impact on children of all stations and extended social control to places beyond the parents' reach.

> The English Ladies are most suitable for the task of education, because the Ladies of the Institute are themselves noble and thus can instill in noble as well as common children a noble, well-mannered way of life, which should be rather desirable for the parents; and also, because the English Ladies lack claustration, they have incomparably more opportunity to offer a guiding hand to the dear youth, to follow and look after them so that the young will never stray from the eyesight and supervision of their elders, which means keeping the young with gentle force forever in the bounds of decorum and honor.[93]

When early modern authorities entrusted the English Ladies with teaching all students a "noble, well-mannered way of life," social equalization was not what they had in mind. Rather the rules for the institute's schools show the institution as an arena in which class distinctions were produced and reproduced. English Ladies arranged the regular public processions of their pupils to church according to the fine calibrations of social status: noble girls came first, followed by the female offspring of the lesser nobility, down to the burghers' daughters and girls of poorer backgrounds. Parents and local authorities joined forces in pushing for the observation of social rank on those and other occasions, especially in the Bavarian capital where burghers' daughters began to attend the institute in increasing numbers in the eighteenth century.[94]

A set of discriminatory house rules established visible class distinctions within each institute as well. The divisions in a boarding school and an external school split the pool of pupils according to social rank. Girls from the nobility dined at separate tables, and some brought their chambermaids into the boarding school.[95] Again, church authorities pushed for maintaining and even rigidifying these hierarchies. Internal guidelines in theory stipulated equal treatment of pupils in cases of rule infractions, yet ecclesiastics urged the English Ladies to draw clear distinctions between students of different class backgrounds. The bishop of Augsburg, for example, requested that "as far as possible, noble students [should] not be punished with words or blows in front of nonnoble students."[96]

A look at the curricula for students of lower rank further reveals the pedagogical interest in perpetuating class differences. The express purpose of instructing the girls from the home for poor girls (*Armemädchenhaus*) was to equip them for life at a lower station. Teachers strove to keep the needs and wants of these pupils at a minimum, putting the educational emphasis on the type of manual labor the girls would in all likelihood perform in adult life.[97] The underlying concept was not social mobility but social stability, which should be achieved through preparing students for their future station and occupation.[98]

In other respects, too, the schools of the English Ladies functioned as vehicles of public order. Parents enrolling their children in the external school were informed about the conditions of acceptance and reasons for expulsion. Schoolchildren were not allowed to come barefoot or in disheveled appearance. The reasons for dismissal were threefold: theft, profligacy, and begging.[99] It is telling that this triad of offenses—against property, sexual mores, and the work ethic of a Christian household—mirrored the main targets of the state's criminal legislation.[100]

If early critics of women's education raised the specter of social upheaval, the English Ladies, as latter-day practitioners, in large part worked toward the opposite objective: securing stability through the preparation of girls for their social roles. Instead of turning their pupils into learned women unsuitable for marriage and in danger of promiscuity, the English Ladies taught domestic skills, religious values, and morals that made for good wives and tied women back into the world of male-headed households. This course marked a departure from the scholarly orientation of Mary Ward's days.

Insofar as the institute's pedagogical practice stressed domestic skills and pursued an ideal of women's social contribution, it anticipated later theories on women's education, notably of Fénelon.[101] When there was more and more talk among educational theorists, in the second half of the eighteenth century, about the supposed incompatibility between female knowledge and being a wife and mother, the English Ladies were well positioned to meet the changing pedagogical needs of this time and alleviate fears of educated women.[102] Enlightenment pedagogues in Bavaria and elsewhere touted the principle of useful knowledge according to gender, using the "female professions" of marriage and cloister as the sole yardstick for an adequate female education.[103] Long before they systematized and theorized this pedagogical agenda, English Ladies had prefigured the program in practice. In the end, the English Ladies' success derived from serving precisely the gender system and household model advocated by church and state: Ward's followers prepared young women equally well for marriage or cloister. In this respect, the state had successfully pushed the institute's work toward domesticity. The English Ladies' public role consisted of preparing girls for their public role— which was to be private.

Yet this is only half of the story. While the English Ladies accommodated themselves to the needs of state and society and contributed to the social reproduction of gender and class hierarchies, they also broadened the range of acceptable female identities. In the midst of restrictions imposed on women's choices, Ward and her followers succeeded in opening up an entirely modern trajectory for female lives: teaching careers.

As much as the Church blocked the efforts of the English Ladies, it also unwittingly helped their cause. Since the Council of Trent, religious education took a prominent place among pious works, opening up a whole new sphere of activity.[104] Trent moreover inaugurated a period of heightened concern about sexual propriety and sweeping efforts to regulate behavior in all areas of social life. In 1680, the papacy issued a ban on having male teachers instruct girls along with boys to prevent possible improprieties. The very prohibition created an instantaneous demand for female teachers in Europe's Catholic polities, including Bavaria.[105] While the Protestant territories adjacent to Bavaria had coed schools, Catholic theologians made a strong case for gender segregation and continued to do so on the basis of women's purported special needs long after the papal ban.[106]

In this cultural climate and with the sponsorship of the Bavarian state, the revamped teaching Institute of English Ladies obtained papal confirmation in the eighteenth century. Although the official fiat was given for a pious institute with simple vows, which did not bind members permanently, and not for the female order Ward had pursued, it was tantamount to blazing a new trail for female apostolic activity within the institutional church.[107] Papal approval, deliberately vague on some issues, did extend to the distinct structure of governance and the lack of enclosure that characterized the female apostolic mission envisioned by Ward.

The institute enjoyed the spiritual and economic privileges attached to religious houses, yet its members were not bound by the sequestration and permanent vows that structured life in religious houses after Trent.[108] The superior general's authority became written into canonical law, allowing her to receive the vows of new members and to transfer women from one house to another. The members of the institute retained a good measure of independence from local ordinaries, certainly more than nuns affiliated with religious orders. These enabling legal provisions set the precedent for future legislation on new foundations of apostolic religious women's communities until 1900.[109]

Innovative not just on the level of norms but in the domain of practice, the English Ladies further blurred the Tridentine boundaries between the sacred and the secular through their manner of life. If solemn vows were the marker of the truly religious, the English Ladies, strictly speaking, were not part of that group. Their everyday existence, however, very much set them apart from secular people. As women who devoted themselves to perpetual chastity they strayed from the beaten path of marriage and veered toward the religious estate. Novices were required to bring religious paraphernalia to the Paradeiserhaus.[110] Members of the institute followed a rhythm of prayers and engaged in the study and instruction of religion. Similar to Munich's cloistered nuns, they housed holy corpses in their churches for devotional purposes.[111]

Although they could only take simple vows, they treated them with a reverence reminiscent of the gravity attached to solemn vows. In 1705, a new member was about to swallow the eucharist during her profession when the host fell on the ground, began to bleed, and left stains on a linen cloth that resisted the priest's repeated removal attempts. Community members interpreted the incident as an expression of God's disapproving of her lack of sincerity and his concern for the vows of the new institute. For want of seriousness about her vows, the story had it, the novice in question departed from the community shortly afterward. Only the stains on the cloth remained permanent.[112]

The life of the English Ladies thus was religious in crucial aspects but not in name. While their refusal to accept enclosure cost them the nomenclature, it did not, however, forestall completely the possibility of living the kind of life Mary Ward had charted. For these women, the third way between the cloister wall (*murus*) and the husband (*maritus*) was a religious life under secular cover. This quasi-privatized religiosity was possible because it remained peripheral and did not interfere with the pedagogical work sanctioned by the state interest.

Bavaria's English Ladies resembled the filles seculières in Counter-Reformation France whose imperceptible subversions of Tridentine norms Elisabeth Rapley has analyzed. Discouraged by the ecclesiastical backlash against the Ursulines and other uncloistered groups of religious women, the filles seculières contented themselves with a secular status. Yet over time their "secular" life of piety approximated the religious life in every possible respect. As Rapley pointedly sums it up, "Nuns were being made where no nuns were supposed to exist."[113] In the French case as well as in the case of Bavaria, the key to successful camouflage lay in fulfilling social needs.

Perhaps the most graphic illustration of the ambiguous status of the English Ladies is an early eighteenth-century etching of the Munich institute. The image is evocative in its likeness to the enclosed garden of a cloister. It depicts an imposing oblong with its invisible inner court closed off by high walls. A spirelike turret peaking above the front entrance reinforces the school's resemblance to a convent, and the artist played up the institutional parallel by adding two female figures in religious habit that approach the dwelling from the right. The confounding of convent life with the institute's school in art offers a reflection of the confusion that surrounded the status of the English Ladies in real life. Whether the members of the institute qualified in any way as religious or were merely secular remained a debated issue among some church and state authorities in Bavaria into the eighteenth century and beyond.[114]

The English Ladies' ambiguous status betwixt and between the religious and the laity represented a flexible and hence resilient position in an early modern world in which church and state with regularity contested the boundaries between secular and sacred. It was the basis on which the institute could create tremendous opportunities for female teachers and their female students. To begin with, the visible successes of the unenclosed English Ladies enticed the Wittelsbachs to sponsor cloistered teaching orders as well. Together with these enclosed female teachers, the English Ladies laid the foundations for the development of women's higher education in the territory. The Salesiannerinnen came to the Bavarian capital at the invitation of the court in 1662. The Servitinnen followed in 1717 and the Ladies of Notre Dame in 1731.[115]

Teaching became a professional option for women, and the Munich institute evolved into a seminary for female teachers.[116] The rise of the female teaching profession was of particular significance because it coincided with the overall decline in well-renumerated and reputable work opportunities for women in Bavaria.[117] Recurrent shortages of female teachers created openings for women in general and a vehicle for social mobility for some lower-class women in particular.[118]

Despite the fact that curricula were based on considerations of rank at institute schools, girls from all social strata did get to enjoy some kind of education. More important still, the Institute of the English Ladies was the only institution where girls from all social strata mingled for female self-improvement. The so-called open schools brought young women of every social class together under one roof, thus creating an entirely new kind of honorable, unenclosed house of women (*Frauenhaus*) in the public

Fig. 6.   Eighteenth-century etching of the Institute of English Ladies. (By Michael Wening. Original in Bildarchiv, Bayerische Staatsbibliothek, Munich.)

sphere.[119] *Open* denoted both the lack of enclosure (*offen*) as well as the public nature (*öffentlich*) of the English Ladies' pedagogical work, qualities that distinguished the institute from contemplative cloistered nunneries.

At last, the English Ladies, unlike their cloistered sisters whose mystical abilities placed them into more ethereal realms, literally embodied a religious femininity that was anchored in the world. The spiritual labor of the mystic required a porous and permeable corporeality that could serve as a conduit between heaven and earth. The English Ladies' activist piety, on the other hand, called for a solid and healthy body. The institute's requirements of physical discipline were minimal, yet the regulations included provisions for bodily hygiene.[120] It was obligatory to fast on Fridays, otherwise members—in consultation with their confessor and female superior—could decide on their own regimen of mortification and diet.[121] While Munich's cloistered nuns drew on Franciscan understandings of the body as object of physical mortification and vehicle of mystical experience, the English Ladies worked out of an Ignatian concept of the disciplined body as an instrument that one had to cultivate, even strengthen, to be fit for social service.[122]

Even though Ward's Institute of English Ladies began as a marginal and doctrinally subversive enterprise within the Counter-Reformation church, it had many unplanned ripple effects and gradually moved to the very center of the Catholic state's program of public education. One slanderous image from the institute's early days captures the great odds against this particular historical outcome: some of Ward's critics claimed that she engaged in sexual relations with her Jesuit confessor, crossdressed as a Jesuit, and inhabited a collegium of the Society of Jesus.[123] Cast as the wanton woman, who at once breached sexual decorum and clerical celibacy, this phantom Ward personifies the rejection of Trent's twofold prescription of cloister/chastity or marriage/monogamy for female lives. She appropriates not only a man's guise but the clerical garb and thus blurs two differences that the Tridentine church and the centralizing state posited as absolutes: the difference between the sexes and the difference between laity and clergy.

And the foundress of the English Ladies crossed yet another boundary in the cultural imaginary of early moderns by entering the male-designated domain of the Society of Jesus. The image of Ward as a sexually active female, dwelling among the learned elite in male disguise and engaged in their intellectual and educational pursuits, amounted to an erosion of the ideological foundation of church and state. The intellectual pursuits and the Latin training in collegia and universities were inextricably bound up with officialdom, internationalism, and participation in the expanding political public. Women as a group were barred from these public arenas, and purportedly promiscuous women represented the nemesis of the sociopolitical order from the viewpoint of early modern authorities.

The rumor freezes in time the multiple layers of transgression that contemporary critics associated with Ward. That she and her English Ladies did achieve their most important goals in spite of these adverse circumstances was due, in no small part, to the women's ability to mobilize the emancipatory potential of Catholicism's ideal of female virginity and the support of secular forces.

In contrast to the Protestant polities that advocated marriage and motherhood for every woman, Catholic territories like Bavaria continued to reserve a space in the sociopolitical and cultural order of things for unwed women who were religious and chaste. Mary Ward and her English Ladies were able to claim this space and assuage fears of unbridled female sexuality. Their upper-class background lent the English Ladies an aura of trustworthiness not accorded to lower-class women, and it enabled them to access the patronage networks of Europe's courts.

In addition, the women exhibited great ingenuity in dealing with constraints and in bypassing barriers. Sacrificing some ambitions while capitalizing on the ideals and needs of their time, they gave up their plan to found a religious order of unenclosed women and contented themselves with a pious institute instead. In so doing, the English Ladies left Tridentine ideology intact. Yet, living as religious women in the world and engaged in self-development and the development of other women through education, they eroded this ideology in practice, all the while waiting for an opportune moment to receive official recognition.

By blurring the lines between theological prescriptions and social meanings of religion, the English Ladies gained the protection of the ruling secular elite and maintained this patronage throughout the centuries. When the education of girls for their role in Catholic society became a central component of the early modern state's public religiosity drive, the English Ladies had the flexibility, mobility, and credibility to move to the forefront of this program. As long as they served the common good, the state supported the English Ladies and, regardless of church regulations, sanctioned their personal expressions of religiosity and their unenclosed way of life.

Over time, the ruling elite pushed the English Ladies to tailor their pedagogy to the new demands of female domesticity. State officials defined women's contribution to public order more sharply in terms of serving as guardians of religion and morality within privatized households headed by male citizens. Ward's original vision of preparing women for a life in the larger world was co-opted on one level, insofar as the English Ladies did participate in the domestication of women in Catholic states. On another level, however, Ward's vision took on a life of its own. The English Ladies still achieved many of their educational goals. Moreover, their compromise position allowed them to develop into an enduring movement and create the identity of the honorable single woman.

Conclusion and Epilogue

Developments in sixteenth- and seventeenth-century Bavaria reveal that neither Catholicism nor female virginity was a medieval residue that the state had to overcome in order to centralize, secularize, and modernize. Instead, Catholicism supplied the state with a storehouse of legal, institutional, and ideological means that authorities could raid for the modernization of political life. Catholicism also furnished an idiom of meaning, behavioral prescriptions, and moral orientations through which rulers as well as ruled acquired and experienced their respective subjectivities. Such is the power of religion.

At this stage in the formation of central government, it was impossible for the state to marginalize religion in the manner assumed by Weberian modernization and rationalization narratives. There was no strategic position outside or beyond religion from which the state could have operated against it. At once more and less than an ideology, religion shaped every aspect of life without determining its specific uses by historical actors, including the agents of state power. The success of the modernizing state consisted in claiming aspects of religion—institutions, practices, and attitudes—that were useful to its centralizing project and defining them as matters of the common good and therefore subject to state control.

Even the Catholic preference for chastity, its most outdated and otherworldly feature from the Protestant reformers' (and a Weberian) viewpoint, could be marshaled to complement the workings of the modernizing state. Bavarian state authorities recruited female virgins to demarcate legitimate and illegitimate forms of sexuality, to maintain hierarchies of gender and class, and to endow power politics with the aura of the sacred and natural.

Every lower-class woman who renounced sexual relations with men at the same time ended up supporting the state's anti-profligacy campaign and its political vision of a society of propertied, married householders. When religious virgins gave up sexual reproduction and embraced the con-

173

templative life behind cloister walls, they put their pure bodies in the service of the spiritual reproduction of a body politic and underwrote the power of the state authorities that headed it. Teaching Bavaria's young women not only how to read and write but also how to be devoted wives or devout nuns, the chaste English Ladies simultaneously schooled their pupils in the type of female citizenship favored by state authorities.

Mothers and wives have stood in the limelight of scholarship on the early modern domestication of women, and feminist historians have done much to illuminate their role. The virgins surrounding the mothers and wives of early modern society, however, were equally central to the process of political centralization. An exploration of their position in culture and society makes plain that state formation entailed not only women's domestication but also the production of the female body as a sexual body. By concentrating on mothers and wives or, differently put, on progressive state control of sexual reproduction, we reinscribe and leave unexamined the problematic association of women and procreation that arose out of the very process we seek to understand. We naturalize the female body as a sexualized body.

By contrast, this study has explored the historical genesis of the modern female body by differentiating between gender and sexuality and by treating virginity as a historical phenomenon. It has documented how virginity and convents were pulled into the same expanding regulation of sexuality that appears to have accompanied confessional state building everywhere and that, as Lyndal Roper has shown, transformed marriage and prostitution, too.[1] During the confessional age, virginity's meanings and implications were thus transformed along with the institutional landscape that made up the state. The consequences of this process, this study has stressed, differed considerably according to class. Like the male bodies of different socioeconomic backgrounds who feature in Isabel Hull's account of state control of sexuality, the female bodies presented in this book all experienced state regulation and its sexualizing effects, yet they experienced them in socially distinct ways.[2] Virginity's radical reconfiguration was taxing for all women, but it still extracted the highest toll from lowerclass women.

Prior to the Protestant Reformation, virginity represented a distinct position in a system of sex and gender classification that was more fluid than the sexual dimorphism that evolved afterward. Virginity could be understood as a psychological as well as a physiological state; it was not (yet) exclusively defined by the absence of sexual relations. Subsequently, the women who made the virginal life their destiny also chose a gender identity that diverged from the gender of women who renounced virginity. Throughout the Middle Ages, Catholicism's religious virgins could constitute a "third gender" of sorts, neither conventionally male nor conventionally female.

That is not to say that there were not also competing discourses already in place in the high and late Middle Ages that pointed toward a more gendered and sexualized understanding of female virginity. Some medieval critics of uncloistered female religious communities invoked the dangers of women's sexuality to argue for the intensification of ecclesiastical control and the implementation of effective enclosure.[3] Many female mystics, on the other hand, voluntarily and wholeheartedly embraced key aspects of their culture's understanding of the feminine. As Caroline Bynum has argued persuasively, these women (and their male supporters) identified the feminine with Christ's suffering humanity and therefore considered the feminine a site of sanctification.[4]

With the coming of the Reformation, the discursive ground on which sexual desire and gender identities could be debated, imagined, and experienced shifted in ways that privileged gendered and sexualized notions of female virginity. The reformers made the existence of a divinely ordained and hence natural sex drive plausible, and they constructed (marital) heterosexuality as everyone's destiny. As a result, virginity became the lower half in an unstable hierarchical pairing with sexuality, a tenuous state always on the brink of tipping into its more "natural" opposite—an active sex life—and an unequivocally corporeal condition. On this new ground, the sexualization and gendering of female virginity could be consolidated.

The female gender was reclassified accordingly, now encompassing natural wives and mothers as well as morally endangered virginal brides, sexually repressed nuns, and "unnaturally" rapacious prostitutes. The institutional results of this reclassification and their connection to Protestant state building are generally familiar: public control of marriage formation, intensified persecution of nonmarital sexuality, abolition of brothels, and closings of convents. Less familiar features, such as the reformers' transformation of some convents into female *Zuchthäuser,* institutions of discipline and decorum for unmarried virgins, indicate that women's chastity, albeit no longer a religious ideal, retained its sociopolitical importance in Protestant polities.

Part of my purpose has been to show that Catholic reconfigurations of marriage and sexuality differed from their Protestant counterparts in style rather than in substance. Bavaria's Catholic authorities, who responded to the reformers' doctrinal, institutional, and discursive changes while pursuing a reform agenda of their own, ultimately followed more faithfully in the Protestant footsteps than they set out to do. In part, this was the case because much of the discursive groundwork was already accomplished within the Church prior to the Reformation. Not merely

matrimony, but sexual intimacy within marriage experienced a revaloriza-
tion within Catholicism itself, echoing the Protestant redefinition of sexual
desire's role in the making of social order. Catholics also pushed for public control over marriage formation and for the eradication of all forms of
nonmarital sex. They too shut down urban brothels.

Even the Catholic celibate ideal, which on the surface set it apart from
Protestantism, changed its contours in the wake of the Reformation. So
did the gender order and the notions of sexuality that Catholicism authorized. Most tellingly, the drive toward the enclosure of religious virgins
(while their male counterparts retained their freedom of movement) highlights a post-Reformation unease among Catholics about the possibilities
of lifelong virginity. Literally every female body had become a sexual body
with potentially unruly desires; a life of virginity was now tantamount to a
life of sexual repression.

The reform discourses among Protestants and Catholics unleashed
their own dynamic, driving one another throughout the confessional age.
They are therefore best understood not as ripples on the surface of "real"
history but rather as part of the very "history of events."[5] Other events and
deeper structural developments were equally significant factors, as we
have seen. Most notably, the Thirty Years' War and the sustained socioeconomic crises originating in the 1620s accelerated the pace of historical
change. The disturbing experiences of warfare, hunger, and disease pried
open the political as well as the psychological space in which material conditions and reform discourses entered into a complex and consequential
dialectic. The result was not only an overall increase in state regulation
but, more specifically, the emergence of gender and sexual norms that were
to remain in place long after the war years and their crises were over.

Understandings of sexuality and gender appear to be among the most
far-reaching and long-term effects of the German confessionalization
process. Looking back, one finds that conceptions of women's place in
society that became recognizable in the seemingly more secular context of
the nineteenth century had already taken root in the overtly religious culture of the sixteenth and seventeenth centuries. This points to the need for
scholarship on gender, sexuality, religion, and the state that straddles the
traditional boundary between the early modern and the modern and oper-
ates with a notion of religion that transcends belief and ritual to consider
questions of cultural identity.[6]

In Bavaria, for instance, early modern anti-profligacy legislation
marked a key phase in the state-initiated creation of the poor unmarried
mother of ill repute, a much-debated social problem of the nineteenth century. Although the state decriminalized pregnancies outside of wedlock in
1808, the lower-class women who historically had suffered most from the

criminalization of nonmarital consensual sex during the early modern period derived no benefit. Rather, the state transferred the regulation of sexuality—together with control over marriage formation—to the police, who operated relatively unchecked within the old parameters of absolutist sexual disciplining. Police cracked down especially hard on women for pregnancies outside of wedlock, yet they no longer made any attempt to track down the men who had impregnated lower-class women.[7]

Correspondingly, in the sphere of civil law, state-sanctioned legal reform further obstructed the possibilities for legal redress for women who became pregnant outside of marriage. Nineteenth-century law codes sought to protect the freedom and privacy of the male citizen whose precious resources were supposedly best spent on marriage and legitimate children. The foil to this new male victim was a new type of offender: the *Dirne* or greedy lower-class seductress out to harm men's reputation and livelihood. Unsure of the identity of her child's father, this promiscuous woman was prone to level accusations at any man. Within this scheme of things, the law above all had to protect the man as the potentially wronged party; it did not have to protect the child, and most certainly not the woman, who was the likely culprit. The lower-class *Dirne* as danger to a civil society composed of propertied married men thus loomed large in the legal and bureaucratic imaginary.[8] The state discourse of early modern profligacy, while steeped in religious moralism, prefigured these post-Enlightenment anxieties and cultural prejudices about the polluting powers of lower-class women's sexuality.

Similarly, the measures that the Bavarian state undertook vis-à-vis female religious institutions in the confessional context of the Thirty Years' War did not unleash their full force until religion ceased to be a primary mechanism of legitimating state rule in the wake of the Enlightenment. In the second half of the nineteenth century, the Institute of English Ladies emerged as the leading force in the burgeoning field of women's education. At this historical moment, the church's rejection of Mary Ward's bid for a female order in the seventeenth century turned out to be beneficial. It had forced the English Ladies to form strong ties with state authorities, to prove their usefulness to civil society by providing pedagogical services, and to be engaged with the larger world. In the changed context of the nineteenth century, the English Ladies came to represent the moral dimension of religion that could facilitate the functioning of a modern society, unlike the mystical escapism and pious naïveté ascribed to nuns. Even liberals skeptical of Catholic influence in public life could feel comfortable with the English Ladies' pedagogical presence because the women were merely a congregation and not a legitimate religious order.[9]

The growing importance of the English Ladies contrasted sharply with the dramatic decline in significance that Bavaria's cloistered and contemplative communities experienced over time. The female cloisters' strength in the early modern period—their alleged ability to channel divine grace upon individuals, communities, and the state—became a liability for their inhabitants following the Enlightenment. State-sponsored enclosure in the seventeenth century stripped these religious houses of key social functions for the sake of spiritual efficacy. In so doing, the state ushered in their demise in the long run. Once contemplative prayer was no longer a persuasive justification for the existence of female religious houses, religious virgins had little to offer to state and society. Not surprisingly, over 4,000 of the 5,054 women who lived in Bavarian convents in 1879 worked in the area of female education and eschewed the contemplative life.[10]

In the guise of identity, morality, and culture, religion apparently shaped the sociopolitical and sexual order as well as gender relations in Bavaria long after the putative deconfessionalization associated with the end of the Thirty Years' War. This raises pointed questions about how we classify periods and how modern the "modern" truly was. Recent scholarship on the nineteenth century has already delivered irrefutable evidence of the abiding importance of religious beliefs, idioms, and practices and their intersection with gender identities and sexual norms even in a secularizing and modernizing context.[11] Tracing lines of continuities between the seventeenth and the nineteenth centuries, the divide between early modern and modern history appears even more porous and arbitrary. If we take religion seriously as a category of historical analysis and broaden our understanding of religion to encompass questions of identity—which are always questions of gender and sexuality—new directions for research come into view that inevitably point across the conventional border between the early modern and the modern. Traversing this boundary should enable us both to recognize more fully the modernizing power of early modern Catholicism and to perceive "the nineteenth century as a confessional century."[12]

The abiding public presence of Munich's Virgin on the pillar (Mariensäule) testifies to religion's deep and durable impact on Bavaria's cultural and social life. Raised as a monument to the victory of Catholicism and its values during the Thirty Years' War, the Virgin has remained a towering figure in the centuries following open confessional conflict. She served as the point of reference for measuring geographic distances until some time in the twentieth century.[13] And to this day she lends her name to Munich's central square and its subway station (Marienplatz). Even though throngs of tourists by and large have replaced the crowds of believers who gathered around her in centuries past, the Virgin clearly continues to maintain her place in the heart of the modern polity.

Notes

INTRODUCTION

1. Georg Schwaiger, "München—Eine geistliche Stadt," in *Monachium Sacrum: Festschrift zur 500-Jahr-Feier der Metropolitankirche zu Unserer Lieben Frau in München*, vol. 1, ed. Georg Schwaiger (Munich: Deutscher Kunstverlag, 1994), 126.

2. Reinhard Heydenreuter, "Der Magistrat als Befehlsempfänger: Die Disziplinierung der Stadtobrigkeit 1579–1651," in *Geschichte der Stadt München*, ed. Richard Bauer (Munich: C. H. Beck, 1992), 189–210.

3. Benno Hubensteiner, *Vom Geist des Barock: Kultur und Frömmigkeit im alten Bayern* (Munich: Süddeutscher Verlag, 1978), 117.

4. Karl-Ludwig Ay, *Land und Fürst im alten Bayern* (Regensburg: Verlag Friedrich Pustet, 1988), 195.

5. David Lederer, "Reforming the Spirit: Confession, Madness and Suicide in Bavaria, 1517–1809" (Ph.D. diss., New York University, 1995), 70.

6. Wolfgang Behringer, *Witchcraft Persecutions in Bavaria: Popular Magic, Religious Zealotry and Reason of the State in Early Modern Europe* (Cambridge: Cambridge University Press, 1997), 106–8.

7. Michael Schattenhofer, *Die Mariensäule in München* (Munich: Schnell und Steiner, 1970), 32.

8. The spelling of names has been modernized to the extent to which it was possible without distortion. The early modern German suffix "-in" used to indicate the female gender (e.g., Maria Jausin) has been dropped throughout (e.g., Maria Jaus).

9. All details pertaining to this case are gleaned from Protokoll des Oberrichters, Stadtarchiv München, Bestand Stadtgericht, 868/5 73r–75v.

10. See, for example, the report of 1639, Bayerisches Hauptstaatsarchiv München, GR Fasz. 322, Tomus "Leichtfertigkeit und Gotteslästerung betr.," Nr. 9.

11. One of the first measures Maximilian took upon assuming office was to stiffen already existing punishments for nonmarital sexuality and to intensify the prosecution of offenders. Felix Stieve, *Das kirchliche Polizeiregiment in Baiern*

unter Maximilian I. 1595–1651 (Munich: Verlag der M. Rieger'schen Universitäts-Buchhandlung, 1876), 37–39.

12. On Germany, see the pathbreaking study of Isabel Hull. This study builds on and expands her narrative by adding virginity to the picture. Hull, *Sexuality, State and Civil Society in Germany, 1700–1815* (Ithaca: Cornell University Press, 1996).

13. Jutta Gisela Sperling, *Convent and the Body Politic in Late Renaissance Venice* (Chicago: University of Chicago Press, 1999), 72–114.

14. Ulinka Rublack, "Wench and Maiden: Women, War, and the Pictorial Function of the Feminine in German Cities in the Early Modern Period," *History Workshop Journal* 44 (1997): 1–21.

15. Benno Hubensteiner, *Bayerische Geschichte* (1992; reprint, Munich: Süddeutscher Verlag, 1994), 232.

16. Aegidius Albertinus, *Haußpolizey* (Munich: Nicolaus Henricus, 1602). The treatise has a tripartite division reflecting the three (sexual) estates contemporaries viewed as constitutive of Catholic society: female virginity, marriage, and clerical celibacy.

17. Max Weber, *Staatssoziologie,* ed. Johannes Winckelmann (Berlin: Duncker und Humblot, 1956). See also Max Weber, *Economy and Society,* vol. 2, ed. Guenther Roth and Claus Wittich (Berkeley: University of California Press, 1978), especially 956–1001, "Bureaucracy," and 1070–1104, "Feudalism, Ständestaat and Patrimonialism."

18. Max Weber, *Die protestantische Ethik und der Geist des Kapitalismus,* ed. Johannes Winckelmann (Gütersloh: Mohn, 1981–82).

19. Because of the great complexity of Weber's work a summary statement of this kind inevitably appears somewhat reductionist. Yet the interpretation I offer responds to the prevalent theoretical strand in Weber's own reflections on the topic and those of his many commentators. Weberians, often much more strongly than Weber, have foregrounded this particular modulation of the argument about Protestantism's modernity.

20. Heinz Schilling, "Between the Territorial State and Urban Liberty: Lutheranism and Calvinism in the County of Lippe," in *The German People and the Reformation,* ed. R. Po-Chia Hsia (Ithaca: Cornell University Press, 1988), 263–84, quote from 266. See also Schilling's article "Die Konfessionalisierung im Reich," *Historische Zeitschrift* 246 (1988): 1–45. One good example of Wolfgang Reinhard's work on the issue is "Zwang zur Konfessionalisierung? Prolegomena zu einer Theorie des konfessionellen Zeitalters," *Zeitschrift für historische Forschung* 10 (1983): 257–77. Insofar as the confessionalization paradigm zooms in on the creation of obedient subjects whose reliable docility was facilitated by religious conformity and based on an internalized ethics of submissiveness to god-given rule, the paradigm intersects with two other large-scale theories: Gerhard Oestreich's "Sozialdisziplinierung" and Norbert Elias's "Zivilisationsprozeß." Oestreich, "Strukturprobleme des europäischen Absolutismus," *Vierteljahrschrift für Sozial- und Wirtschaftsgeschichte* 55 (1968): 319–47. Oestreich did not take account of gender in his analysis of modern rule. Norbert Elias's *Über den Prozeß der Zivilisation: Soziogenetische und psychogenetische Untersuchungen,* 2d ed.

(Bern: Francke, 1969), is characterized by the same oversight, yet Elias addressed questions of relations between the sexes elsewhere. He actually took up the issue of sexual inequality in a manuscript that was destroyed by accident in 1971. In 1986 he reconstructed some of his thoughts on the topic in an article on ancient Rome. Stephen Mennell, *Norbert Elias: Civilization and the Human Self-Image* (Oxford: Basil Blackwell, 1989), 25, 131–36.

21. For example, Pierre Bourdieu, *An Outline of a Theory of Practice* (Cambridge: Cambridge University Press, 1977); Michel Foucault, *Power/Knowledge: Selected Interviews and Other Writings* (New York: Pantheon, 1980).

22. Heinz Schilling, "Die frühneuzeitliche Formierung und Disziplinierung von Ehe, Familie und Erziehung im Spiegel calvinistischer Kirchenratsprotokolle," in *Glaube und Eid. Treueformel, Glaubensbekenntnisse und Sozialdisziplinierung zwischen Mittelalter und Neuzeit,* ed. Paolo Prodi (Munich: Oldenbourg, 1993), 199–235.

23. Friedrich Engels, *Der Ursprung der Familie, des Privateigentums und des Staates,* 19th ed. (Stuttgart: Dietz, 1920).

24. On this issue, including the problematic legacy of Engels and critiques thereof in recent anthropological studies based on fieldwork in non-Western countries, see the literature survey by Irene Silverblatt, "Women in States," *Annual Review of Anthropology* 17 (1988): 427–60.

25. Ibid. See also Barbara Watson Andaya, ed., *Other Pasts: Women, Gender, and History in Early Modern Southeast Asia* (Honolulu: Center for Southeast Asian Studies, University of Hawaii, 2000).

26. See, for example, Ida Blom, Karen Hagemann, and Catherine Hall, eds., *Gendered Nations: Nationalism and Gender Order in the Long Nineteenth Century* (Oxford: Berg, 2000). For a thought-provoking account of changing forms of patriarchal governance between the early modern and the modern period, see Pavla Miller, *Transformations of Patriarchy in the West, 1500–1900* (Bloomington: Indiana University Press, 1998).

27. Heide Wunder has developed this argument in *'Er ist die Sonn', sie ist der Mond.' Frauen in der Frühen Neuzeit* (Munich: C. H. Beck, 1992).

28. Hull.

29. Heide Wunder, "Herrschaft und öffentliches Handeln von Frauen in der Frühen Neuzeit," in *Frauen in der Geschichte des Rechts. Von der Frühen Neuzeit bis zur Gegenwart,* ed. Ute Gerhard (Munich: C. H. Beck, 1997), 27–54.

30. Heide Wunder's work is the exception to this rule.

31. Lyndal Roper, *The Holy Household: Women and Morals in Reformation Augsburg* (Oxford: Clarendon Press, 1989). In this narrative on the "domestication" of women in Protestant Augsburg, Protestantism remains the primary agent of change on the eve of modernity, an analytical act in line with Weber's special emphasis on Protestantism. Another example of the quasi-Weberian privileging of Protestantism in the explanatory models of feminist historians of early modern Europe is Siegrid Westphal, *Frau und lutherische Konfessionalisierung. Eine Untersuchung zum Fürstentum Pfalz-Neuburg, 1542–1614* (Frankfurt am Main: P. Lang, 1994). The process of "domestication," however, created new problems, since male householders were both empowered and also more controlled by governing

authorities. On the tension between normative masculinities and patriarchal claims of householders, see Lyndal Roper, "Blood and Codpieces: Masculinity in the Early Modern Town," in *Oedipus and the Devil: Witchcraft, Sexuality, and Religion in Early Modern Europe* (London and New York: Routledge, 1994), 107–24. For the complexities of patriarchal authority in England, see Susan Amussen, *An Ordered Society: Gender and Class in Early Modern England* (Oxford and New York: Basil Blackwell, 1988).

32. Sarah Hanley, "Engendering the State: Family Formation and State Building in Early Modern Europe," *French Historical Studies* 16, no. 1 (spring 1989): 4–27.

33. Beate Schuster, *Die freien Frauen: Dirnen und Frauenhäuser im 15. und 16. Jahrhundert* (Frankfurt am Main: Campus Verlag, 1995).

34. Susanna Burghartz, "Jungfräulichkeit oder Reinheit? Zur Änderung von Argumentationsmustern vor dem Basler Ehegericht im 16. und 17. Jahrhundert," in *Dynamik der Tradition,* ed. Richard van Dülmen (Frankfurt am Main: Fischer, 1992), 13–40.

35. Roper, *Holy Household.*

36. Joan Kelly, "Did Women Have a Renaissance?" in *Women, History, and Theory: The Essays of Joan Kelly* (Chicago: University of Chicago Press, 1984), 19–50.

37. See, for example, Elizabeth Rapley, *The Dévotes: Women and Church in Seventeenth-Century France* (Montreal: McGill-Queen's University Press, 1990); Craig Monson, *Disembodied Voices: Music and Culture in an Early Modern Italian Convent* (Berkeley: University of California Press, 1995); Anne Conrad, *Zwischen Kloster und Welt: Ursulinen und Jesuitinnen in der katholischen Reformbewegung des 16./17. Jahrhunderts* (Mainz: Zabern, 1991).

38. In a number of cases the abolition of female religious houses proved so tricky that Protestants acquiesced to the conversion of the entire religious community, leaving us with a historical contradiction in terms: a Protestant nunnery. Ironically, some of Germany's most powerful women were the abbesses of the Protestant monastic establishments, institutions whose existence defies conventional analytical categories and has therefore generally been overlooked. Merry Wiesner-Hanks, "Ideology Meets the Empire: Reformed Convents and the Reformation," in *Germania Illustrata: Essays on Early Modern Germany Presented to Gerald Strauss,* ed. Andrew C. Fix and Susan C. Karant-Nunn (Kirksville, Mo.: Sixteenth Century Journal, 1992), 181–96.

39. On the role of confessional rivalry in producing parallel sociopolitical developments, see Susanna Burghartz, *Zeiten der Reinheit—Orte der Unzucht. Ehe und Sexualität in Basel während der Frühen Neuzeit* (Paderborn: Schöningh Verlag, 1999).

40. Helmut Puff, "'. . . ein schul / darinn wir allerlay Christliche tugend vnd zucht lernen.' Ein Vergleich zweier ehedidaktischer Schriften des 16. Jahrhunderts," in Rüdiger Schnell, ed., *Geschlechterbeziehungen und Textfunktionen. Studien zu Eheschriften der Frühen Neuzeit* (Tübingen: M. Niemeyer, 1998), 59–88.

41. It is important to keep in mind that the reconfiguration of clerical celibacy

in Protestant and Catholic polities set new parameters for masculine self-understandings and male behavior as well. The nature of such changes and their implication for the male gender warrant an in-depth analysis that goes beyond the scope of this book.

42. For analyses of virginity in the Middle Ages, see among others Clarissa W. Atkinson, "Precious Balm in a Fragile Glass: The Ideology of Virginity in the Later Middle Ages," *Journal of Family History* 8 (1983): 131–43; Jane Tibbetts Schulenburg, *Forgetful of Their Sex: Female Sanctity and Society, ca. 500–1100* (Chicago: University of Chicago Press, 1998); Cindy L. Carlson and Angela Jane Weisl, eds., *Constructions of Widowhood and Virginity in the Middle Ages* (New York: St. Martin's Press, 1999). Discussions of early Christian ideas about chastity include Peter Brown, *The Body and Society: Men, Women, and Sexual Renunciation in Early Christianity* (New York: Columbia University Press, 1988), and Susanna Elm, *Virgins of God: The Making of Asceticism in Late Antiquity* (Oxford: Oxford University Press, 1994).

43. Sigrun Haude's current project on the effect that Wittelsbach social disciplining had across the entire territory of Bavaria will shed more light on this issue. Preliminary findings indicate that the success of the Wittelsbachs was uneven. See Sigrun Haude, "War—A Fortuitous Occasion for Social Disciplining and Political Centralization? The Case of Bavaria under Maximilian I," paper delivered at Sixteenth Century Studies Conference, San Antonio, Texas, October 2002. I would like to thank Sigrun Haude for providing me with a copy of her paper.

44. Merry E. Wiesner, *Working Women in Renaissance Germany* (New Brunswick, N.J.: Rutgers University Press, 1986), 16.

45. Werner Schultheiß, *Die Münchner Gewerbeverfassung im Mittelalter* (Munich: Beck'sche Verlagsbuchhandlung, 1936), 94, 145.

46. Helmuth Stahleder, "Konsolidierung und Ausbau der bürgerlichen Stadt: München im 15. Jahrhundert," in *Geschichte der Stadt München*, ed. Richard Bauer, 120–47, 133.

47. Ibid., 144.

48. Ingo Schwab, "Zeiten der Teuerung: Versorgungprobleme in der zweiten Hälfte des 16. Jahrhunderts," in *Geschichte der Stadt München*, ed. Richard Bauer, 166–88, 167. Schwab considers 10,000—the population number commonly reported in the secondary literature—a somewhat high estimate.

49. The trend toward an independent court economy had begun already in the closing decades of the fifteenth century, but started to have a serious impact only after the political changes of the sixteenth century. On the late-fifteenth-century development, see Stahleder, 144–45. On the developments from 1506 onward, see Joachim Hecker, "Um Glaube und Recht: Die fürstliche Stadt 1505 bis 1561," in *Geschichte der Stadt München*, ed. Richard Bauer, 148–65, 148–49.

50. Ay, 86. As early as 1480s court officials, on the basis of papal privileges, carried out extensive cloister visitations in Bavaria's monastic houses. Maximilian Lanzinner, *Fürst, Räte und Landstände. Die Entstehung der Zentralbehörden in Bayern 1511–1598* (Göttingen: Vandenhoeck und Ruprecht, 1980), 82.

51. On the role of courts in the emergence of modern government see Ronald

G. Asch and Adolf M. Birke, *Princes, Patronage, and the Nobility: The Court at the Beginning of the Modern Age, c. 1450–1650* (Oxford: Oxford University Press, 1991).

52. Lanzinner, 11.

53. Schwaiger, "München—Eine geistliche Stadt," 73, 75–76, 80.

54. Lanzinner, 156.

55. Schwaiger, "München—Eine geistliche Stadt," 77–79. Bavarian officials took this oath until the end of the eighteenth century.

56. Lanzinner, 159.

57. Hecker, 150–55. Schwaiger, "München—Eine geistliche Stadt," 73–74. The standard monograph on Protestantism in the diocese of Freising is Hans Rößler, *Geschichte und Strukturen der evangelischen Bewegung im Bistum Freising (1520–1571)* (Nuremberg, 1966). On Protestants in Munich, Ernst Dorn's study remains classic: *Der Sang der Wittenberg Nachtigall in München. Eine Geschichte des Protestantismus in Bayerns Hauptstadt in der Zeit der Reformation und Gegenreformation des 16. Jahrhunderts* (Munich, 1917).

58. Hecker, 155–56.

59. Ibid., 159.

60. Albrecht reorganized the tribunal into a permanent Ecclesiastical Council (*Geistlicher Rat*), an institutional body that exercised control and disciplinary powers in matters pertaining to religious reform and education in Bavaria until the end of the eighteenth century. Schwaiger, "Geistliche Stadt," 94; Rößler, 61–77. Rößler reports that a total of forty-eight people were exiled, eleven women and thirty-seven men. Although they only amounted to 1.3 percent of the city's taxpayers, they generated more than 5 percent of the city's revenue. Magistrate complaints to the court about the economic loss were to no avail. Hecker, "Glaube und Recht," 160–61. Extensive records of the tribunals can be found in Bayerisches Hauptstaatsarchiv München, Kurbayern Äusseres Archiv, 4208, 416ff.

61. Andreas Kraus, *Maximilian I. Bayerns großer Kurfürst* (Graz: Verlag Styria; Regensburg: Pustet, 1990), 23.

62. On this issue see Paul Münch, "Die 'Obrigkeit im Vaterstand,'" *Daphnis* 11 (1982): 15–40.

63. Kraus, 25.

64. Heydenreuter, "Magistrat als Befehlsempfänger," esp. 189–91.

65. Lanzinner, 253.

66. Ay, 52–56.

67. Schwab, "Zeiten der Teuerung," 167.

68. Lanzinner, 236–37.

69. Finally, as more and more patricians transferred from city government to court service, Maximilian could replace them with officials of his choice to whom he in turn awarded patrician status. Heydenreuter, "Magistrat als Befehlsempfänger," 196–98.

70. On Maximilian's use of Munich as a test ground for his police ordinances, see Reinhard Heydenreuter, *Der landesherrliche Hofrat unter Herzog und Kurfürst Maximilian I. von Bayern (1598–1651)* (Munich: C. H. Beck, 1981), 231–68. On state formation and police ordinances in general see Marc Raeff, *The Well-*

Ordered Police State: Social and Institutional Change through Law in the Germanies and Russia, 1600–1800 (New Haven: Yale University Press, 1983).

71. On the criminal prosecution of moral crimes, see Wolfgang Behringer, "Mörder, Diebe, Ehebrecher: Verbrechen und Strafen in Kurbayern vom 16. bis 18. Jahrhundert," in *Kultur der einfachen Leute,* ed. Richard van Dülmen (Munich, 1983), 87–132.

72. The socioeconomic and political crises of the war years also explain the peak in witchcraft prosecutions in Bavaria in the late 1620s. The witch-hunts were another instrument the state used to extend its power from the center to the periphery. Behringer, *Witchcraft Persecution in Bavaria.*

73. Wiesner, *Working Women,* 16.

74. Compare Burghartz, *Zeiten der Reinheit—Orte der Unzucht.*

75. Sperling, 134.

CHAPTER 1

1. Stadtarchiv München, Bestand Stadtgericht, 867/8 65r.

2. Stadtarchiv München, Bestand Stadtgericht, 867/9 102r–105r.

3. Rainer Beck, "Illegitimität und voreheliche Sexualität auf dem Land," in *Kultur der einfachen Leute: Bayerisches Volksleben vom 16. bis zum 19. Jahrhundert,* ed. Richard van Dülmen, 112–50 (Munich: Verlag C. H. Beck, 1983); Sandra Cavallo and Simona Cerutti, "Female Honor and the Social Control of Reproduction in Piedmont between 1600–1800," in *Sex and Gender in Historical Perspective,* ed. Edward Muir and Guido Ruggiero (Baltimore: Johns Hopkins University Press, 1990), 80–109.

4. On the nexus of marriage regulation and state power see, for example, Michela De Giorgio and Christiane Klapisch-Zuber, eds., *Storia del matrimonio* (Rome and Bari: Laterza, 1996).

5. Reinhard Heydenreuter, *Der landesherrliche Hofrat unter Herzog und Kurfürst Maximilian I. von Bayern (1598–1651)* (Munich: C. H. Beck, 1981), 231–68.

6. Rüdiger Schnell posits that this greater valorization of marriage already emerged in late medieval theology, in *Frauendiskurs, Männerdiskurs, Ehediskurs: Textsorten und Geschlechterkonzepte in Mittelalter und Früher Neuzeit* (Frankfurt am Main and New York: Campus Verlag, 1998).

7. Bernward Deneke, *Hochzeit* (Munich: Prestel-Verlag, 1971), 10, 16.

8. Ibid., 13.

9. See the example of Florence in Christiane Klapisch-Zuber, "Zacharias or the Ousted Father: Nuptial Rites in Tuscany between Giotto and the Council of Trent," in *Women, Family, and Ritual in Renaissance Italy,* trans. Lydia G. Cochrane (Chicago: University of Chicago Press, 1985), 178–212, especially 193.

10. For example, salaries for and licensing of "Notarien/Stuel unnd andern Schreibern in Stoeten unnd Maerckten" were regulated in *Baierische Lanndtsordnung,* Getruckt in unser Stat Ingolstadt 1553, 2. Buch, 8. Titul, 1. Articul, XXXVIv.

11. These festivities might spill over into the wedding itself and continue after-

ward as well. Neuordnung der Hochzeiten, 12.5.1535, Stadtarchiv München, Zimelie 11, 11r.

12. Deneke, 55.

13. Interestingly, the number of female guests was the primary indicator of membership in a particular class. Munich's wealthiest residents had permission to invite 52 women, as compared to the 16 women whom the lowest class could host. Hans Moser, "Aufriß zur Geschichte des Münchner Faschings," *Bayerisches Jahrbuch für Volkskunde* (1988): 42; also Moser, *Volksbräuche im geschichtlichen Wandel. Ergebnisse aus fünfzig Jahren volkskundlicher Quellenforschung* (Deutscher Kunstverlag, 1985), 103.

14. Cited in Deneke, 55.

15. Various proverbs encapsulate the legal significance of covering spouses with a blanket: "Ist das Bett beschritten, ist das Recht erstritten;" or "Ist die Decke über dem Kopf, so sind die Eheleute gleich reich." Lutz Röhrich, *Lexikon der sprichwörtlichen Redensarten*, vol. 1, 3d ed. (Freiburg: Herder Verlag, 1974) 310, s.v. "Decke."

16. Deneke, 130–31.

17. Thomas M. Safley, *Let No Man Put Asunder: The Control of Marriage in the German Southwest: A Comparative Study, 1550–1600* (Kirksville, Mo.: Sixteenth Century Journal, 1984), 17.

18. Safely, 15–16; Joel Harrington, *Reordering Marriage and Society in Reformation Germany* (Cambridge: Cambridge University Press, 1995), 53–57; James A. Brundage, *Law, Sex, and Christian Society in Medieval Europe* (Chicago and London: University of Chicago Press, 1987), 236–37, 264–70.

19. Brundage, 333–34; Harrington, 57.

20. Harrington, 55–57.

21. Safley, 16.

22. Brundage, 362; Harrington, 57.

23. Heide Wunder, *'Er ist die Sonn', sie ist der Mond.' Frauen in der Frühen Neuzeit* (Munich: C. H. Beck, 1992), 62.

24. Harrington, 172–73, 177.

25. Ibid., 122.

26. Lucia Ferrante documents how women in early modern Bologna used the church's support of the free choice of spouses to counter their parents' attempts to coerce them into marriages. Lucia Ferrante, "Marriage and Women's Subjectivity in a Patrilineal System: The Case of Early Modern Bologna," in *Gender, Kinship, and Power: A Comparative and Interdisciplinary History*, ed. Mary Jo Maynes et al. (New York and London: Routledge, 1996), 115–29.

27. Michael Schröter, "Staatsbildung und Triebkontrolle. Zur Regulierung des Sexualverhaltens vom 13. bis 16. Jahrhundert," in *Macht und Zivilisation. Materialien zu Norbert Elias Zivilisationstheorie*, ed. P. Gleichmann et al. (Frankfurt am Main, 1984), 148–92. The church's commitment to enforcing the obligation that arose from a consensual marriage promise was held in the balance by its equally strong commitment to uphold the freedom of marriage. The decision over how much persuasive "force" should be applied in each case was left to the discretion of individual judges. Daniela Lombardi, "Interventions by Church and State

in Marriage Disputes in Sixteenth- and Seventeenth-Century Florence," in *Crime, Society, and the Law in Renaissance Italy,* ed. Trevor Dean and K. J. P. Lowe (Cambridge: Cambridge University Press, 1994), 146–48.

28. Harrington, 12, 28–30, 94.

29. Lyndal Roper, *The Holy Household: Women and Morals in Reformation Augsburg* (Oxford: Clarendon Press, 1989).

30. Ibid., especially 132–64. For more on city-run marriage courts, see Walther Köhler, *Zürcher Ehegericht und Genfer Konsistorium* (Leipzig: Vol. 1, 1932; vol. 2, 1942).

31. Neuordnung der Hochtzeiten 12.5.1535, Stadtarchiv München, Zimelie 11, 9v–10r.

32. Stadtarchiv München, Zimelie 11, 10r.

33. Stadtarchiv München, Zimelie 11, 10r–10v (on betrothal and wedding invitations), 12r (on gift giving), 11r–11v (prohibition of additional festivities).

34. Wilhelm Smets, *Des hochheiligen, ökumenischen und allgemeinen Concils von Trient Canones und Beschlüsse* (Bielefeld: Velhagen und Klasing, 1869; Fotomechanischer Nachdruck, erschienen im Sankt Meinrad Verlag für Theologie, Christine Maria Esser, Sinzing, 1989), "Doctrina de Sacramento Matrimonii," 138.

35. Ibid., 140.

36. Harrington, 95–96.

37. Smets, 141.

38. Ibid., 142; John Bossy, "The Counter-Reformation and the People of Catholic Europe," *Past and Present* 47 (May 1970): 51–70.

39. Smets, 141.

40. Ibid., 142.

41. Stefan Breit, *"Leichtfertigkeit" und ländliche Gesellschaft. Voreheliche Sexualität in der frühen Neuzeit* (Munich: Oldenbourg Verlag, 1991).

42. Patricia Seed, *To Love, Honor, and Obey in Colonial Mexico: Conflicts over Marriage Choice, 1574–1821* (Stanford: Stanford University Press, 1988).

43. Sarah Hanley, "Engendering the State: Family Formation and State Building in Early Modern France," in *French Historical Studies* 16, no. 1 (spring 1989): 4–27.

44. Geminianus compiled his sermons and published them in the form of a guidebook. Geminianus Monacensis, *Geistlicher Weeg-Weiser gen Himmel/ Catholische Predigen über alle Sonn: und Feyrtägliche Evangelia.* Gedruckt und verlegt/Durch Johann Jaecklin/Churfuerstlichen Freysingischen und Regens-purgischen Hof-Buchdruckern. Munich, 1679, 182–84. For further information about him and his sermons as source materials for the study of popular culture see Elfriede Moser-Rath, "Münchner Volksprediger der Barockzeit," *Bayerisches Jahrbuch für Volkskunde* (1958): 85–102.

45. Both the Pauline position, which was closely tied to the idea of sexuality as pollution, and the focus on the reproductive function of marriage were present within Christian theology throughout the Middle Ages; the latter, however, became progressively more important from the twelfth century onward. A third position, which stressed the beneficial effect of satisfying sex on marital intimacy,

already found some advocates during late medieval times, but became virulent with the Protestant Reformation. Tridentine Catholicism subsequently also displayed a greater openness toward sexual enjoyment within marriage and encouraged pleasure as long as it led to the ultimate goal of proper intercourse and reproduction. Brundage, 579–82, 565–67.

46. Geminianus, 185.

47. Safley, 17.

48. "Ermahnung den zweyen Eheleuten vor der Zusammengebung zuthun," in *Pastorale ad Usum Romanum Accomodatum. Canones et Ritus Ecclesiasticos qui ad Sacramentorum administrationem aliaque Pastorali Officia in Diocesi Frisingensi, rite obeunda pertinent complectens* (Ingolstadt: Ex Officina Ederiana apud Andream Angermanium, 1612), 146–47.

49. Susan Karant-Nunn, "Kinder, Küche, Kirche: Social Ideology in the Wedding Sermons of Johannes Mathesius," in *Germania Illustrata: Essays on Early Modern Germany Presented to Gerald Strauss,* ed. Andrew C. Fix and Susan C. Karant-Nunn, 121–40 (Kirksville, Mo.: Sixteenth Century Journal, 1992), 127.

50. See reason number 4 in *Pastorale,* 148.

51. Geminianus, 191–94.

52. *Pastorale,* 151.

53. Karant-Nunn, especially 131–35.

54. Geminianus, 189.

55. Ibid., 191.

56. Deneke, 88.

57. At least their bishop requested such monthly readings and explications in 1580. *Decretum contra clandestina matrimonia,* Diözesanarchiv des Erzbistums München-Freising, Generalien 1501–1650, 113 ff.

58. Diözesanarchiv des Erzbistums München-Freising, Geistliche Raths-Missiv Protokolle, 1.2.1597.

59. Diözesanarchiv des Erzbistums München-Freising, Geistliche Raths-Missiv Protokolle, 439.

60. Diözesanarchiv des Erzbistums München-Freising, Geistliche Raths-Missiv Protokolle, 302, 522. This type of popular resistance to church ceremonies was a phenomenon that cut across confessional boundaries. Harrington finds evidence for avoidance and lack of punctuality in the Lutheran city of Speyer, the Calvinist Palatine-Electorate, and the Catholic Prince-Bishopric of Speyer. Harrington, 213.

61. Diözesanarchiv des Erzbistums München-Freising, Offizialatsprotokolle, H 243; 1.10.1625.

62. Cited in Johann Andreas Schmeller, *Bayerisches Wörterbuch* (Munich: Oldenbourg, 1983), 4 (reprint of 2d ed. by G. Karl Fromman [Munich, 1872–77], 753).

63. Smets, 140; Breit, 56.

64. Harrington, 177–78.

65. Diözesanarchiv des Erzbistums München-Freising, Offizialatsprotokolle, H 241, H 241a, H 243. Bayerisches Hauptstaatsarchiv, HL Freising 243.

66. Stadtarchiv München, Bürgermeister und Rat, B8, 674v.

67. Stadtarchiv München, Bürgermeister und Rat, B8, 675.

68. Research on Bavaria's countryside has shown that church courts frequently sided with women in cases of broken marriage promises from 1670 to the nineteenth century. See Breit and Beck. It has yet to be determined whether these findings are the result of the later time frame of the respective studies or of a profound difference between countryside and city, especially the state capital.

69. In 1594 Balthasar Heymedaler sued Maria Strickl, a single brewer, before the civic judge. Heymedaler claimed the woman kept accusing him of promising marriage to her and that she threatened to put a curse on him should he not take her into matrimony. He hoped that the judge would force Strickl to leave him alone "with words and deeds." Strickl, on the other hand, denied having threatened him with either poisoned food or bewitchment. Instead she called the judge's attention to male ways of dealing with women's claims: violence. Heymedaler had beaten her up three times, and Strickl stressed how she too wanted "peace and security." In the end, Heymedaler was actually sentenced to paying 2 Gulden for his mistreatment of Strickl, and both parties were ordered to keep the peace. Stadtarchiv München, Stadtgericht 867/3, 88r.

70. Stadtarchiv München, Stadtgericht, 867/22; 13.7. and 14.7.1610 (unpaginated volume).

71. Stadtarchiv München, Stadtgericht 867/19, 31v–32r.

72. See discussion below.

73. For an example from Upper Austria see Hermann Rebel, *Peasant Classes: The Bureaucratization of Property and Family Relations under Early Habsburg Absolutism, 1511–1636* (Princeton: Princeton University Press, 1983). More generally, see Pavla Miller, *Transformations of Patriarchy in the West, 1500–1900* (Bloomington: Indiana University Press, 1998).

74. Hanley, "Engendering the State."

75. *Bairische Lanndtsordnung* 1553, 4. Buch, 12. Titul, 5. Articul, CX and CXv.

76. State law also urged families to set up marriage contracts following mandatory standardized forms. *Landrecht/Policey: Gerichts- Malefiz und andere Ordnungen der Fürstenthumben Obern und Nidern Bayrn* (Munich: 1616), 1. Titul, 18. Articul, 211. The nobility was exempted from the obligatory use of standardized marriage contracts. Unlike other contracts, marriage contracts required not just two or three but a total of five witnesses to be valid (Ibid., 19. Art.). By 1671 the state required official registration of marriage contracts for legal validity. Stadtarchiv München, Bürgermeister und Rat, 60 B2, 22. October 1671.

77. *Bairische Lanndtsordnung* 1553, 4. Buch, 12. Titul, 2. Articul, CVIIIv–CIXv. Bavarian law allotted to both sons and daughters a "Heiratsgut" (dowry). According to Munich's tax ordinance from 1606 and 1616, dowries for female and male offspring could come in various forms, not just cash: "as happens often, [in the form of] a house, a piece of land, a small field, rents [ewig gelt], or similar things, which are given instead of cash." Stadtarchiv München, Steueramt 630, Steuerordnung von 1606, Art. 66; 14v–15r.

78. The French edict of 1556 "lengthened minority age from twenty to thirty

years for males, from seventeen to twenty-five years for females." Hanley, "Engendering the State," 9.

79. *Bairische Lanndtsordnung* 1553, 4. Buch, 12. Titul, 1. Articul, CVIII–CVIIv.

80. "Bad, profligate, or of ill repute." "Landrecht der Fürstenthumben Obern und Nidern Bayern" (Munich: Nicolaus Henricus, 1616) in *Landrecht* 1616, 40. Titul, 9. Articul, 372.

81. This applied to daughters under the age of twenty-five and sons under the age of thirty who had been offered honorable marriages of good standing (or whose parents at least did not get in the way of such a marriage). *Landrecht* 1616, 40. Titul, 9. Articul, 372.

82. *Landrecht* 1616, 40. Titul, 9. Articul, 372.

83. If she had already forsaken her right to inheritance for a certain amount of dowry payments—which was apparently common in families of certain classes—she received half of that amount at her parents' death. *Landrecht* 1616, 40. Titul, 9. Articul, 372.

84. *Landrecht* 1616, 40. Titul, 9. Articul, 373.

85. The dowry system and its implication for inheritance laws and gender relations has been analyzed for the case of Florence by Christian Klapisch-Zuber. Christiane Klapisch-Zuber, "The Griselda Complex: Dowry and Marriage Gifts in the Quattrocento," in *Women, Family, and Ritual,* 213–46, especially 213–16. See also Thomas Kuehn's work on Italian city-states and the mandatory "exclusio propter dotem" of women. Thomas Kuehn, "Some Ambiguities of Female Inheritance Ideology in the Renaissance," in his *Law, Family, and Women: Toward a Legal Anthropology of Renaissance Italy* (Chicago: University of Chicago Press, 1991), 238–57.

86. See *Landrecht* 1616, 40. Titul, 9. Articul, 372. The acquisition of this right was one of the results of the patriciate's effort to emulate the nobility and reach comparable social standing. Michael Schattenhofer, "Das Münchner Patriziat," *Beiträge zur Geschichte der Stadt München: Oberbayerisches Archiv* 109 (1984): 35. In this and other respects, the Bavarian nobility represented the most patrilineal class, an agnatic emphasis that blended well with using female dowries for the disinheritance of women. Diane Owen Hughes has traced the shift from a kinship and inheritance system based on the brideprice to one based on the dowry. She evaluates the establishment of the dowry in the medieval Mediterranean world in the context of an increasingly patrilineal kinship system. Hughes associates the morning gift—which was also part of the Bavarian kinship system and more integrally so than the disinheritance of dowered women—with bilateral descent and an emphasis on the conjugal couple. Diane Owen Hughes, "From Brideprice to Dowry in Mediterranean Europe," *Journal of Family History* 3 (1978): 262–96.

87. The law of the land labeled these various types of parental subsidies "Heuratgut," "Fertigung," or "Haimsteuer." It is extremely difficult to reconstruct the exact meaning of these different types of "dowry."

88. *Landrecht* 1616, 2. Titul, 1. Articul, 212.

89. In Reformation Augsburg the economic partnership between spouses was also built on the triple foundation of dowry, matching, and morning gift, yet the

latter seems to have been a less substantial contribution than in Munich. Roper, *Holy Household,* 144, 148.

90. *Landrecht* 1616, 1. Titul, 3. Articul, 202. Regulations of this kind can be found in the *Landrecht* of 1518 (reissued in 1588) and in the *Landrecht* of 1616. I am gleaning my information from the 1616 version, because it represents the culmination of legislation on the economic aspects of marriage, but I will record significant deviations from previous *Landrechte* in the notes.

91. However, there existed a legal possibility for a woman to reserve administrative rights over some of their property. If she did not explicitly make use of this right, the husband assumed economic control as previously described. *Landrecht* 1616, 1. Titul, 16. Articul, 210. According to the *Landrecht* of 1518 and that of 1588, a husband could also represent his wife in court unless legal matters pertained to her dowry or any property she had inherited. A wife, in turn, could not represent her husband except with his explicit permission. *Reformation der Bayrischen Landrecht nach Christi unsers Haylmachers Geburd.* [1518]... *widerumben nachgedruckt M.D. LXXX VIII* (Munich). 5. Titul, 10. and 11. Articul, xxv.

92. See category "Vätterliche Gewalt," *Landrecht* 1616, 3. Titul, 215 ff. The *Landrechte* of 1518/1588 do not contain anything about "Vätterliche Gewalt."

93. Yan Thomas, "The Division of the Sexes in Roman Law," in *A History of Women: From Ancient Goddesses to Christian Saints,* ed. Pauline Schmitt Pantel (Cambridge: Belknap Press of Harvard University Press, 1992), 83–137.

94. *Landrecht* 1616, 3. Titul, 215–16.

95. The clause condemned profligate domestics for abandoning their masters and setting up "clandestine shelters." In the eyes of state authorities, this practice was the cause of soaring salaries for servants and the reason why many day laborers became incapable of supporting their numerous offspring. *Bairische Lanndtsordnung* 1553, 5. Buch, 12. Titul, 5. Articul, fol. CLVIIIv–CLIV.

96. Breit, 79.

97. Isabel Hull, *Sexuality, State, and Civil Society in Germany, 1700–1815* (Ithaca: Cornell University Press, 1996), especially 29–52. Rainer Beck, *Naturale Ökonomie. Unterfinning: Bäuerliche Wirtschaft in einem oberbayrischen Dorf des 18. Jahrhunderts* (Munich, 1989). Miller, *Transformations of Patriarchy.*

98. Reinhard Heydenreuter, *Herrschen durch Strafen: Zur Entwicklung des frühneuzeitlichen Staates im Herzogtum und Kurfürstentum Bayern (1150–1650),* manuscript, 342–43. I would like to thank Reinhard Heydenreuter for making parts of this manuscript available to me prior to its publication.

99. Harrington, 130, 162. The Concordant regulated church-state relations in Bavaria during the seventeenth and eighteenth centuries, even though its stipulations remained subject to ongoing contestation; Georg Schwaiger, "Die Haupt- und Residenzstadt München im Zeitalter der Glaubenskämpfe," in *Monachium Sacrum: Festschrift zur 500-Jahr-Feier der Metropolitankirche zu Unserer Lieben Frau in München,* ed. Georg Schwaiger, vol. 1 (Munich: Deutscher Kunstverlag, 1994), 80.

100. Harrington, 153, quote from 162.

101. Pueßordnung von 1587, Stadtarchiv München, Stadtgericht, Bußamt 922, 3r–3v.

102. Anton Fischer, "Die Verwaltungsorganisation Münchens im 16. und 17. Jahrhundert" (Diss., München, maschinenschriftliches Exemplar, 1951, Bibliothek des Stadtarchivs München), 153.

103. Ibid., 154. Although this ordinance of 1578 is lost, it is possible to reconstruct parts of it from deliberations held by the civic Kammerrat. This political body met on January 3, 1602, for the purpose of "improving" the ordinance. See the minutes of this meeting in Stadtarchiv München, Kammeratsprotokolle, Kämmerei 107/1, 30r–32r.

104. Fischer, 154.

105. Ibid., 162.

106. Ibid., 153.

107. If an applicant was rejected, he or she had to leave Munich within a fortnight. Ibid., 162.

108. This practice is outlined in a report to the court in 1619. Stadtarchiv München, Einwohneramt Nr. 195.

109. Ibid.

110. Fischer, 155.

111. Stadtarchiv München, Einwohneramt Nr. 195.

112. Fischer, 155.

113. Stadtarchiv München, Kammeratsprotokolle, Kämmerei 107/1, 30r, Nr. 2.

114. Stadtarchiv München, Kammeratsprotokolle, Kämmerei 107/1, 32r, Nr. 17.

115. Stadtarchiv München, Kammeratsprotokolle, Kämmerei 107/1, 30r, Nr. 6.

116. Stadtarchiv München, Kammeratsprotokolle, Kämmerei 107/1, 30r, Nr. 1.

117. See the oath he took upon assuming office. Stadtarchiv München, Zimelie 16, Eidbuch, 40r.

118. Stadtarchiv München, Kammeratsprotokolle, 30r, Nr. 1.

119. Stadtarchiv München, Kammeratsprotokolle, Kämmerei 107/1, 31v, Nr. 1, 2, and 3.

120. Stadtarchiv München, Kammeratsprotokolle, Kämmerei 107/1 31r, Nr. 5.

121. Fischer, 159–60.

122. Stefan Breit makes the analogous point for Bavaria's late-seventeenth-century rural population. Breit, 5.

123. Cited in Merry Wiesner, *Working Women in Renaissance Germany* (New Brunswick, N.J.: Rutgers University Press, 1986), 88.

124. This was not unusual. Many contemporary ordinances were patterned after the regulations of Augsburg. Harrington, 190.

125. "Honorability" was key to the civic guild ethos so that admission into one of Munich's guilds presupposed not only appropriate training but also proof of legitimate birth and the prospect of getting married. Fischer, 160–61. While there existed a possibility of marriage for journeymen of select guilds in the sixteenth century, the revisions of the *Hochzeitsordnung* of 1602 outlawed the practice and limited marriage to masters. Stadtarchiv München, Kammeratsprotokolle, Kämmerei 107/1, 31v, Nr. 8. On guild notions of honor and marriage in medieval Munich, see Werner Schultheiß, *Die Münchner Gewerbeverfassung im Mittelalter* (Munich: Beck'sche Verlagsbuchhandlung, 1936), especially 97–98, 113–15.

CHAPTER 2

1. Otto Titan von Hefner, "Original Bilder aus der Vorzeit Münchens," *Oberbairisches Archiv für vaterländische Geschichte* 13 (1852): 25; Schattenhofer reports 1595. Michael Schattenhofer, "Henker, Hexen und Huren," *Oberbairisches Archiv* 109, no. 1 (1984): 138.

2. Beate Schuster, *Die freien Frauen: Dirnen und Frauenhäuser im 15. und 16. Jahrhundert* (Frankfurt am Main: Campus Verlag, 1995), 88–91. Schuster's imaginative work has very much shaped my thinking on this topic.

3. The city fathers of Landsberg gave this explanation when they established their dowry foundation (*Jungfernstiftung*) in 1437; it became the model for the foundation in Munich. Georg Lammert, *Zur Geschichte des bürgerlichen Lebens und der öffentlichen Gesundheitspflege sowie insbesondere der Sanitätsanstalten in Süddeutschland* (Regensburg, 1880), 163.

4. Schuster, *Die freien Frauen*, 178–79; James A. Brundage, *Law, Sex, and Christian Society in Medieval Europe* (Chicago and London: University of Chicago Press, 1987), 522.

5. Cited in Fridolin Solleder, *München im Mittelalter* (Aalen: Scientia Verlag, Nachdruck der Ausgabe München 1938), 402, fn.1.

6. Stadtarchiv München, Zimelie 52, Eidbuch II 1488.

7. Schuster, *Die freien Frauen*, 51.

8. Schattenhofer, "Huren," 136.

9. Ruth Mazzo Karras, "Sex and the Singlewoman," in *Singlewomen in the European Past, 1250–1800*, ed. Judith M. Bennett and Amy M. Froide (Philadelphia: University of Pennsylvania Press, 1999), 133.

10. Schattenhofer, "Huren," 136.

11. Schuster, *Die freien Frauen*, 14, 195.

12. Karras, 127–45.

13. Schuster, *Die freien Frauen*, 228–30.

14. Ibid., 204–5, 236, 239, 244–45, 247–50.

15. Lyndal Roper, *The Holy Household: Women and Morals in Reformation Augsburg* (Oxford: Clarendon Press, 1989).

16. Schuster, *Die freien Frauen*, 335–38.

17. Schattenhofer, "Huren," 136.

18. Hefner, 26.

19. Schuster, *Die freien Frauen*, 88–91.

20. Lyndal Roper, "Luther: Sex, Marriage and Motherhood," *History Today* 33 (1983): 33–38, esp. 35.

21. Susanna Burghartz, *Zeiten der Reinheit—Orte der Unzucht. Ehe und Sexualität in Basel während der Frühen Neuzeit* (Paderborn: Schöningh, 1999).

22. Roper, "Luther: Sex, Marriage and Motherhood," 34.

23. Guild notions of honor and sexuality slowly filtered into Munich's magistrate. Similar to many other German cities, Munich experienced a guild revolt in the late fourteenth century, leading to an ultimately short-lived guild rule in the Bavarian capital. Although the guilds were pushed out of political government in 1403, their expulsion brought the de facto institutionalization of lasting guild

influence. The guilds were relegated to the status of strictly economic institutions, and the city council reserved for itself jurisdictional and disciplinary powers over the guilds, including market inspections. In dealing with the directly subordinated guilds the council relied extensively on guild members themselves to serve as auxiliary civic officials, conducting market inspections and reporting on guild affairs. Because guild members constituted a significant portion of the city's staff, a steady influx of guild ideas from below was inevitable. Werner Schultheiß, *Die Münchner Gewerbeverfassung im Mittelalter* (Munich: Beck'sche Verlagsbuchhandlung, 1936), 94, 112, 145.

24. Stadtarchiv München, Zimelie 11, "Ordnung wider die Laster," 17v–19v, quote from 18r–18v.

25. Peter Schuster speculates that this use of brothels as instruments of discipline and deterrence was common in all of Germany around this time. Peter Schuster, "Hinaus oder ins Frauenhaus. Weibliche Sexualität und gesellschaftliche Kontrolle an der Wende vom Mittelalter zur Neuzeit," in *Mit den Waffen der Justiz. Zur Kriminalitätsgeschichte des späten Mittelalters und der Frühen Neuzeit,* ed. Andreas Blauert and Gerd Schwerhoff (Frankfurt am Main: Fischer Verlag, 1993), 17–31.

26. Schattenhofer, "Huren," 136, 137 (on use of Munich brothel for moral improvement).

27. Schattenhofer, "Huren," 138.

28. Anton Fischer, "Die Verwaltungsorganisation Münchens im 16. und 17. Jahrhundert" (Diss., München, 1951), 204, 210 fn. 32.

29. Schuster, *Die freien Frauen,* 14, 191, 401.

30. Elisabeth Schepers, *Als der Bettel in Bayern abgeschafft werden sollte: staatliche Armenfürsorge in Bayern im 16. und 17. Jahrhundert* (Regensburg: F. Pustet, 2000).

31. Stadtarchiv München, Ratsprotokolle 1596; 172r–172v. The case of Anna Seyfrid from 1600 shows the council following its own guidelines. Seyfrid, under suspicion of profligacy, was made to promise that she would leave the city. The council threatened her with forced expulsion in case of her return. Stadtarchiv München, Ratsprotkolle; 1600, 27v.

32. Cited in Merry Wiesner, "Having Her Own Smoke: Employment and Independence for Singlewomen in Germany, 1400–1750," in *Singlewomen,* 197.

33. Merry Wiesner, *Working Women in Renaissance Germany* (New Brunswick, N.J.: Rutgers University Press, 1986).

34. Statistics in Bernd Roeck, "Bayern und der Dreißigjährige Krieg," *Geschichte und Gesellschaft* 17 (1991): 448–49, 453.

35. Beate Schuster's study makes this process plain.

36. Stadtarchiv München, Ratsprotokolle, Stadtschreiberserie 1613, February 12, 1614, 103.

37. Max Hufnagel, "Das Franziskanerinnenkloster der Ridlerschwestern zu St. Johannes auf der Stiege in München," in *Bavaria Franciscana Antiqua,* vol. 3, ed. bayerische Franziskanerprovinz (Munich: Lentner'sche Buchhandlung, 1957), 310.

38. Georg Schwaiger, "München—Eine geistliche Stadt," in *Monachium*

Sacrum: Festschrift zur 500-Jahr-Feier der Metropolitankirche zu Unserer Lieben Frau in München, vol. 1, ed. Georg Schwaiger (Munich: Deutscher Kunstverlag, 1994), 43.

39. Some time in the first half of the thirteenth century the small assembly of (later) Pütrich sisters commenced their communal life. Max Hufnagel, "Das Franziskanerinnenkloster der Pütrichschwestern z. Hl. Christophorus in München," in *Bavaria Franciscana Antiqua,* vol. 3, ed. bayerische Franziskanerprovinz (Munich: Lentner'sche Buchhandlung, 1957), 275–76. The Pütrich first appear in the role of sponsors in 1284. Eleven years later, in 1295, Heinrich Ridler endowed a house for the sisters who were to constitute the Ridler soul-house. Schwaiger, 53.

40. Wolfgang Burgmair, "Das Pütrich-Kloster in München," in *Festschrift für Prof. Dr. Hans Rall* (Munich: "Die Gurke," 1987), 5–6. It is possible that there existed a division of labor between different soul-houses with respect to these various tasks. Because the physical and spiritual care of the sick and dying is closely related, however, it seems more plausible that each house carried out the entire range of tasks.

41. They also made provisions for oil, wax, stones, and wood. Fortunatus Hueber, *Lob-, Danck-, und Ehrenreiche Gedaechtnuss/Von dem Geist- und Loeblichen Jungfrau-Closter des III. Ordens S. Francisci Bey den zweyen Heiligen Joannes, dem Tauffer und dem Evangelisten, Auff der Stiegen (deren Ridler genamselt) zu München in Bayern an der Chur-Fürstlichen Residenz* (Munich: Sebastian Rauch, 1695), hereafter cited as *Gedaechtnuss,* 5.

42. Fridolin Solleder, *München im Mittelalter* (Aalen: Scientia Verlag, Nachdruck der Ausgabe München, 1938), 384.

43. Wiesner, *Working Women.*

44. Another offshoot of ducal patronage was the presence of widows and unmarried women in the convent who sometimes stayed simply as prebendaries. Johannes Gatz, "Klarissen-Kloster St. Jakob am Anger in München," in *Bavaria Franciscana Antiqua,* vol. 3, ed. bayr. Franziskanerprovinz (Munich: Lentner'sche Buchhandlung, 1957), 199–200.

45. Hufnagel does not specify what kinds of annoyance prompted the duke to take action. Hufnagel, "Pütrichschwestern," 276. We do not know the precise set of circumstances under which the Ridler sisters became tertiaries. But their community, too, underwent the change from a loose congregation of soul-nuns to a house for Franciscan tertiaries sometime before 1369. Hufnagel, "Ridlerschwestern," 312.

46. The rules for the Ridler convent of 1369 and those for the Pütrich community of 1387 were virtually identical. Hufnagel, "Ridlerschwestern," 312, fn. 7.

47. Ridler gave permission to the sisters to use jewelry and money freely as long as they were part of the community. If a sister decided to leave, however, her property was to change into the hands of the convent except for several items of clothing (including one fur coat). Sisters could not will property to anyone other than poor relatives. Upon their death, the lion's share fell to the soul-house. Burgmair, 11; Hufnagel, "Pütrichschwestern," 279.

48. *Gedaechtnuss,* 14.

49. For Italian examples, albeit from the fifteenth century, see Gabriella Zarri, "Gender, Religious Institutions, and Social Discipline: The Reform of the Regulars," in *Gender and Society in Renaissance Italy,* ed. Judith Brown and Robert C. Davis (London and New York: Longman, 1998), 195–96.

50. Johannes Gatz, "Franziskanerkloster St. Antonius in München," in *Bavaria Franciscana,* vol. 3, ed. bayr. Franziskanerprovinz (Munich: Lentner'sche Buchhandlung Dr. E. K. Stahl, München, 1957), 59, 62, on the issue of property; 62–67, on initial resistance and ultimate defeat of the Franciscans subscribing to a more permissible notion of apostolic poverty.

51. Gatz, "Klarissen-Kloster," 235–39.

52. The orthodoxy of the Poor Clares was one reason for choosing the *Angerkloster* as the site of Mary Ward's imprisonment. See chapter 5.

53. *Bittrich voll des himlischen Manna und Süssen Morgen-Thau. Das ist: Historischer Discurs/Von dem Ursprung, Fundation, Auffnamb/glücklichen Fortgang/ Tugend-Wandel/und andern denckwürdigen Sachen Deß Löbl. Frauen-Closters/ Ordens der dritten Regul des heil. Francisci/Bey Sanct Christophen im Bittrich genannt/In der Chur-Fürstlichen Residenz-Stadt München mit Erlaubnis der Obern* (Munich: Johann Lucas Straud, 1721), 63. Hereafter cited as *Manna.*

54. *Gedaechtnuss,* 20. Hufnagel, "Ridlerschwestern," 314.

55. "At the time only five recalcitrant sisters were dismissed from and locked out of the *Regelhaus." Gedaechtnuss,* 20. Hufnagel, "Ridlerschwestern," 314.

56. *Manna,* 113–14.

57. Hufnagel, "Pütrichschwestern," 280.

58. Solleder, 385–86.

59. On the parallels between nuns and whores and the long history of associating these two groups of unmarried women, see Amy Leonard, "Nuns as Whores: A Common Trope" (manuscript in preparation). I would like to thank Amy Leonard for making her fascinating manuscript available to me prior to its publication.

60. Cited in Ulrike Strasser, "Brides of Christ, Daughters of Men: Nuremberg Poor Clares in Defense of Their Identity (1524–1529)," *Magistra: Journal of Women's Spirituality in History* 1, no. 2 (1995): 234–35.

61. Ibid., 235.

62. Ibid., 237.

63. Merry Wiesner-Hanks, "Ideology Meets the Empire: Reformed Convents and the Reformation," in *Germania Illustrata: Essays on Early Modern Germany Presented to Gerald Strauss,* ed. Andrew Fix and Susan Karant-Nunn (Kirksville, Mo.: Sixteenth Century Journal, 1992), 181–96, and "Gender and Power in Early Modern Europe: The Empire Strikes Back," in *The Graph of Sex and the German Text: Gendered Culture in Early Modern Germany, 1500–1700* (Chloe: Beihefte zum Daphnis Band 19), ed. Lynne Tatlock (Amsterdam and Atlanta: Rodopi, 1994), 201–23.

64. Amy Leonard, "Nails in the Wall: Dominican Nuns in Reformation Strasbourg" (Ph.D. diss., University of California, Berkeley, 1999), 123.

65. Ibid., 75, including note 1.

66. Ibid., 234–43.

67. See (among others) Jane Tibbetts Schulenburg, *Forgetful of Their Sex: Female Sanctity and Society, ca. 500–1100* (Chicago: University of Chicago Press, 1998).

68. Wilhelm Smets, *Des hochheiligen, ökumenischen und allgemeinen Concils von Trient Canones und Beschlüsse* (Bielefeld, Velhagen und Klasing 1869: Fotomechanischer Nachdruck, erschienen im Sankt Meinrad Verlag für Theologie, Christine Maria Esser, Sinzing 1989), 168.

69. Smets, 175.

70. Ibid., 174.

71. Ibid., 175.

72. Ibid., 167–79.

73. Zarri, "Gender, Religious Institutions and Social Discipline," 207.

74. Peter Schuster, *Das Frauenhaus: Städtische Bordelle in Deutschland (1350–1600)* (Paderborn: Schöningh Verlag, 1992), 199–202.

75. Elizabeth Rapley, *The Dévotes: Women and Church in Seventeenth-Century France* (Montreal, Kingston, London, and Buffalo: McGill-Queen's University Press, 1990), 28. She views this difference in treatment as the most revealing illustration of the difference in perception between male and female religious.

76. Zarri, "Gender, Religious Institutions, and Social Discipline," 212.

77. Smets, 169–70.

78. Only episcopal permission could overrule these regulations, *indulta* and privileges could not. Ibid., 170.

79. Ibid.

80. Pius V's *Circa Pastoralis* of 1566 made Tridentine cloister mandatory for all tertiaries. There was no "grandfathering" clause for those who had already entered tertiary communities but rather the conditions of entry were invalidated retroactively. Ruth P. Liebowitz, "Virgins in the Service of Christ: The Dispute over an Active Apostolate for Women during the Counter-Reformation," in *Women of Spirit: Female Leadership in the Jewish and Christian Tradition,* ed. Rosemary Ruether and Eleanor McLaughlin (New York: Simon and Schuster, 1979), 150, endnote 27.

81. Elizabeth Makowski, *Canon Law and Cloistered Women. Periculoso and Its Commentators, 1298–1545* (Washington, D.C.: Catholic University of America Press, 1977).

82. Amy Leonard, "Female Religious Orders," in *A Companion to the World of the Reformation,* ed. R. Po-Chia Hsia (Oxford: Blackwell, 2003), 237–54.

83. The distinction between "active" and "contemplative" is less clear-cut than it seems at first glance. On the complexities of these categories, see Craig Harline, "Actives and Contemplatives: The Female Religious of the Low Countries Before and After Trent," *Catholic Historical Review* 89, no. 4 (October 1995): 541–67.

84. For examples from Catalonia, see H. Kamen, *The Phoenix and the Flame: Catalonia and the Counter Reformation* (New Haven: Yale University Press, 1993), 336–39. For Italian examples, see Jutta Sperling, *Convents and the Body Politic in Late Renaissance Venice* (Chicago: University of Chicago Press, 1999), and Mary R. Laven,"Venetian Nunneries in the Counter-Reformation, 1550–1630" (Ph.D.

diss., University of Leicester, 1997). I would like to thank Mary Laven for providing me with a copy of her dissertation.

85. *Manna,* 28.

86. Ibid., 54. Her collection of relics had been a gift bestowed upon her by Emperor Maximilian I, her brother, during a visit to the convent; ibid., 45; ibid., 38, on Christ dolls.

87. Ibid., 57. Wilhelm took a particular liking to the Ridler sisters; Hufnagel, "Ridlerschwestern," 316.

88. *Manna,* 58.

89. Archiv des Erzbistums, Klostersachen Fasz. 265. I have not been able to ascertain when in the first half of the sixteenth century these sickrooms were set up.

90. Unpaginated letter, Bayerisches Hauptstaatsarchiv München, KL Fasz. 423/2 Nr. 5.

91. Giovanni Morone's ecclesiastical career reached a height with his appointment to the presidency over the Council of Trent in 1559 (after it had dropped to the nadir of imprisonment for alleged sympathies with the Protestant cause in 1557). For biographical information see *Nouvelle biographie général depuis les temps plus reculés jusqu'à jours* publiée par MM. Firmin Didot Frères sous la direction de M. Le Dr. Hoefer, vol. 36 (Paris, 1865), 634 under "Morone."

92. Albrecht's letter to Morone indicates that a visitation (by Nas?) had taken place in the tertiary houses by 1576. Albrecht urged the Cardinal not to clamp down on the entire community "ob unius sororis morositatem." Bayerisches Hauptstaatsarchiv, Äußeres Archiv, 4115, f. 210r–213v; quote from 213.

93. Bayerisches Hauptstaatsarchiv München, Äußeres Archiv, 4115, 211v.

94. Bayerisches Hauptstaatsarchiv München, Äußeres Archiv, 4115, 211v–212r.

95. Karl Schellhass, *Der Dominikaner Felician Ninguarda und die Gegenreformation in Süddeutschland und Österreich 1560–1583,* vol. 2, "Felician Ninguarda als Nuntius 1578–1580" (Rome: W. Regenberg, 1939), 238, 242–43.

96. Ibid., 216.

97. *Manna,* 77.

98. *Gedaechtnuss,* 41. Ninguarda made the statement in reference to the Ridler community but his attenuated reforms in the Pütrich house document a virtually identical assessment in this case.

99. "Item to hold the 'Jahrtage'/to which you are bound by obligation." *Gedaechtnuss,* 41. "So that you may go to the Church of Our Lady or also to other churches in the city, foremost because of the 'Jahrtage.'" *Manna,* 79.

100. Ibid., 80.

101. Ibid., 81.

102. Printed in Ibid., 84–85. This edition features the pages 83 and 84 twice. The quotation is taken from the second 84.

103. Ibid., 84 (second 84—see previous note).

104. *Gedaechtnuss,* 41; *Manna,* 79.

105. *Manna,* 79.

106. *Gedaechtnuss,* 45.

107. Ibid., 42.

108. Ibid., 44–45.
109. Ibid., 27–32.
110. Ibid., 45.
111. Ibid., 42.
112. "Dann vor Jahren wurden die heylige Junckfrawen von den Lewen mit Gewalt gezogen ins unzuechtige Frauwen Hauß/Aber an ietzo werden Sie mit Mauren und Schloessern gleichsamb mit Gewalt bewart/damit sie versichert seyen von den Schendern. Sehet/den unterschid der zeit unnd Sitten/ Dann damals doerfften sie ihres gefallens nicht keuschlich leben/an ietzo wird den unsrigen nicht erlaubt/ires gefallens etwas unkeusches zu begehen." Aegidius Albertinus, *Haußpolizey* (Munich, 1602), 10r–10v.
113. "O grosses greuel/O grosse vermessenheit/O grosse schmach/das nemlich ein Junckfrau/welche mit sollchen herlichen Solemniteten und misterien der religion/ist consecriert und geheiligt/wird zu einem Schlepsack unnd Cloac und Pfuetzen der Unreinigkeiten. Und was war es vonnoeten euch zu bedecken und mit hohen Mawren zuversperren: Seytemal wir/leider/sehen/dass an etlichen orten durch den Unfleis der hirten/die heylige Cloester verkehrt und verendert werden in schendtlich heuser." Ibid., 13.
114. Sherrill Cohen, *The Evolution of Women's Asylums since 1500: From Refuges for Ex-Prostitutes to Shelters for Battered Women* (Oxford and New York: Oxford University Press, 1992).
115. Harline, "Actives and Contemplatives."
116. Burghartz, *Zeiten der Reinheit—Orte der Unzucht.*

CHAPTER 3

1. For all details regarding this case, see Stadtarchiv München, Bestand Stadtgericht, 867/2, 52r.
2. Stadtarchiv München, Bestand Stadtgericht, 868/9; 73r–74r. Unfortunately, the verdict for this case is missing.
3. Legal and judicial sources are integral to the proliferation of discourses on "sexuality" outlined in Michel Foucault, *The History of Sexuality,* vol. 1, *An Introduction,* translated from the French by Robert Hurley (1976; reprint, New York: Vintage Books, 1990). Lyndal Roper has highlighted the gender-specific restrictions of legal language, allowing the expression of male but not female will (among other things). Lyndal Roper, "Will and Honour: Sex, Words, and Power in Augsburg Criminal Trials," in *Oedipus and the Devil: Witchcraft, Sexuality and Religion in Early Modern Europe* (New York, London: Routledge, 1994), 53–79. For a discussion of the limits of narrative control by authorities and of how individuals and communities co-author legal discourses, see Ulrike Gleixner, *"Das Mensch" und "der Kerl". Die Konstruktion von Geschlecht in Unzuchtsverfahren der Frühen Neuzeit (1700–1760)* (Frankfurt am Main and New York: Campus Verlag, 1994).
4. On the harsher treatment of female offenders, see Ulinka Rublack, *Magd, Metz' oder Mörderin. Frauen vor frühneuzeitlichen Gerichten* (Frankfurt am Main: Fischer-Taschenbuch-Verlag, 1998), esp. 130–33 and 211–14. On the frequency of

shaming and banishment of maidservants and their consequences, see Renate Dürr, *Mägde in der Stadt. Das Beispiel Schwäbisch Hall in der Frühen Neuzeit* (Frankfurt am Main and New York: Campus Verlag, 1995), 229–45. On the "feminization" of particular forms of public shaming, see Gleixner, 58–59. Also see Isabel Hull, who points out that single women, due to their often more limited means, were more likely to opt for conversion of fines into public humiliation, further tightening the connection between shame, sexual honor, and femininity. Moreover, once state authorities began to use work rather than imprisonment or exile as a form of punishment, greater numbers of women were sentenced to public humiliation since they were deemed less capable of strenuous physical labor. Isabel Hull, *State, Sex, and Civil Society in Germany, 1700–1815* (Ithaca: Cornell University Press, 1996), 87, 97.

5. The cases are contained in the "Gerichtsbücher des Oberrichters" ("Oberrichteramtsprotokolle" after 1634), Stadtarchiv München, Bestand Stadtgericht.

6. Klaus Schreiner and Gerd Schwerhoff, eds., *Verletzte Ehre: Ehrkonflikte in Gesellschaften des Mittelalters und der Frühen Neuzeit* (Cologne, Weimar, and Vienna: Böhlau, 1995); Sibylle Backmann et al., eds., *Ehrkonzepte in der Frühen Neuzeit: Identitäten und Abgrenzungen* (Berlin: Akademie Verlag, 1998).

7. Susanna Burghartz, "Rechte Jungfrauen oder unverschämte Töchter? Zur weiblichen Ehre im 16. Jahrhundert," in *Frauengeschichte, Geschlechtergeschichte,* ed. Karin Hausen and Heide Wunder (Frankfurt am Main: Campus Verlag, 1992), 173–83.

8. For a discussion of informal mechanisms of social control, see chapter 1. Also, Sandra Cavallo and Simona Cerutti, "Female Honor and the Social Control of Reproduction in Piedmont between 1600 and 1800," in *Sex and Gender in Historical Perspective,* ed. Edward Muir and Guido Ruggiero (Baltimore: Johns Hopkins University Press, 1990), 73–109.

9. Heide Wunder, *'Er ist die Sonn', sie ist der Mond.' Frauen in der Frühen Neuzeit* (Munich: Verlag C. H. Beck, 1992), 61–62; Michael Schröter, "Staatsbildung und Triebkontrolle. Zur Regulierung des Sexualverhaltens vom 13. bis 16. Jahrhundert," in *Macht und Zivilisation. Materialien zu Norbert Elias Zivilisationstheorie,* ed. P. Gleichmann et al. (Frankfurt am Main: Suhrkamp Verlag, 1984), 148–92.

10. Cavallo and Cerrutti, 90–92.

11. At least 65 percent of the plaintiffs had migrated to the Bavarian capital from other places. Only 45 women are recorded as residents of Munich or the so-called Au (a bordering settlement).

12. Civic sumptuary laws of 1626 mention four social classes. The majority of female plaintiffs before the civic court stemmed from the lowest to second lowest class. Michael Schattenhofer, "Das Münchner Patriziat," *Beiträge zur Geschichte der Stadt München, Oberbairisches Archiv* 109, no. 1 (1984), 48.

13. Burghers apparently resorted to different mechanisms to solve the types of conflicts that arose in conjunction with marriage promises or nonmarital impregnations. If daughters of burghers took their cases to court, they were often represented by parents, other kin, guardians, or a procurator.

14. See chapter 1.

15. Reinhard Heydenreuter, *Der landesherrliche Hofrat unter Herzog und Kurfürst Maximilian I. von Bayern (1598–1651)* (Munich, 1981), 231–68.

16. "Landespoliceyordnung," in *Landrecht/Policey: Gerichts: Malefiz: und andere Ordnungen. Der Fürstenthumben Obern und Nidern Bayrn* (Munich, 1616), 5. Buch, 9. Titul, 18. Articul, 709–10.

17. Anton Fischer, "Die Verwaltungsorganisation Münchens im 16. und 17. Jahrhundert" (Diss., München, maschinenschriftliches Exemplar, 1951, Bibliothek des Stadtarchivs München), 210, note 32.

18. Stadtarchiv München, Stadtgericht 867/7, 42r–45r.

19. Stadtarchiv München, Stadtgericht 867/7, 103r. Hülmayer was ordered to take responsibility for the child unless he could prove that he was not the father, i.e., bring the true father before the civic judge.

20. Stadtarchiv München, Stadtgericht 867/17; 63v–64v.

21. Stadtarchiv München, Stadtgericht 867/23; 10.2.1612.

22. Stadtarchiv München, Stadtgericht 867/27; 306r–307r.

23. Stadtarchiv München, Stadtgericht 867/27, 306r–308r.

24. Stadtarchiv München, Stadtgericht 867/24, 77r.

25. Stadtarchiv München, Stadtgericht 867/8, 41r–42r.

26. Stadtarchiv München, Stadtgericht, 867/9, 132r.

27. If, on the other hand, the judge meted out an *ex officio* punishment for profligacy, the records reported that the guilty man "had erred in profligacy" (*sich in Leichtfertigkeit vergriffen*) whereas the guilty woman was "weakened" (*geschwecht*) by profligacy. Men's sexuality was thus conceptualized as active engagement in profligacy, whereas women appear as the passive recipients of the profligate act.

28. Stadtarchiv München, Stadtgericht, 867/5, 148.

29. My findings in this respect parallel those of Thomas Safley, *Let No Man Put Asunder: The Control of Marriage in the German Southwest, a Comparative Study, 1550–1600* (Kirksville, Mo.: Sixteenth Century Journal, 1984), 67.

30. Stadtarchiv München, Stadtgericht, 867/5, 148.

31. Reinhard Heydenreuter, "Der Magistrat als Befehlsempfänger. Die Disziplinierung der Stadtobrigkeit 1579 bis 1651," in *Geschichte der Stadt München,* ed. Richard Bauer (Munich: C. H. Beck, 1992), 200.

32. Ingo Schwab, "Zeiten der Teuerung: Versorgungsprobleme in der zweiten Hälfte des 16. Jahrhunderts," in *Geschichte der Stadt München,* ed. Richard Bauer (Munich: C. H. Beck, 1992), 168–69, 173.

33. Maurus Friesenegger, *Tagebuch aus dem 30jährigen Krieg,* ed. P. Willibald Mathäser (1627–1648; reprint, Munich: Hugendubel, 1996), 141. I would like to thank Hans Medick for calling my attention to this rich eyewitness account.

34. Schwab, 181.

35. Aegidius Albertinus, *Haußpolizey* (Munich, 1602), 144r–144v, 148v.

36. Stadtarchiv München, Bürgermeister und Rat, 62, 57v–58v.

37. Stadtarchiv München, Bürgermeister und Rat, 60 B3, 19v.

38. Stefan Breit, *"Leichtfertigkeit" und ländliche Gesellschaft. Voreheliche Sexualität in der Frühen Neuzeit* (Munich: Oldenbourg Verlag, 1991), 236.

39. Stadtgericht, 867/23; 24.7.1612.

40. Heydenreuter, "Der landesherrliche Hofrat," 253.

41. Ibid., 252.

42. Heydenreuter, "Magistrat als Befehlsempfänger," 201. Maximilian apparently encountered stronger resistance in the rest of his territory, and he had fewer means to counter it there. The devastation of the war years at times also undermined the prince's attempts at social discipline and political centralization, even if the war generally provided Maximilian with powerful justification for his regulatory actions. Sigrun Haude, "War—A Fortuitous Occasion for Social Disciplining and Political Centralization? The Case of Bavaria under Maximilian I." Paper delivered at Sixteenth Century Studies Conference, San Antonio, Texas, October 2002.

43. Stadtarchiv München, "Bürgermeister und Rat," B6, Decretum Ducis October 1626.

44. Stadtarchiv München, "Bürgermeister und Rat," 60 B7, 262–63.

45. Stadtarchiv München, "Bürgermeister und Rat," 60 B3, 18 (Bleistift-Nummerierung).

46. Hull also makes this point, speaking of an "involuntary and *public* form of self-incrimination." She compares this public quality and its authorizing function for state prosecutors to the Constitutio Criminalis Carolina's redefinition of adultery as a "public act," which enabled state intervention in a previously personal arena. Hull, 100–101.

47. Wolfgang Behringer, "Mörder, Diebe, Ehebrecher: Verbrechen und Strafen in Kurbayern vom 16. bis 18. Jahrhundert," in *Kultur der einfachen Leute,* ed. Richard van Dülmen (Munich: C. H. Beck, 1983), 100–102.

48. Ulinka Rublack, "Wench and Maiden: Women, War and the Pictorial Function of the Feminine in German Cities in the Early Modern Period," *History Workshop Journal* 44 (1997): 1–21.

49. Merry Wiesner, "War, Work, and Wealth: The Bases of Citizenship in Early Modern German Cities," in *Gender, Church, and State in Early Modern Germany* (New York and London: Longman, 1998), 114–30.

50. Matthias Rogg, "'Wol auff mit mir, du schoenes weyb,' Anmerkungen zur Konstruktion von Männlichkeit im Soldatenbild des 16. Jahrhunderts," in *Landsknechte, Soldatenfrauen und Nationalkrieger. Militär, Krieg und Geschlechterordnung im historischen Wandel,* ed. Karen Hagemann and Ralf Pröve (Frankfurt am Main: Campus Verlag, 1998), 51–73.

51. These ideological representations masked the very real and much-needed presence of lower-class women among troops. As procurers and preparers of food, nurses, trench workers, and companions, women were indispensable to the organization of an early modern army. Christiane Andersson, "Von 'Metzen' und 'Dirnen'. Frauenbilder in Kriegsdarstellungen der Frühen Neuzeit," in Hagemann and Pröve, 171–98; Bernhard R. Kroener, "'. . . und ist der jammer nit zu beschreiben'. Geschlechterbeziehungen und Überlebensstrategien in der Lagergesellschaft des Dreißigjährigen Krieges," in Ibid., 279–96.

52. Rublack cites examples from Konstanz and Memmingen. Rublack, "Wench and Maiden," 11.

53. Stadtarchiv München, Ratsberichtsprotokolle 56 A 16; 30.3.1626, 245–46.

54. Fischer, 538.

55. Stadtarchiv München, Eidbuch 1686, Zimelie 29, 13v. Also, in 1644 the

council exhorted the midwives "with seriousness that they report more industriously than has happened in the past the single women's extra-marital children . . . to the *Stadtoberrichter;* in the opposite case one would proceed against them [the midwives] with exemplary punishment." Stadtarchiv München, Ratsprotokolle, Unterrichterserie 13.4.1644; 117v. On the part midwives played in the detection of nonmarital pregnancies in early modern German cities, including Munich, see Merry Wiesner, *Working Women in Renaissance Germany* (New Brunswick, N.J.: Rutgers University Press, 1986), 55–73, especially 70.

56. Bayerisches Haupstaatsarchiv München, GR Fasz. 321 Nr. 7, Decretum Konzept 1.2.1629 Konzept; Reinschrift 3.2.1629.

57. Heydenreuter, "Magistrat als Befehlsempfänger," 195–96.

58. Stadtarchiv München, Ratsprotokoll 1629; Stadtschreiberserie, 190r–190v. The growing intolerance toward nonmarital sex soon encouraged a climate of denunciation. In 1630 Maria Albl relayed to the magistrate that Barbara Meisegger, recipient of a dowry from the *Jungfernstiftung,* had carried a child out of wedlock seventeen years ago. The council immediately deprived Meisegger of the award and made Maria Albl the beneficiary of the redistribution of Meisegger's dowry. Ratsprotokolle; Unterrichterserie; 15.11.1630, 286r–286v.

59. Stadtarchiv München, Stadtgericht 867/29; 369r–370r.

60. Stadtarchiv München, Stadtgericht 867/29; 205r–206r.

61. Behringer, "Mörder, Diebe, Ehebrecher," 100–102.

62. Stadtarchiv München, Stadtgericht 868/2; 31v.

63. Bayerisches Hauptstaatsarchiv München, GR, Fasz. 321, Nr. 7. For a different interpretation of the 1635 mandate and its treatment of female nonmarital sexuality, see Hull, 82–84.

64. Existing studies on the actual punishments, which authorities meted out to offenders in fornication cases, indicate that women received harsher penalties than men. Furthermore, punishment for women, maidservants in particular, tended to be more consequential, including measures such as exile. Rublack, 130–33; 211–14; Dürr, 229–45.

65. Susanna Burghartz finds that in Protestant Basel, too, a judicial notion of female virginity as a state of physical purity over time replaced an older understanding of female virginity as contextually defined. Susanna Burghartz, "Jungfräulichkeit oder Reinheit? Zur Änderung von Argumentationsmustern vor dem Basler Ehegericht im 16. und 17. Jahrhundert," in *Dynamik der Tradition,* ed. Richard van Dülmen (Frankfurt am Main: Fischer, 1992), 13–40, especially 39–40.

66. Stadtarchiv München, Stadtgericht 868/3; 120r–120v and 868/9; 18r.

67. Stadtarchiv München, Stadtgericht 868/13; 7r.

68. For example, Stadtarchiv München, Stadtgericht 868/10; 53v. Stadtarchiv München, Stadtgericht 868/13; 55r. Stadtarchiv München, Stadtgericht 868/13; 143v.

69. Thanks go to Erik Jensen for making me consider this.

70. Stadtarchiv München, Stadtgericht 868/2, fol. 193r–195r.

71. Stadtarchiv, Stadtgericht 868/9, 169r–170v.

72. For example, in 1648 Christoph Weinman asked to be let off the hook "because truthfully he had no means." The court ordered a settlement at a later date, and Weinman wound up in prison for a few days. He ended up paying for the

pregnancy and child support. The plaintiff's requests regarding the marriage promise and the loss of virginity, however, remained unmet, at least for the time being. Stadtarchiv München, Stadtgericht 868/15; 123v–125r.

73. Stadtarchiv München, Stadtgericht 868/10, 53v–54r.

74. Cavallo and Cerrutti, 98–99, 108 endnote 68.

75. Burghartz, "Jungfräulichkeit oder Reinheit?" 21.

76. Susanna Burghartz, "Tales of Seduction, Tales of Violence: Argumentative Strategies before the Basel Marriage Court," in *German History* 17, no. 1 (1999): 41–56.

77. Dürr, 223–45.

78. Susanna Burghartz, *Zeiten der Reinheit—Orte der Unzucht: Ehe und Sexualität in Basel während der Frühen Neuzeit* (Paderborn: Schöningh Verlag, 1999).

79. Stadtarchiv München, Bürgermeister und Rat, 60 B2, 738r–738v.

80. Stadtarchiv München, Bürgermeister und Rat, 60 B3, 144r.

81. Hull, 86; 107.

82. Stadtarchiv München, Bürgermeister und Rat, 62, 18v.

83. Ibid.

84. Stadtarchiv München, Stadtgericht 868/6, 45v.

85. Stadtarchiv München, Stadtgericht 867/5; 34r.

86. Stadtarchiv München, Stadtgericht, 868/16; 11r.

87. Martin Airnschmaltz, for instance, agreed in 1607 to pay a monthly allowance and give clothing until the child could "earn their own bread and reached marriageable age." Stadtarchiv München, Stadtgericht, 867/19; 32r. Benedict Maerzen gave the mother of his child enough money "to raise . . . and dower the child," Stadtarchiv München, Stadtgericht 867/6; 43r.

88. For example, Stadtarchiv München, Stadtgericht 867/7; 123–24.

89. See also Ulrike Gleixner, who points out that some female plaintiffs tried—usually in vain—to direct judicial attention to men impregnating other women outside of wedlock before them. Gleixner, 101.

90. Stadtarchiv München, Stadtgericht 868/16; 10r–11v.

91. Hull, 103.

92. Richard van Dülmen, *Frauen vor Gericht. Kindsmord in der frühen Neuzeit* (Frankfurt am Main: Fischer-Taschenbuch-Verlag, 1991). On the moralization of infanticide during the sixteenth and seventeenth centuries see 17–24; quote from 24.

93. Stadtarchiv München, Bürgermeister und Rat, Landesherrliche Spezialmandate Nr. 62, 99r–99v.

94. Ibid.

95. Behringer, "Mörder, Diebe, Ehebrecher."

96. Calculations based on table by Adalbert Huhn, *Geschichte des Spitales, der Kirche und der Pfarrei zum heiligen Geiste in München, 2 Bde.* (Munich: Verlag der JJ Lentner'schen Buchhandlung, 1893), 238–39.

97. Stadtarchiv München, Stadtgericht 868/11; 31r–32r.

98. Huhn, 240.

99. Most recently, Hull, 280–81.

100. Kathy Stuart, *Defiled Trades and Social Outcasts: Honor and Ritual Pollution in Early Modern Germany* (Cambridge: Cambridge University Press, 1999).

101. This is Wolfgang Behringer's explanation for the increase in infanticide cases tried before the privy council. Behringer, "Mörder, Diebe, Ehebrecher."

102. Gleixner, 74–75.

103. Hull, 115–16.

CHAPTER 4

1. Michel de Certeau, *The Practice of Everyday Life* (Berkeley: University of California Press, 1984), xviii–xix.

2. *Beschreibung von ainer alten schwester aus unseren den pittrich closter bey St. Christoph was sich von ao: 1620 bis dreissigsten Jahr mit der andern Reformation maistens die Clausur betrf: zuegetragen.* May 3, 1620. Bayerisches Hauptstaatsarchiv, Klosterliteralien Fasz. 423, Nr. 3; unpaginated manuscript. Hereafter cited as *Beschreibung* plus respective date of entry.

3. Felix Stieve, *Das kirchliche Polizeiregiment in Baiern unter Maximilian I. 1595–1651* (Munich: Verlag der M. Rieger'schen Universitäts-Buchhandlung, 1876). Reinhard Heydenreuter, "Der Magistrat als Befehlsempfänger: Die Disziplinierung der Stadtobrigkeit 1579–1651," in *Geschichte der Stadt München,* ed. Richard Bauer (Munich, 1994), 189–210.

4. Gabriella Zarri, "Pieta' e profezia alle corti padane: le pie consigliere dei principi," in *Le sante vive. Profezie di corte e devozione femminile tra '400 e '500* (Turin: Rosenberg e Sellier, 1990), 51–85, and Gabrielle Zarri, "Le sante vive," in Ibid., 87–163.

5. Benno Hubensteiner, *Vom Geist des Barock: Kultur und Frömmigkeit im alten Bayern* (1967; reprint, Munich: Süddeutscher Verlag, 1978), 90.

6. Hubensteiner, *Vom Geist des Barock,* 89.

7. Georg Schwaiger, "München—Eine geistliche Stadt," in *Monachium Sacrum: Festschrift zur 500-Jahr-Feier der Metropolitankirche zu Unserer Lieben Frau in München,* vol. 1, ed. Georg Schwaiger (Munich: Deutscher Kunstverlag, 1994), 107. For a comparative perspective see Jutta Sperling's work on Venice. She details how state-sponsored monastic reform entailed the development of new governmental institutions that could supplant traditional networks of power, such as monastic orders and private families. Jutta Sperling, *Convents and the Body Politic in Late Renaissance Venice* (Chicago: University of Chicago Press, 1999).

8. *Beschreibung,* May 1620–March 1621.

9. Johannes Gatz, "Franziskanerkloster St. Antonius in München," in *Bavaria Franciscana Antiqua,* vol. 3, ed. bayr. Franziskanerprovinz (Munich: Lentner'sche Buchhandlung, 1957), 93–94.

10. *Beschreibung,* 21.11.1622.

11. *Bittrich voll des Himmlischen Manna und Süssen Morgen-Thau. Das ist: Historischer Discurs/Von dem Ursprung, Fundation, Auffnamb/glücklichen Fortgang/Tugend-Wandel/und andern denckwürdigen Sachen Deß Löbl. Frauen-*

Closters/Ordens der dritten Regul des heil. Francisci/Bey Sanct Christophen im Bitt-rich genannt/In der Chur-Fürstlichen Residenz-Stadt München mit Erlaubnis der Obern (Munich: Johann Lucas Straud, 1721), 113–14. Hereafter cited as *Manna.*

12. *Manna,* 98; Fortunatus Hueber, *Lob-, Danck-, und Ehrenreiche Gedaecht-nuss/Von dem Geist- und Loeblichen Jungfrau-Closter des III. Ordens S. Francisci Bey den zweyen Heiligen Joannes, dem Tauffer und dem Evangelisten, Auff der Stiegen (deren Ridler genamselt) zu München in Bayern an der Chur-Fürstlichen Residenz* (Munich: Sebastian Rauch, 1695), 56. Hereafter cited as *Gedaechtnuss.*

13. *Manna,* 98.

14. The two churches were torn down in the nineteenth century, and it is impossible to reconstruct their exact layout from archival materials. The Ridler church apparently had a Janus-faced altar in the middle with one side reaching into the nuns' choir, the other into the nave; see Max Hufnagel, "Franziskanerinnen-kloster der Ridlerschwestern zu St. Johannes auf der Stiege in München," in *Bavaria Franciscana Antiqua,* vol. 3, ed. bayr. Franziskanerprovinz (Munich: Lent-ner'sche Buchhandlung, 1957), 337.

15. Gabriella Zarri, "Gender, Religious Institutions and Social Discipline: The Reform of the Regulars," in *Gender and Society in Renaissance Italy,* ed. Judith Brown and Robert C. Davis (London and New York: Longman, 1998), 210–11.

16. *Manna,* 101.

17. David Myers, *"Poor Sinning Folk": Confession and Conscience in Counter-Reformation Germany* (Ithaca: Cornell University Press, 1996).

18. Reports of these exams can be found in Diözesanarchiv des Erbistums München-Freising, Klosterliteralien Fasz. 235.

19. *Beschreibung,* January 1622.

20. Galbiato promulgated a special set of statutes for each group of sisters. Both sets are preserved in Bayerisches Haupstaatsarchiv München, Klosterlite-ralien 461, Nr.1.

21. "On April 6 of this year of 1627 six virgins were admitted, two into the choir and four laysisters, the first being . . . the daughter of a peasant, the second . . . also a daughter of a peasant, those two served us, the third was the daughter of a baker . . . the fourth also the daughter of a peasant." *Beschreibung,* April 6, 1627.

22. Ibid., May 10, 1626.

23. See *Necrologue of the Pütrich Sisters,* Archiv Kloster Reutberg, Schublade 59/9.

24. Bayerisches Hauptstaatsarchiv München, Klosterliteralien 423, Nr.3 ULF; question number 8.

25. Sabine John, "'Mit Behutsamkeit vnd Reverentz zu tractieren': Die Katakombenheiligen im Münchner Pütrichkloster—Arbeit und Frömmigkeit," *Bayerisches Jahrbuch für Volkskunde* (1995), 8.

26. Contemporary Munich composers dedicated music to the sisters in the Pütrich, Ridler, and Anger convents. See Hufnagel, "Ridlerschwestern," 321–22, note 31.

27. Gabriella Zarri, "Ursula and Catherine: The Marriage of Virgins in the Sixteenth Century," in *Creative Women in Medieval and Early Modern Italy: A*

Religious and Artistic Renaissance, ed. Ann Matter and John Coakley (Philadelphia: University of Pennsylvania Press, 1994), 262–63; Zarri, "Gender, Religious Institutions and Social Discipline," 203–4.

28. Bayerisches Hauptstaatsarchiv München, Klosterliteralien, Fasz. 423, Nr. 3, Hofkammer 1: letter of April 4, 1626.

29. The lay sisters "were not as dressed up on their wedding day as are the choir sisters but rather, as befits their station, they walk with a small wreath and their braids down." *Beschreibung,* June 20, 1627.

30. Horst Heres, ed.: *Kulturgeschichte des Dachauer Landes* (Dachau: Museumsverein Dachau e. V., 1994), 109–11; illustrations on 109 for status-related differences in headdress.

31. The most spectacular example is the spiritual wedding of Sister Emanuela Theresia (formerly Maria Anna Karolina), the daughter of Elector Maximilian Emanuel. She entered Munich's most ascetic and austere cloister of Poor Clares, the *Angerkloster,* in 1719. Anton Freiherr von Om, "Einkleidung der Prinzessin Maria Anna Karolina im Clarissenkloster zu München (1719)," *Altbayerische Monatsschrift* 2 (1900): 145.

32. Bayerisches Hauptstaatsarchiv München, Klosterliteralien, Fasz. 423, Nr. 3, ULF; question number 6.

33. Hufnagel, "Ridlerschwestern," 319–20, emphasis added.

34. For examples from Catalonia, see H. Kamen, *The Phoenix and the Flame: Catalonia and the Counter Reformation* (New Haven: Yale University Press, 1993), 336–39.

35. *Beschreibung,* December 1621.

36. Ibid., November 21, 1622.

37. James Scott, *The Weapons of the Weak: Everyday Forms of Peasant Resistance* (New Haven: Yale University Press, 1985).

38. *Gedaechtnuss,* 58.

39. Bayerisches Hauptstaatsarchiv München, Klosterliteralien, Fasz. 423, Nr. 1: 32r–33r, esp. 33r.

40. A copy of Maximiliana's *vita* written by a nun and friend can be found in Bayerisches Hauptstaatsarchiv München, Klosterliteralien Fasz. 423, Nr. 5. It is entitled "Description of numerous things about our Dear Mother M. Maximiliana." Hereafter cited as *Maximiliana.*

41. *Maximiliana,* 5.

42. Ibid., 5–6.

43. *Beschreibung,* April 17, 1627.

44. *Maximiliana,* 12.

45. Ibid., 11–12.

46. Bayerisches Hauptstaatsarchiv München, Klosterliteralien 16, Bericht, 233.

47. *Maximiliana,* 14.

48. Ibid., 15.

49. Ibid., 20.

50. Ibid., 20.

51. Caroline Walker Bynum, *Holy Feast and Holy Fast: The Religious Significance of Food to Medieval Women* (Berkeley: University of California Press, 1987).

52. *Maximiliana,* 21.

53. Ibid., 22.

54. Ibid., 23.

55. Ibid., 22.

56. Jodi Bilinkoff, *The Avila of Saint Teresa* (Ithaca: Cornell University Press, 1989), 50–52.

57. Bilinkoff, 137.

58. Claire Walker, "Combining Martha and Mary: Gender and Work in Seventeenth-Century English Cloisters," *Sixteenth Century Journal: The Journal of Early Modern Studies* 30, no. 2 (summer 1999): 399–404.

59. Ibid., 404–8, 416–17.

60. See the incomplete list of dowries of the Pütrich convent in Bayerisches Haupstaatsarchiv München, Klosterliteralien 423/1. Dowry payments for choir sisters ranged from 300 to 3,000 florins. The record also contains other information about financial dealings "in this difficult time," including a note that the convent "begged" Maximiliana to give 500 florins supposedly toward the restoration of church and altar. The prince granted the request.

61. Letter of December 12, 1632, by Mother Superior Elisabeth Zehendtner to Elector Maximilian, asking him to help with the collection of interest. Bayerisches Haupstaatsarchiv München, Klosterliteralien Fasz. 461, Nr. 1, "Hofkammer."

62. *Gedaechtnuss,* 58.

63. *Manna,* 101; *Gedaechtnuss,* 58.

64. On enclosure as "an additional hymen" and post-Trent legal attempts to stabilize traditionally unstable meanings of virginity and clausura so that nuns could serve their communities as efficacious protectors, see also Sperling, esp. 134–41.

65. Wilhelm Smets, *Des hochheiligen, ökumenischen, und allgemeinen Concils von Trient Canones und Beschlüsse* (Bielefeld, Velhagen und Klasing 1869: Fotomechanischer Nachdruck, erschienen im Sankt Meinrad Verlag für Theologie, Christine Maria Esser, Sinzing 1989), 165.

66. Philip Soergel, *Wondrous in His Saints: Counter-Reformation Propaganda in Bavaria* (Berkeley: University of California Press, 1993), 121.

67. Wilhelm Liebhart, "'Die Seelen haben einen großen Trost verloren . . .': Die 'gottselige' Klara Hortulana Empacher im Münchner Angerkloster," *Amperland* 31 (1995): 36–39.

68. Clara's assignment for each sister included attending communion 5 times, attending 27 extra masses, singing the psalms of David 15 times, "300 Lord's prayers in honor of the anxiety and bloody sweat shed at the Mount Olives, 500 Hail Mary in honor of the Mother of God in her holy compassion," praying the "litany of Christ's suffering" 12 times, keeping total silence for 3 days and 3 nights, and fasting with "a little bit of water and bread" for a day. Liebhart, "Seelen," 38.

69. Natalie Zemon Davis, "Ghosts, Kin and Progeny: Some Features of Family Life in Early Modern France," *Daedalus* 106, no. 2 (1977): 87–114, esp. 92–96.

70. Liebhart, "Seelen," 38, 36. The Empacher were an influential patrician family in Munich.

71. Ibid., 38.

72. Klara Reischl was related to the (then) late Caecilia Reischl from the Pütrich convent. Ibid., 38.

73. Mother Barbara Morat from the Ridler convent pleaded with papal officials for thirteen years to be granted the Lateran indulgence of St. Johannes for the cloister church "so that not only the members of the order, but also all secular people" could partake of its spiritual benefits. *Gedaechtnuss,* 93.

74. For each mass said at any one of the altars in the Ridler church, a soul was supposed to be released from purgatory. *Gedaechtnuss,* 93–94. In the Pütrich cloister, dead nuns and their consanguineous kin of the first and second degree received complete remission of their sins whenever mass was celebrated on the high altar on Fridays and during the week of the Feast of Corpus Christi. *Manna,* 190.

75. Electress Henriette Adelaide initiated the installment of the stairs in the cloister in 1655. *Gedaechtnuss,* 94; *Manna,* 189; Hufnagel, "Ridlerschwestern," 336–37.

76. John also notes this transition. John, "Katakombenheiligen," 8.

77. *Manna,* 126.

78. John, "Katakombenheiligen," 11.

79. Hansjakob Achermann, *Die Katakombenheiligen und ihre Translationen in der schweizerischen Quart des Bistums Konstanz* (Stans: Hist. Verein Nidwal, 1979), 9–17, esp. 12.

80. Soergel, 181–91.

81. Ibid., esp. 160–61, 182–83.

82. Peter Brown, *Cult of the Saints: Its Rise and Function in Latin Christianity* (Chicago: University of Chicago Press, 1981), in particular chapters 1 and 2.

83. Smets, 166.

84. *Ordentliche Beschreibung Des gantzen verlauffs, wie die H.H. Reliquien und Cörper S. Hyacinthij Martyrers und S.Dorothea Martyrin, wie auch vier benandten Stuekh Heilthumber Der H.H. Martyrer Si. Calisti, Si. Concordij, Si. Elpistij, und Si: Demetrj mit Authentischen Brieffen und Sigill von Rom herauss in Diss würdige Gottshaus und Closster Si. Christophori gebracht: Dernach von dem Durchleuchtigisten hochwürdigisten Fürsten und Herrn Herrn [sic] Alberto Sigismundo Bischoffen zu Freysingen, als ordinario Loci, appropriert und mit dessen genedigisten Consens zu oeffentlicher verehrung, und algemainen Trost der Christglaubigen In unnser Closterkürchen transferriert und beygesetzt worden.* Kloster Reutberg, Archiv, Schublade 63/6. All details and quotes pertaining to the story of the corpse of St. Dorothea are taken from this source unless otherwise noted.

85. Bayerisches Haupstaatsarchiv München, Klosterliteralien 423/3, Nr. 5. During a meeting of the General Chapter of the Reformati province the "nuns were forbidden to have small children enter into enclosure, regardless of how young they are, because nothing but upheaval and impropriety comes of it."

86. Merry Wiesner, "Women's Defense of Their Public Role," in *Women in the Middle Ages and the Renaissance,* ed. Mary Beth Rose (Syracuse: Syracuse University Press, 1986), 1–27, esp. 21.

87. Ibid.

88. Smets, 167.

89. John, "Katakombenheiligen," 3.

90. Hufnagel, "Ridlerschwestern," 334, 336.

91. John discusses the procession in "Katakombenheiligen," 13–16. She offers a slightly more positive interpretation of its meaning for the nuns' self-understandings than I do.

92. *Manna,* 142. Also cited in John, "Katakombenheiligen," 14.

93. According to the chronicle, "this holy corpse [Dorothea] enkindled in the sisters the love and veneration of holy relics to such a degree" that they asked Modestus Reichart to obtain another one on his journey to Rome in 1664. *Manna,* 147. Perhaps the request was also a means to make good on the faux pas with the Capuchin buyer. By the end of the seventeenth century the convent housed the bodies of Dorothea, Hyacinth, Geminus, Felicitas, and Victorinus. The chronicle tells about these acquisitions and also gives a list of other holy treasures. *Manna,* 190–94.

94. The Ridler sisters obtained the body of St. Perpetua in 1663 and the body of St. Columbus in 1666. The Ridler chronicle relates that "of the bones of holy apostles, martyrs, confessors, virgins and penitents a great number was presented for public veneration" in the cloister church. *Gedaechtnuss,* 92. The chronicler for the Angerkloster tells us that Munich's convent of Poor Clares housed in its church "several whole holy corpses [i.e., those] of S. Antigonus, M.S. Faustus, M.S. Justinus, M.S. Justina V, M.S. Eleutheria and S. Eutichia all of them artistically and preciously framed together with many other renowned relics and bones of God's saints." See Barnabas Kirchhuber: *Der Gnaden-und Tugend-reiche Anger/Das ist: Die sonderbare grosse Gnaden/tugendsame Leben/vnd andere denck-vnd lob-würdige Begebenheiten/So in dem Uhr-alten vnd hochberühmten Gotts-Hauß/vnd jungfräulichen Closter S. Clarae Ordens in München bey S. Jacob am ANGER biß in die 480. Jahr verschlossen/vnd verborgen gelegen/nunmehr angemerckt vnd eröffnen.* Getruckt zu München /bey Maria Magdalena Rauchin/Wittib. Im Jahr 1701, 19. Hereafter cited as *Gnaden-Anger.*

95. John, "Katakombenheiligen," 22–23.

96. The need for advertisement also explains the detailed descriptions of the convent treasures in the printed chronicles.

97. John, "Katakombenheiligen," 17f.

98. Lyndal Roper, "Exorcism and the Theology of the Body," in *Oedipus and the Devil: Witchcraft, Sexuality and Religion in Early Modern Europe* (New York and London: Routledge, 1994), 171–98.

99. Caroline Walker Bynum, *Jesus as Mother: Studies in the Spirituality of the High Middle Ages* (Berkeley: University of California Press, 1982); Bynum, *Fragmentation and Redemption: Essays on Gender and the Human Body in Medieval Religion* (New York: Zone Books, 1992); also Bynum, *Holy Feast and Holy Fast.*

100. On the "hypostasization of pain" underlying sorcery practices and its counterpart in the physical experience of the suffering of Christ, see Roper, "Exorcism," 183.

101. *Gedaechtnuss,* 83.

102. "Inter alia virtutum exercitia flagravit desiderio Martyrij et Sanguinem suum pro amore Jesu fundendi, quod iterato Confessario suo multis suspicijs aperuit, sed cum hic illam ad internum Martyrium semper adhortabatur, ipsa contra non cessavit a Deo pro gratia etiam externi Martyrij rogare, quam et mirabiliter impetravit, et quia ab hominibus hanc gratiam habere non posset ob impedimentum Clausurae, per diabolum impetravit, dum hic ex Divina permissione hanc benedictam Virginem ab eminenti loci praecipitavit, e quo lapsu tam copiose capit sanguinem emittere." Bayerisches Hauptstaatsarchiv München, Klosterliteralien 3561, Nr. 1/62.

103. Kirchhuber, *Gnaden-Anger,* 64–65, 66.

104. For example, David Lan, *Guns and Rain: Guerrillas and Spirit Mediums in Zimbabwe* (Berkeley: University of California Press, 1985).

105. John, "Katakombenheiligen," 4.

CHAPTER 5

This chapter is dedicated to the memory of Leah C. Kirker. She was working on a dissertation entitled "Women's Education and the State: Mary Ward and the English Ladies in Bavaria, 1630–1806" when a tragic accident took her life. Leah C. Kirker and I never met. Tom Brady, her adviser at the University of California, Berkeley, generously made her research notes and photocopies available to me. In looking through the material, I found out that she and I had used many of the same sources. I also learned about some new resources because of Leah C. Kirker's research, for which I am very grateful.

1. Cited in Mathilde Köhler, *Maria Ward: Ein Frauenschicksal des 17. Jahrhunderts* (Munich: Kösel-Verlag, 1985), 222.

2. The story of Mary Ward has been retold many times. According to Mary Katherine Elizabeth Chambers, at least twelve biographies exist, starting with the first biography in manuscript written by Ward's companions Winefrid Wigmore and Mary Poyntz in the seventeenth century. One of the first accounts that went to press is a two-volume study by Marcus Fridl. See Marcus Fridl, *Englische Tugend-Schul* (Augsburg, 1732). An incomplete manuscript version of Fridl's biography can be found in the Bayerisches Hauptstaatsarchiv München Klosterliteralien, Fasz. 432. Fridl used many primary sources, some of which he cites at length. The general intent of his work, however, is leaning toward the hagiographic. For information on the various biographies, see the introduction to Chambers, *The Life of Mary Ward in Two Volumes,* ed. Henry James Coleridge (London: Burns and Oates, 1882, 1885). This is the first modern-style work that appeared after centuries of silence about Mary Ward. Modern scholarship continues to draw extensively on Chambers's prolix study. For recent research, see Mathilde Köhler, *Maria Ward: Ein Frauenschicksal des 17. Jahrhunderts* (Munich: Kösel-Verlag, 1985), and Henriette Peters, *Maria Ward: Ihre Persönlichkeit und ihr Institut* (Vienna and Innsbruck: Tyrolia-Verlag, 1991). For a useful short introduction, see Sylvia Rösner-Zimmermann, "<Maria Ward> Vorkämpferin einer 'Emanzipation' der Frau in der Kirche," in *Aus Schwaben und Altbayern: Festschrift für Pankraz Fried zum 60. Geburtstag,* ed. Peter Fassl, Wilhelm Liebhart, and Wolfgang Wüst (Sigmaringen:

Jan Thorbecke Verlag, 1991), 203–17. Josef Grisar has explored the Roman reaction to Mary Ward and her proposed female order. Among other works see his *Maria Wards Institut vor römischen Kongregationen (1616–1630), Miscellanea Historiae Pontificiae,* vol. 27 (Rome: Pontifica Universita Gregoriana, 1966). There is considerably less research done on the workings of the institute itself. Its social history by and large remains to be written. For Bavaria in particular, the following two pieces offer some information: Johann Nepomuk Buchinger, "Erinnerungen an die Gründung und erste Verbreitung des Instituts der englischen Fräulein in Bayern," *Oberbayerisches Archiv für vaterländische Geschichte,* vol. 17 (Munich, 1857), 116–73; and Maria Theodolinde Winkler, *Maria Ward und das Institut der Englischen Fräulein in Bayern von der Gründung des Hauses in München bis zur Säkularisation desselben. 1626–1810* (Munich: Druck und Kommissionsverlag Carl Aug. Seyfried und Comp., 1926).

3. The papal privilege did not preclude close interactions with pious women on a local level, and Jesuits generally paid great attention to female believers. The Jesuits' inviting attitude ended, however, at the institutional boundary of their Society. See Anne Conrad, *Zwischen Kloster und Welt. Ursulinen und Jesuitinnen in der katholischen Reformbewegung des 16./17. Jahrhunderts* (Mainz: Verlag Philipp von Zabern, 1991), especially 65–66.

4. Robert Bireley, *Maximilian von Bayern, Adam Contzen S.J. und die Gegenreformation in Deutschland 1624–1635* (Göttingen: Vandenhoeck und Ruprecht, 1975).

5. Ward outlined her quest for a fitting arena of piety in a letter of 1620 to the papal nuncio Albergati. I cite from a German copy of the letter in the Bavarian State Archive. The letter is unpaginated. All translations are mine. Bayerisches Hauptstaatsarchiv München, Klosterliteralien, Faszikel 432/1.

6. Letter to Albergati, Bayerisches Hauptstaatsarchiv München, Klosterliteralien, Faszikel 432/1. Conrad, who also cites this letter, surmises that the men were Jesuits. Conrad, 86.

7. "I understood clearly, not because of a voice but intellectually, the following words: take the same as the Society." Letter to Albergati, Bayerisches Hauptstaatsarchiv München, Klosterliteralien, Faszikel, 432/1.

8. The three different versions of a constitution for the English Ladies— Schola Beatae Mariae (1611/12), Ratio Instituti (1615), Institutum (1620)—display a progressive approximation of the Society's institutional structure. Grisar, 19–21. Conrad, 87–92.

9. Chambers, *Life of Mary Ward,* vol. 1, 409.

10. Chambers, *Life of Mary Ward,* vol. 1, 410.

11. Elizabeth Rapley, *The Dévotes: Women and Church in Seventeenth-Century France* (Montreal and Kingston: McGill-Queen's University Press, 1990), 28. She views this difference in treatment as the most revealing illustration of the difference in perception between male and female religious.

12. Mary Wright, *Mary Ward's Institute: The Struggle for Identity* (Sydney: Crossing Press, 1997), 74.

13. Urban VIII's bull of suppression explicitly made the connection: "in eiusque Superiorem, ac praetensae Congregationis suae Generalem indito prae-

posita titulo, et attributis facultatibus benvisis constituissent, in illiusque manibus paupertatis, castitatis, et obedientiae vota, ad instar solemnium emitterer, clausuraeque legibus non districtae pro libitu divagari." *Annullatio,* Bayerisches Hauptstaatsarchiv München, MK 22106.

14. Two Munich women, Anna Maria Grainwald and Anna Redl, took their vows by taking Ward's hand. Peters, 755.

15. The canonist Suarez viewed this judicial prerogative as part of the "usum clavium" generally denied to the laity and to women. On Suarez's distinction between the different forms of governance within religious orders and the respective competencies of men and women, see Conrad, 259–60.

16. The beguines were important forerunners to the English Ladies with respect to both teaching activities and the refusal of enclosure. It is probably no accident that Mary Ward embarked upon her educational enterprise in St. Omer, a traditional center of beguine activity. Like the English Ladies, beguines attracted severe criticism for their pedagogical aspirations and uncloistered way of life. Unlike the English Ladies, they never strove to establish a new religious order, but they became subject to stricter rules of enclosure over time. Walter Simons, *Cities of Ladies: Beguine Communities in the Medieval Low Countries, 1200–1565* (Philadelphia: University of Pennsylvania Press, 2001).

17. Merry Wiesner, *Women and Gender in Early Modern Europe* (Cambridge: Cambridge University Press, 1993; reprint, 1998) 132.

18. Patricia Labalme, ed., *Beyond Their Sex: Learned Women of the European Past* (New York, 1980).

19. Margaret King, *Women of the Renaissance* (Chicago: University of Chicago Press, 1991), 164–218.

20. Wiesner, *Women and Gender,* 121–23. The Ursuline concept of charitable work in the world originally included the instruction of girls. In the early seventeenth century, church authorities forced them to accept cloister and narrow their range of charitable activities to education within convent walls. Rapley, 48–49, 59.

21. Conrad, 91; for example, Ward concluded a letter from 1627 to Winefrid Bedingfield in Munich: "Commend me to all your scholars." Chambers, *Life of Mary Ward,* vol. 2, 238.

22. See Conrad, 91; the bull of dissolution states: "aedificia in collegiorum formam redegissent, domos probationum erexissent." *Annullatio.*

23. In Ong's words: "For well over a thousand years, it [Latin] was sex-linked, a language written and spoken only by males, learned outside the home in a tribal setting which was in effect a male puberty rite, complete with physical punishment and other kinds of deliberately imposed hardships. It had no direct connection with anyone's unconscious of the sort that mother tongues, learned in infancy, always have. . . . Learned Latin was a striking exemplification of the power of writing for isolating discourse and of the unparalleled productivity of such isolation." Cited in *Medieval Women's Visionary Literature,* ed. Elizabeth A. Petroff (New York and Oxford: Oxford University Press, 1986), 29 (introduction by Petroff). Petroff points out that numerous medieval women writers did indeed have knowledge of Latin but it stemmed from familiarity with the liturgy rather than from systematic study. Ibid., 29–30.

24. Wiesner, *Women and Gender,* 126–27.

25. Karl-Ludwig Ay, *Land und Fürst im alten Bayern* (Regensburg: Verlag Friedrich Pustet, 1988), 204.

26. Joseph Gebele, *Das Schulwesen der königlich bayrischen Haupt- und Residenzstadt München* (Munich: M. Kellerer's h. b. Hof-, Buch-, und Kunsthandlung, 1896), 4–8.

27. Georg Schwaiger, "München—Eine geistliche Stadt," in *Monachium Sacrum,* vol. 1, ed. Schwaiger (Munich: Deutscher Kunstverlag, 1994), 100–102.

28. Köhler, 70.

29. The annual payments to Lüttich amounted to 10,000 Gulden; the payments to Cologne peaked at 30,000 Gulden. Ibid., 167.

30. Winkler, 14.

31. Ibid., 16.

32. Peters, 675.

33. Anton Fischer, "Der Verwaltungsaufbau der Stadt München im 16. und 17. Jahrhundert" (Diss., München, 1951), 557.

34. Male guild members filed a complaint against them with the city council in the early seventeenth century. We know from this document that one of the women, Anna Rizl, "taught boys as well as girls." Cited in Gebele, 11; see page 6 on the foundation of the teachers' guild. Rizl was cognizant of her precarious position and also of the city council's interest in keeping widows off the list of alms recipients. When the guild submitted a complaint to the council, voicing grievances over pecuniary difficulties, Rizl was the only one who asserted "that she . . . had no complaints." Cited in Ibid., 12.

35. Grisar, 282.

36. Ibid., 281.

37. In 1690, these were still rented out. Winkler, 15.

38. Köhler, 176.

39. Grisar, 282, fn. 17.

40. Köhler, 174.

41. Jeanne Cover, *Love: The Driving Force* (Milwaukee: Marquette University Press, 1997), 13.

42. Grisar, 306, fn. 74.

43. Wolfgang Behringer, *Hexenverfolgung in Bayern: Volksmagie und Staatsräson in der Frühen Neuzeit* (Munich: Oldenbourg Verlag, 1987), 249–50.

44. Vitelleschi regularly intervened on Ward's behalf. Grisar, 286, fn. 25.

45. Köhler, 179.

46. Gisar, 285 including fn. 22.

47. Köhler, 180.

48. Grisar outlines this in great detail in his study.

49. Peters, 793–95.

50. *Annullatio.*

51. "Et quae viri sacrarum litterarum scientia, rerum usu, vitaeque innocentia spectatissimis, difficile admodum, et non nis magna circumspectione adhibita aggrediuntur." *Annullatio.*

52. *Annullatio.*

53. Cited in Peters, 861, fn. 39.

54. Fridl, 2. Buch, 16. Kapitel, 338–40. In the course of her imprisonment Ward developed something akin to a friendship with the abbess of the *Angerkloster*, Katharina Bernardine Gräf. Gräf actually had looked forward to housing Ward in her convent. Ward reports in a letter that the abbess "is full of my writings. She hath been in some hopes to have me here. She tells me my first vow was St. Clare's Order." Chambers, *Life of Mary Ward*, vol. 2, 355.

55. Peters, 867, fn. 58.

56. Mary Ward relates this in a letter from prison dated February 13, 1631: "Our door chained and double locked and never opened but at the only entrance and departure of our two keepers, and the Lady Abbess who is our chief guardian. We were conducted in by the three same within and two Franciscans who speak Italian, and the night, or rather hour, we came were placed beds near to our door, where night and day four nuns keep guardia." Cited in Chambers, *Life of Mary Ward*, vol. 2, 356.

57. Chambers, *Life of Mary Ward*, vol. 2, 370.

58. Urban VIII had no knowledge of Ward's imprisonment and ordered her immediate release upon finding out about her detainment. Ibid. Her return to the Paradeiserhaus took place in a carriage provided by Electress Elisabeth and in front of a cheering crowd. Köhler, 265.

59. The missives have entered research under the category of "Limonenbriefe" or "lemon letters." They were written with lemon juice because the juice remains invisible unless held over a flame.

60. Chambers, *Life of Mary Ward*, vol. 2, 358–59.

61. Ibid., 391.

62. The statement comes from a letter Ward sent out to all members of her institute regarding the bull of suppression. Ibid., 360. According to Fridl, Ward said they could "serve God better" in a secular estate. Fridl, 2. Buch, 16. Kapitel, 358. Chambers, who is consistently thorough, bases her version on manuscript evidence.

63. During a particularly severe bout of illness, she wrote: "If God give health, we shall find another way to serve Him than by becoming Ursulines." Chambers, *Life of Mary Ward*, vol. 2, 363.

64. Winkler, 19–20.

65. Mary Ward reported in one of her prison letters that Munich's most influential Jesuit made "braggs that he hath done this deed." Chambers, *Life of Mary Ward*, vol. 2, 353.

66. Fridl, 2; Buch, 13; Kapitel, 315.

67. Buchinger, 122–23.

68. Ward wrote to Francis Brooksby: "In Paradise our friends still live, and there you will be most welcome." Chambers, *Life of Mary Ward*, vol. 2, 396. On the Vienna community, see Chambers, *Life of Mary Ward*, vol. 2, 395.

69. Ibid., 407.

70. Köhler, 281.

71. "Daß sie die jungen weibs Persohnen, in den Jenigen sachen, so dennselben Zulehrnen gebürt, Und wies sonsten under denen weltlichen Persohnen alhie

gebreuchig, Instruirn Unnd Underweisen auch dergestalt Ihren Undhalt suech mögen." Cited in Winkler, 22.

72. Christl Knauer, *Frauen unter dem Einfluss von Kirche und Staat* (Munich, 1995).

73. Fridl, 2; Buch, 10; Kapitel, 224.

74. Winkler, 98–99.

75. The English Ladies invested the capital and drew annual interest. Buchinger, 152.

76. Winkler, 27.

77. Buchinger, 158–73.

78. Winkler, 60.

79. From an inventory of rooms needed, see Bayerisches Hauptstaatsarchiv München, Klosterliteralien, Faszikel 432/1 I.

80. Winkler, 23.

81. Buchinger, 144.

82. This was true not just of Mary Ward but also of other "Jesuitesses" like Alix Le Clercs or Anne de Xainctonge. Conrad, 216–17.

83. Winkler, 81–82.

84. Ward had Bedingfield forward the works of the two students to Vienna. Chambers, *Life of Mary Ward,* vol. 2, 237–38. In the same letter Ward congratulated Bedingfield "on the unexpected progress of your Latin school."

85. Winkler, 56; Knauer, 32.

86. Institutes of English Ladies that were founded after 1700 do not include any mention of languages other than French in their curricula. Winkler, 82–83.

87. Peter Petschauer, *The Education of Women in Eighteenth-Century Germany: New Directions from the German Female Perspective* (Lewiston, N.Y.: E. Mellen Press, 1989)

88. Winkler, 53.

89. Archival records of these arrangements are available in Bayerisches Hauptstaatsarchiv München, KL, Fasz. 437/17.

90. Buchinger, 162.

91. Cited in Winkler, 51.

92. Ibid., 76.

93. Cited in ibid., 59.

94. Ibid., 77, 65.

95. Ibid., 66. The presence of chambermaids becomes apparent from a bill issued by the community in Augsburg to three countesses in 1691. Ibid., 72 fn. 139.

96. Cited in Ibid., 78.

97. Ibid., 102.

98. The only exception to this are a few grants that the Elector offered to talented poorer girls who wished to attend the boarding school.

99. Winkler, 93.

100. On the role of schooling in the consolidation of state rule in general see Pavla Miller, *Transformations of Patriarchy in the West, 1500–1900* (Bloomington: Indiana University Press, 1998).

101. Winkler, 50, 80.

102. Knauer, 46–47.

103. Ibid., 49.

104. The council tried to bar women from religious instruction, yet the shortage of priests in many geographic areas eventually opened up opportunities for female participation. Rapley, 72, 117.

105. Mary Jo Maynes, *Schooling for the People* (New York: Holmes and Meier, 1985), 74.

106. Knauer, 59.

107. Pope Clemens XI confirmed the rules in 1703. In 1749, Pope Benedict XIV gave the new institute its constitution but also renewed Urban's bull of condemnation from 1631. The latter implied an express prohibition against claiming Mary Ward as the foundress. Ward was not rehabilitated until the early twentieth century. Rösner-Zimmermann, 203. In the 1970s, the papacy granted the institute the Jesuit constitution for which Ward asked in the early seventeenth century.

108. Mary Wright, *Mary Ward's Institute: The Struggle for Identity* (Sydney: Crossing Press, 1997), 60.

109. Wright, 75–77.

110. See the inventory of required equipment for the year of 1701, preserved in the Bayerisches Hauptstaatsarchiv München, KL 1.

111. The English Ladies possessed the holy corpses of the boy martyr Mercurius and the girl martyr Margaritha, "both very beautiful and luxuriously adorned for the special veneration of the school youth." The Capuchin Adrian Aham had procured the bodies for the institute. His sister was among the members there. Fridl, *Tugend-Schul,* 4; Buch, 15; Kapitel, 614–15.

112. Father Tobias Lohner, the community's confessor at the time of the miracle, included the tale in his *Das Gottselige Leben und die fürtrefflichen Tugenden Donna Maria Della Guardia* (1689), Maschinenschriftliche Kopie, Archiv der Englischen Fräulein, München-Nymphenburg, 40–41. See also Chambers, *Life of Mary Ward,* vol. 2, 537.

113. Rapley, 111–12, quote from 112.

114. Grisar, 89.

115. Westenrieder, *Beschreibung der Haupt- und Residenzstadt München* (Johann Baptist Strobl, 1728). Facsimile reprint, Munich: Carl Gerber Verlag GmbH, 1984, 203–4.

116. Winkler, 55.

117. Knauer, 453.

118. Such was the case in the eighteenth century when a shortage of teachers gained some women who came from the lower social classes admission into the teaching seminary. Ibid., 62.

119. Ibid., 29.

120. Wright, 68.

121. Lohner, 37, Nr. 11.

122. On the related issue of Ursuline concepts of physical mortification and their relationship to Ignatian ideas see Marie Florine Bruneau, *Women Mystics Confront the Modern World* (Albany: State University of New York Press, 1998).

123. Rapley, 31.

CONCLUSION

1. Lyndal Roper, *The Holy Household: Women and Morals in Reformation Augsburg* (Oxford: Clarendon Press, 1989).

2. Isabel Hull, *Sexuality, State, and Civil Society in Germany, 1700–1815* (Ithaca: Cornell University Press, 1996).

3. Thanks to Amy Hollywood for making me think about these continuities. Elizabeth Makowski, *Canon Law and Cloistered Women: Periculoso and Its Commentators, 1298–1545* (Washington, D.C.: Catholic University of America Press, 1977). Walter Simons, *Cities of Ladies: Beguine Communities in the Medieval Low Countries, 1200–1565* (Philadelphia: University of Pennsylvania Press, 2001). Herbert Grundmann, *Religiöse Bewegungen im Mittelalter. Untersuchungen über die geschichtlichen Zusammenhänge zwischen der Ketzerei, den Bettelorden und der religiösen Frauenbewegung im 12. und 13. Jahrhundert und über die geschichtlichen Grundlagen der deutschen Mystik,* 2d ed. (Darmstadt: Wissenschaftliche Buchgesellschaft, 1961).

4. Caroline Walker Bynum, *Holy Feast and Holy Fast: The Religious Significance of Food to Medieval Women* (Berkeley: University of California Press, 1987); and *Jesus as Mother: Studies in the Spirituality of the High Middle Ages* (Berkeley: University of California Press, 1982).

5. On "Diskursgeschichte als Ereignisgeschichte," see Susanna Burghartz, *Zeiten der Reinheit—Orte der Unzucht: Ehe und Sexualität in Basel während der Frühen Neuzeit* (Paderborn: Schöningh Verlag, 1999)

6. On the conceptual challenges and promises of this type of approach, see Joel F. Harrington and Helmut Walser Smith, "Confessionalization, Community, and State Building in Germany, 1555–1870," *Journal of Modern History* 69, no. 1 (March 1997): 77–101. The authors do not include either gender or sexuality in their discussion.

7. Hull, 333–59.

8. Hull, 360–71, 403–4.

9. Christl Knauer, *Frauen unter dem Einfluss von Kirche und Staat* (Munich, 1995), 453.

10. Knauer, 461.

11. Among others, Dagmar Herzog, *Intimacy and Exclusion: Religious Politics in Pre-Revolutionary Baden* (Princeton: Princeton University Press, 1996), Jonathan Sperber, *Popular Catholicism in Nineteenth-Century Germany* (Princeton: Princeton University Press, 1984), David Blackbourn, *Marpingen: Apparitions of the Virgin Mary in Bismarckian Germany* (New York: Oxford University Press, 1993).

12. Helga Schnabel-Schüle, "Vierzig Jahre Konfessionalisierungsforschung—eine Standortbestimmung," in *Konfessionalisierung und Region,* ed. Peer Frieß and Rolf Kießling (Constance: Universitätsverlag Konstanz, 1999), 23–40.

13. David Lederer, *Reforming the Spirit: Society, Madness and Suicide in Central Europe, 1517–1809* (Ph.D. diss., New York University, 1995), 70, fn. 156.

Bibliography

ARCHIVAL SOURCES

Stadtarchiv München
    Bestand "Stadtgericht"
        Gerichtsbücher des Oberrichters
        Oberrichteramtsprotokolle
        Pueßordnung 1587
    Ratsprotokolle/Stadtschreiberserie
    Ratsprotokolle/Unterrichterserie
    Kammerratsprotokolle
    Zimelie 11
    Zimelie 16
    Zimelie 29
    Zimelie 52
    Steueramt 630
    Bürgermeister und Rat: Mandate, Spezialmandate, Dekrete
    Ratsberichtsprotokolle
    Wohltätigkeitsstiftungen
    Einwohneramt Nr. 195

Bayerisches Hauptstaatsarchiv, München
    Klosterliteralien Englische Fräulein
    Klosterliteralien Ridlerkloster
    Klosterliteralien Pütrichkloster
    Bestand "Angerkloster"
    Angerkloster KL 16
    GR Fasz. 321
    GR Fasz. 322, Tomus "Leichtfertigkeit und Gotteslästerung betr."
    GL 68 B
    HL "Freising"
    Äußeres Archiv 4115
    MK 221306

Diözesanarchiv des Erzbistums München-Freising
Offizialatsprotokolle
Kirchenbücher Unser Lieben Frauen, Trauungen 1624–1662
Generalien 1501–1650
Geistliche Raths-Missiv Protokolle
Klosterliteralien
Archiv des Klosters Reutberg
Schublade 59/9
Schublade 63/6

Archiv der Englischen Fräulein München-Nymphenburg Tobias Lohner. *Das Gottselige Leben und die fürtrefflichen Tugenden Donna Maria Della Guardia* (1689), Maschinenschriftliche Kopie.

PRINTED PRIMARY SOURCES

Albertinus, Aegidius. *Haußpolizey.* Munich, 1602.

Bairische Lanndtsordnung, Ingolstadt, 1553.

Bittrich voll des himmlischen Manna und Süssen Morgen-Thau, Das ist: Historischer Discurs/Von dem Ursprung, Fundation, Auffnamb/glücklichen Fortgang/ Tugend-Wandel/und andern denckwürdigen Sachen Deß Löbl. Frauen-Closters/ Ordens der dritten Regul des heil. Francisci/Bey Sanct Christophen im Bittrich genannt/In der Chur-Fürstlichen Residenz-Stadt München mit Erlaubnis der Obern. Munich: Johann Lucas Straud, 1721.

Briefe von, an und über Caritas Pirckheimer. Ed. Josef Pfanner. Landshut: Solanus-Druck, 1966.

Des hochheiligen, ökumenischen und allgemeinen Concils von Trient Canones und Beschlüsse. Ed. Wilhelm Smets. Bielefeld: Velhagen und Klasing, 1869; reprint, erschienen im Sankt Meinrad Verlag für Theologie, Christine Maria Esser, Sinzing, 1989.

Die Denkwürdigkeiten der Äbtissin Caritas Pirckheimer. Ed. Frumentius Renner. St. Ottilien: Eos-Verlag, 1982.

Friesenegger, Maurus. *Tagebuch aus dem 30jährigen Krieg.* Ed. P. Willibald Mathäser. Munich: Süddeutscher Verlag, 1627–48. Reprint, Munich: Hugendubel, 1996.

Geminianus Monacensis. *Geistlicher Weeg-Weiser gen Himmel/Catholische Predigen über alle Sonn: und Feyrtägliche Evangelia.* Gedruckt und verlegt/Durch Johann Jaecklin/Churfuerstlichen Freysingischen und Regenspurgischen Hof-Buchdruckern. Munich, 1679.

Hueber, Fortunatus. *Lob-, Danck-, und Ehrenreiche Gedaechtnuss/Von dem Geist- und Loeblichen Jungfrau-Closter des III. Ordens S. Francisci Bey den zweyen Heiligen Joannes, dem Tauffer und dem Evangelisten, Auff der Stiegen (deren Ridler genamselt) zu München in Bayern an der Chur-Fürstlichen Residenz.* Munich: Sebastian Rauch, 1695.

Kirchhuber, Barnabas. *Der Gnaden-und Tugend-reiche Anger/Das ist: Die sonder-*

bare grosse Gnaden/tugendsame Leben/vnd andere denck-vnd lob-würdige Begebenheiten/So in dem Uhr-alten vnd hochberühmeten Gotts-Hauß/vnd jungfräulichen Closter S. Clarae Ordens in München bey S. Jacob am ANGER biß in die 480. Jahr verschlossen/vnd verborgen gelegen/nunmehr angemerckt vnd eröffnen. Getruckt zu München bey Maria Magdalena Rauchin/Wittib. Im Jahr 1701.

Landrecht/ Policey: Gerichts- Malefiz und andere Ordnungen Der Fürstenthumben Obern und Nidern Bayrn. Munich: 1616.

Landts und Policey Ordnung der Fürstenthumben Obern und Nidern Bayrn. Munich: 1616.

Pastorale ad Usum Romanum Accomodatum. Canones et Ritus Ecclesiasticos qui ad Sacramentorum administrationem aliaque Pastorali Officia in Diocesi Frisingensi, rite obeunda pertinent complectens. Ingolstadt: Ex Officina Ederiana apud Andream Angermanium, 1612.

Reformation der Bayrischen Landrecht nach Christi unsers Haylmachers Geburd . . . [1518] . . . widerumben nachgedruckt. Munich: 1588.

Wening, Michael. *Historico-Topographica descriptio. Das ist: Beschreibung deß Churfürsten- und Hertzogthumbs Ober- und Nidern Bayrn.* Getruckt zu München bey Johann Lucas Straub, 1701–1796.

Westenrieder, Lorenz. *Beschreibung der Haupt- und Residenzstadt München im gegenwärtigen Zustand.* Munich: 1782. Reprint, Munich, 1984.

SECONDARY SOURCES

Achermann, Hansjakob. *Die Katakombenheiligen und ihre Translationen in der schweizerischen Quart des Bistums Konstanz.* Stans: Hist. Verein Nidwal, 1979.

Amussen, Susan. *An Ordered Society: Gender and Class in Early Modern England.* Oxford and New York: Basil Blackwell, 1988.

Andaya, Barbara Watson. *Other Pasts: Women, Gender, and History in Early Modern Southeast Asia.* Honolulu: Center for Southeast Asian Studies, University of Hawaii, 2000.

Andersson, Christiane. "Von 'Metzen' und 'Dirnen'. Frauenbilder in Kriegsdarstellungen der Frühen Neuzeit." In *Landsknechte, Soldatenfrauen und Nationalkrieger. Militär, Krieg und Geschlechterordnung im Historischen Wandel,* ed. Karen Hagemann and Ralf Pröve. Frankfurt am Main: Campus Verlag, 1998.

Asch, Ronald G., and Adolf M. Birke, eds. *Princes, Patronage, and Nobility: The Court at the Beginning of the Modern Age, c. 1450–1650.* Oxford: Oxford University Press, 1991.

Atkinson, Clarissa W. "Precious Balm in a Fragile Glass: The Ideology of Virginity in the Later Middle Ages." *Journal of Family History* 8 (1983): 131–43.

Ay, Karl-Ludwig. *Land und Fürst im alten Bayern.* Regensburg: Verlag Friedrich Pustet, 1988.

Backmann, Sibylle, Hans-Jörg Künast, B. Ann Tlusty, Sabine Ullmann, eds.

Ehrkonzepte in der Frühen Neuzeit. Identitäten und Abgrenzungen. Berlin: Akademie Verlag, 1998.

Bary, Roswitha von. *Herzogsdienst und Bürgerfreiheit: Verfassung und Verwaltung der Stadt München im Mittelalter 1158–1560.* Munich: Hugendubel, 1997.

Beck, Rainer. "Illegitimität und voreheliche Sexualität auf dem Land." In *Kultur der einfachen Leute: Bayerisches Volksleben vom 16. bis zum 19. Jahrhundert,* ed. Richard van Dülmen, 112–50. Munich: C. H. Beck, 1983.

———. *Naturale Ökonomie. Unterfinning: Bäuerliche Wirtschaft in einem oberbayrischen Dorf des 18. Jahrhunderts.* Munich, 1989.

Behringer, Wolfgang. "Mörder, Diebe, Ehebrecher: Verbrechen und Strafen in Kurbayern vom 16. bis 18. Jahrhundert." In *Kultur der einfachen Leute,* ed. Richard van Dülmen, 85–132. Munich: C. H. Beck, 1983.

———. *Hexenverfolgung in Bayern: Volksmagie und Staatsräson in der Frühen Neuzeit.* Munich: Oldenbourg Verlag, 1997.

———. *Witchcraft Persecution in Bavaria: Popular Magic, Religious Zealotry and Reason of the State in Early Modern Europe.* Cambridge: Cambridge University Press, 1987.

Bell, Rudolph. *Holy Anorexia.* Chicago: University of Chicago Press, 1985.

Bennett, Judith M., and Amy Froide, eds. *Singlewomen in the European Past, 1250–1800.* Philadelphia: University of Pennsylvania Press, 1999.

Bilinkoff, Jodi. *The Avila of Saint Teresa.* Ithaca: Cornell University Press, 1989.

Bireley, Robert. *Maximilian von Bayern, Adam Contzen S.J. und die Gegenreformation in Deutschland 1624–1635.* Göttingen: Vandenhoeck und Ruprecht, 1975.

Blackbourn, David. *Marpingen: Apparitions of the Virgin Mary in Bismarckian Germany.* New York: Oxford University Press, 1993.

Blom, Ida, Karen Hagemann, and Catherine Hall, eds. *Gendered Nations: Nationalism and Gender Order in the Long Nineteenth Century.* Oxford: Berg, 2000.

Bossy, John. "The Counter-Reformation and the People of Catholic Europe." *Past and Present* 47 (May 1970): 51–70.

Bourdieu, Pierre. *An Outline of a Theory of Practice.* Cambridge: Cambridge University Press, 1977.

———. "Ökonomisches Kapital, kulturelles Kapital, soziales Kapital." In *Soziale Ungleichheiten,* ed. R. Kreckel, 183–98. Göttingen: Schwartz, 1983.

Breit, Stefan. *"Leichtfertigkeit" und ländliche Gesellschaft: Voreheliche Sexualität in der frühen Neuzeit.* Munich: Oldenbourg Verlag, 1991.

Brown, Peter. *Cult of the Saints: Its Rise and Function in Latin Christianity.* Chicago: University of Chicago Press, 1981.

———. *The Body and Society: Men, Women, and Sexual Renunciation in Early Christianity.* New York: Columbia University Press, 1988.

Brundage, James. *Law, Sex and Christian Society in Medieval Europe.* Chicago: University of Chicago Press, 1987.

Bruneau, Marie Florine. *Women Mystics Confront the Modern World.* Albany: State University of New York Press, 1998.

Buchinger, Johann Nepomuk. "Erinnerungen an die Gründung und erste Verbreitung des Instituts der englischen Fräulein in Bayern." *Oberbayerisches Archiv für vaterländische Geschichte* 17 (1857): 116–73.

Burghartz, Susanna. "Jungfräulichkeit oder Reinheit? Zur Änderung von Argumentationsmustern vor dem Basler Ehegericht im 16. und 17. Jahrhundert." In *Dynamik der Tradition,* ed. Richard van Dülmen, 13–40. Frankfurt am Main: Fischer, 1992.

———. "Rechte Jungfrauen oder unverschämte Töchter? Zur weiblichen Ehre im 16. Jahrhundert." In *Frauengeschichte—Geschlechtergeschichte,* ed. Karin Hausen and Heide Wunder, 173–83. Frankfurt am Main: Campus Verlag, 1992.

———. "Tales of Seduction, Tales of Violence: Argumentative Strategies before the Basel Marriage Court." *German History* 17, no. 1 (1999): 41–56.

———. *Zeiten der Reinheit—Orte der Unzucht: Ehe und Sexualität in Basel während der Frühen Neuzeit.* Paderborn: Schöningh Verlag, 1999.

Burgmair, Wolfgang. "Das Pütrich-Kloster in München." In *Festschrift für Prof. Dr. Hans Rall.* Munich: "Die Gurke," 1987.

Bynum, Caroline Walker. *Jesus as Mother: Studies in the Spirituality of the High Middle Ages.* Berkeley: University of California Press, 1982.

———. *Holy Feast and Holy Fast: The Religious Significance of Food to Medieval Women.* Berkeley: University of California Press, 1987.

———. *Fragmentation and Redemption: Essays on Gender and the Human Body in Medieval Religion.* New York: Zone Books, 1992.

Carlson, Cindy L., and Angela Jane Weisl, eds. *Constructions of Widowhood and Virginity in the Middle Ages.* The New Middle Ages series, ed. Bonnie Wheeler. New York: St. Martin's Press, 1999.

Cavallo, Sandra, and Simona Cerutti. "Female Honor and the Social Control of Reproduction in Piedmont between 1600–1800." In *Sex and Gender in Historical Perspective,* ed. Edward Muir and Guido Ruggiero, 73–109. Baltimore: Johns Hopkins University Press, 1990.

Chambers, Mary Katherine Elizabeth. *The Life of Mary Ward in Two Volumes.* Ed. Henry James Coleridge. 2 vols. London: Burns and Oates, 1882, 1885.

Chojnacki, Stanley. "Dowries and Kinsmen in Early Renaissance Venice." *Journal of Interdisciplinary History* 5 (1975): 571–600.

———. "The Power of Love: Wives and Husbands in Late Medieval Venice." In *Women and Power in the Middle Ages,* ed. Mary Erler and Maryanne Kowaleski, 126–48. Athens: University of Georgia Press, 1988.

———. "The Most Serious Duty: Motherhood, Gender, and Patrician Culture in Renaissance Venice." In *Refiguring Woman: Perspectives on Gender and the Italian Renaissance,* ed. Marilyn Migiel and Juliana Schiesari, 133–54. Ithaca and London: Cornell University Press, 1991.

Ciammitti, Luisa. "One Saint Less: The Story of Angela Mellini, a Bolognese Seamstress (1667–17[?])." In *Sex and Gender in Historical Perspective,* ed. Edward Muir and Guido Ruggiero, 141–76. Baltimore: Johns Hopkins University Press, 1990.

Cohen, Sherrill. *The Evolution of Women's Asylums since 1500: From Refuges for*

Ex-Prostitutes to Shelters for Battered Women. New York and Oxford: Oxford University Press, 1992.

Conrad, Anne. *Zwischen Kloster und Welt: Ursulinen und Jesuitinnen in der katholischen Reformbewegung des 16./17. Jahrhunderts.* Mainz: Verlag Philipp von Zabern, 1991.

———, ed. *"In Christo ist weder man noch weyb": Frauen in der Zeit der Reformation und der katholischen Reform.* Münster: Aschendorff, 1999.

Cover, Jeanne. *Love: The Driving Force.* Milwaukee: Marquette University Press, 1997.

Coyne Kelly, Kathleen, and Marina Leslie, eds. *Menacing Virgins: Representing Virginity in the Middle Ages and Renaissance.* Newark and London: Associated University Presses, 1999.

Davis, Natalie Zemon. *Society and Culture in Early Modern France.* Stanford, Calif.: Stanford University Press, 1975.

———. "Ghosts, Kin, and Progeny: Some Features of Family Life in Early Modern France." *Daedalus* 106, no. 2 (1977): 87–114.

de Certeau, Michel. *The Practice of Everyday Life.* Berkeley: University of California Press, 1984.

Deneke, Bernward. *Hochzeit.* Munich: Prestel-Verlag, 1971.

Deutinger, Martin von, ed. *Die älteren Matrikeln des Bisthums Freysing.* Munich: Verlag der erzbischöflichen Kanzley, 1849.

Dorn, Ernst. *Der Sang der Wittenberger Nachtigall in München. Eine Geschichte des Protestantismus in Bayerns Hauptstadt in der Zeit der Reformation und Gegenreformation des 16. Jahrhunderts.* Munich, 1917.

Dülmen, Richard van. *Frauen vor Gericht: Kindsmord in der frühen Neuzeit.* Frankfurt am Main: Fischer Taschenbuchverlag, 1991.

Dürr, Renate. *Mägde in der Stadt. Das Beispiel Schwäbisch Hall in der Frühen Neuzeit.* Frankfurt am Main and New York: Campus Verlag, 1995.

Elias, Norbert. *Über den Prozeß der Zivilisation: Soziogenetische und psychogenetische Untersuchungen.* Bern and Munich: Francke, 1969.

Elm, Susanna. *Virgins of God: The Making of Asceticism in Late Antiquity.* Oxford: Oxford University Press, 1994.

Engels, Friedrich. *Der Ursprung der Familie, des Privateigentums und des Staates.* 19th ed. Stuttgart: Dietz, 1920.

Farmer, Sharon. "'It Is Not Good That [Wo]Man Should Be Alone': Elite Responses to Singlewomen in High Medieval Paris." In *Singlewomen in the European Past, 1250–1800,* ed. Judith M. Bennett and Amy Froide, 82–105. Philadelphia: University of Pennsylvania Press, 1999.

Farr, James. "The Pure and Disciplined Body: Hierarchy, Morality, and Symbolism in France during the Catholic Reformation." *Journal of Interdisciplinary History* 21, no. 3 (1991): 391–414.

———. *Authority and Sexuality in Early Modern Burgundy, 1550–1730.* New York: Oxford University Press, 1995.

Ferrante, Lucia. "Honor Regained: Women in the Casa Del Soccorso Di San Paolo in Sixteenth-Century Bologna." In *Sex and Gender in Historical Per-*

spective, ed. Edward Muir and Guido Ruggiero, 46–72. Baltimore: Johns Hopkins University Press, 1990.

―――. "Marriage and Women's Subjectivity in a Patrilineal System: The Case of Early Modern Bologna." In *Gender, Kinship, and Power: A Comparative and Interdisciplinary History,* ed. Mary Jo Maynes, Ann Waltner, Birgitte Soland, and Ulrike Strasser, 115–31. New York and London: Routledge, 1996.

Fischer, Anton. "Die Verwaltungsorganisation Münchens im 16. und 17. Jahrhundert." Diss., München, 1951.

Fleischmann, Philipp J. "Sozialtopographie einer Residenzstadt. Die Münchner Sozial- und Wohnstruktur am Vorabend des Dreißigjährigen Krieges." *Oberbayerisches Archiv* 117/118 (1993): 261–88.

Foucault, Michel. *The History of Sexuality.* Vol. 1, *An Introduction.* Trans. Robert Hurley. New York: Vintage Books, 1990.

―――. *Power/Knowledge: Selected Interviews and Other Writings.* New York: Pantheon Books, 1980.

Friedrichs, Christopher. *Urban Society in an Age of War: Nördlingen, 1580–1720.* Princeton: Princeton University Press, 1979.

―――. *The Early Modern City, 1450–1750.* London and New York: Longman, 1995.

―――. "Capitalism, Mobility, and Class Formation in the Early Modern German City." *Past and Present* 69 (November 1975): 24–49.

Gatz, Johannes. "Franziskanerkloster St. Antonius in München." In *Bavaria Franciscana Antiqua,* vol. 3, ed. bayr. Franziskanerprovinz, 17–136. Munich: Lentner'sche Buchhandlung, 1957.

―――. "Klarissen-Kloster St. Jakob am Anger in München." In *Bavaria Franciscana Antiqua,* ed. bayr. Franziskanerprovinz, 195–272. Munich: Lentner'sche Buchhandlung, 1957.

Gebele, Joseph. *Das Schulwesen der königlich bayrischen Haupt- und Residenzstadt München.* Munich: M. Kellerer's h. b. Hof-, Buch-, und Kunsthandlung, 1896.

Ginzburg, Carlo. *The Cheese and the Worms: The Cosmos of a Sixteenth-Century Miller.* Trans. John Tedeschi and Anne Tedeschi. Baltimore: Johns Hopkins University Press, 1980.

―――. "Mikro-Historie. Zwei oder drei Dinge, die ich von ihr weiß." *Historische Anthropologie* 1 (1993): 169–92.

Giorgio, Michela De, and Christine Klapisch Zuber, eds. *Storia del matrimonio.* Rome and Bari: Laterza, 1996.

Gleixner, Ulrike. *"Das Mensch" und "der Kerl." Die Konstruktion von Geschlecht in Unzuchtsverfahren der Frühen Neuzeit (1700–1760).* Frankfurt am Main and New York: Campus Verlag, 1994.

Grisar, Josef. *Maria Wards Institut vor römischen Kongregationen (1616–1630).* Vol. 27, *Miscellanea Historiae Pontificiae.* Rome: Pontifica Universita Gregoriana, 1966.

Grundmann, Herbert. *Religiöse Bewegungen im Mittelalter. Untersuchungen über die geschichtlichen Zusammenhänge zwischen der Ketzerei, den Bettelorden und der religiösen Frauenbewegung im 12. und 13. Jahrhundert und über die geschichtlichen Grundlagen der deutschen Mystik.* 2d ed. Darmstadt: Wissenschaftliche Buchgesellschaft, 1961.

Hanawalt, Barbara. "Patriarchal Provisions for Widows and Orphans in Medieval London." In *Gender, Kinship, and Power: A Comparative and Interdisciplinary History,* ed. Mary Jo Maynes, Ann Waltner, Birgitte Soland, and Ulrike Strasser, 201–13. New York and London: Routledge, 1996.

Hanley, Sarah. "Engendering the State: Family Formation and State Building in Early Modern Europe." *French Historical Review* 16, no. 1 (spring 1989): 4–27.

———. "Social Sites of Political Practice in France: Lawsuits, Civil Rights, and the Separation of Power in Domestic and State Government." *American Historical Review* 102, no. 1 (February 1997): 27–52.

Harline, Craig. "Actives and Contemplatives: The Female Religious of the Low Countries before and after Trent." *Catholic Historical Review* 81, no. 4 (1995): 541–67.

Harrington, Joel. *Reordering Marriage and Society in Reformation Germany.* Cambridge, England, and New York: Cambridge University Press, 1995.

Harrington, Joel, and Helmut Walser Smith. "Confessionalization, Community, and State Building in Germany, 1555–1870." *Journal of Modern History* 69, no. 1 (March 1997): 77–101.

Haude, Sigrun. "War—A Fortuitous Occasion for Social Disciplining and Political Centralization? The Case of Bavaria under Maximilian I." Paper delivered at Sixteenth Century Studies Conference, San Antonio, Texas, October 2002.

Hecker, Joachim. "Um Glaube und Recht: Die fürstliche Stadt 1505 bis 1561." In *Geschichte der Stadt München,* ed. Richard Bauer, 148–65. Munich: C. H. Beck, 1992.

Hefner, Otto Titan. "Original Bilder aus der Vorzeit Münchens." *Oberbairisches Archiv für vaterländische Geschichte* 13 (1852): 3–101.

Helmholz, Richard, ed. *Canon Law in Protestant Lands.* Berlin: Duncker and Humblot, 1992.

Heres, Horst, ed. *Kulturgeschichte des Dachauer Landes.* Vol. 10. Dachau: Museumsverein Dachau e.V., 1994.

Herzog, Dagmar. *Intimacy and Exclusion: Religious Politics in Pre-Revolutionary Baden.* Princeton: Princeton University Press, 1996.

Heydenreuter, Reinhard. *Der landesherrliche Hofrat unter Herzog und Kurfürst Maximilian I. von Bayern (1598–1651).* Munich: C. H. Beck, 1981.

———. "Der Magistrat als Befehlsempfänger: Die Disziplinierung der Stadtobrigkeit 1579–1651." In *Geschichte der Stadt München,* ed. Richard Bauer, 189–210. Munich: C. H. Beck, 1992.

———. *Herrschen durch Strafen: Zur Entwicklung des frühneuzeitlichen Staates im Herzogtum und Kurfürstentum Bayern (1150–1650)* (forthcoming).

Hoefer, M. Le Dr., ed. *Nouvelle biographie général depuis les temps plus reculés jusqu'à jours. Tome Trente-Sixième.* Paris: MM. Firmin Didot, 1865.

Hsia, R. Po-Chia. *The World of Catholic Renewal, 1540–1770.* New Approaches to European History series, ed. William Beik, T. C. W. Blanning, and R. W. Scribner. Cambridge: Cambridge University Press, 1998.

Hubensteiner, Benno. *Vom Geist des Barock: Kultur und Frömmigkeit im alten Bayern.* Reprint, Munich: Süddeutscher Verlag, 1978.

―――. *Bayerische Geschichte.* 1992. Reprint, Munich: Süddeutscher Verlag, 1994.

Hufnagel, Max. "Das Franziskanerinnenkloster der Pütrichschwestern z. hl. Christophorus in München." In *Bavaria Franciscana Antiqua,* ed. bayr. Franziskanerprovinz, 237–307. Munich: Lentner'sche Buchhandlung, 1957.

―――. "Das Franziskanerinnenkloster der Ridlerschwestern zu St. Johannes auf der Stiege in München." In *Bavaria Franciscana Antiqua,* ed. bayr. Franziskanerprovinz, 309–51. Munich: Lentner'sche Buchhandlung, 1957.

Hughes, Diane Owen. "From Brideprice to Dowry in Mediterranean Europe." *Journal of Family History* 3 (1978): 262–96.

Huhn, Adalbert. *Geschichte des Spitales, der Kirche und der Pfarrei zum heiligen Geiste in München.* 2 vols. Munich: Verlag der JJ Lentnerschen Buchhandlung, 1893.

Hull, Isabel. *Sexuality, State, and Civil Society in Germany, 1700–1815.* Ithaca: Cornell University Press, 1996.

John, Sabine. "'. . . Laß mich ein, Du Allerliebstes mein': Von der Christkindverehrung im Münchner Pütrich-Kloster." *Bayernspiegel* 6 (1991): 22–23.

―――. "'. . . mit Behutsambkeit vnd Reverentz zu tractieren': Die Katakombenheiligen im Münchner Pütrichkloster—Arbeit und Frömmigkeit." *Bayerisches Jahrbuch für Volkskunde* (1995): 1–34.

Kamen, H. *The Phoenix and the Flame: Catalonia and the Counter Reformation.* New Haven: Yale University Press, 1993.

Karant-Nunn, Susan. "'Kinder, Küche, Kirche': Social Ideology in the Wedding Sermons of Johannes Mathesius." In *Germania Illustrata: Essays on Early Modern Germany Presented to Gerald Strauss,* ed. Andrew C. Fix and Susan C. Karant-Nunn, 121–40. Kirksville, Mo.: Sixteenth Century Journal, 1992.

Karras, Ruth Mazzo. "Sex and the Singlewoman." In *Singlewomen in the European Past, 1250–1800,* ed. Judith M. Bennett and Amy Froide, 127–45. Philadelphia: University of Pennsylvania Press, 1999.

Kelly, Joan. "Did Women Have a Renaissance?" In *Women, History, and Theory: The Essays of Joan Kelly,* 19–50. Chicago: University of Chicago Press, 1984.

King, Margaret. *Women of the Renaissance.* Chicago: University of Chicago Press, 1991.

Klapisch-Zuber, Christiane. *Women, Family and Ritual in Renaissance Italy.* Trans. Lydia G. Cochrane. Chicago: University of Chicago Press, 1985.

―――. "Zacharias or the Ousted Father: Nuptial Rites in Tuscany between Giotto and the Council of Trent." In *Women, Family and Ritual in Renaissance Italy,* 178–212. Trans. Lydia G. Cochrane. Chicago: University of Chicago Press, 1985.

―――. "The Griselda Complex: Dowry and Marriage Gifts in the Quattrocento." In *Women, Family and Ritual in Renaissance Italy,* 213–46. Trans. Lydia G. Cochrane. Chicago: University of Chicago Press, 1985.

Knauer, Christl. *Frauen unter dem Einfluss von Kirche und Staat.* Munich: Kommissionsverlag UNI-Druck, 1995.

Kobolt, Anton Maria. *Baierisches Gelehrtenlexikon.* Landshut, 1795.

Köhler, Mathilde. *Maria Ward: Ein Frauenschicksal des 17. Jahrhunderts.* Munich: Kösel-Verlag, 1985.

Köhler, Walther. *Zürcher Ehegericht und Genfer Konsistorium.* 2 vols. Leipzig: M. Heinsius Nachfolger, 1932, 1942.

Koller, Fritz. *Der Eid im Münchner Stadtrecht des Mittelalters.* Munich: R. Pflaum, 1953.

Kowaleski, Maryanne. "Singlewomen in Medieval and Early Modern Europe: The Demographic Perspective." In *Singlewomen in the European Past, 1250–1800,* ed. Judith M. Bennett and Amy Froide, 38–81. Philadelphia: University of Pennsylvania Press, 1999.

Kraus, Andreas. *Maximilian I: Bayerns großer Kurfürst.* Graz: Verlag Styria, 1990.

Kroener, Bernhard. "'. . . und ist der jammer nit zu beschreiben'. Geschlechterbeziehungen und Überlebensstrategien in der Lagergesellschaft des Dreißigjährigen Krieges." In *Landsknechte, Soldatenfrauen und Nationalkrieger. Militär, Krieg und Geschlechterordnung im Historischen Wandel,* ed. Karen Hagemann and Ralf Pröve, 279–96. Frankfurt am Main: Campus Verlag, 1998.

Kuehn, Thomas. *Law, Family and Women: Toward a Legal Anthropology of Renaissance Italy.* Chicago: University of Chicago Press, 1991.

Labalme, Patricia, ed. *Beyond Their Sex: Learned Women of the European Past.* New York: New York University Press, 1980.

Lammert, Georg. *Zur Geschichte des bürgerlichen Lebens und der öffentlichen Gesundheitspflege sowie insbesondere der Sanitätsanstalten in Süddeutschland.* Regensburg, 1880.

Lan, David. *Guns and Rain: Guerrillas and Spirit Mediums in Zimbabwe.* Berkeley: University of California Press, 1985.

Lanzinner, Maximilian. *Fürst, Räte und Landstände: Die Entstehung der Zentralbehörden in Bayern 1511–1598.* Göttingen: Vandenhoeck und Ruprecht, 1980.

Laven, Mary. *Virgins of Venice: Broken Vows and Cloistered Lives in the Renaissance Convent.* New York: Viking, 2003.

———. "Venetian Nunneries in the Counter-Reformation, 1550–1630." Diss., University of Leicester, 1997.

Lederer, David. *Madness, Religion and the State in Early Modern Europe: A Bavarian Beacon.* Cambridge: Cambridge University Press, 2006.

———. "Reforming the Spirit: Confession, Madness and Suicide in Bavaria, 1517–1809." Diss., New York University, 1995.

Leonard, Amy. *Nails in the Wall: Catholic Nuns in Reformation Germany.* Chicago and London: University of Chicago Press, 2005.

———. "Nails in the Wall: Dominican Nuns in Reformation Strasbourg." Diss., University of California, Berkeley, 1999.

———. "Nuns as Whores: A Common Trope." Manuscript in preparation.

———. "Female Religious Orders." In *A Companion to the World of the Reformation,* ed. R. Po-Chia Hsia, 237–54. Oxford: Blackwell, 2003.

Lerner, Robert. *The Heresy of the Free Spirit in the Later Middle Ages.* Berkeley: University of California Press, 1972.

Liebhart, Wilhelm. "Die Seelen haben einen großen Trost verloren . . .': Die 'gottselige' Klara Hortulana Empacher im München Angerkloster." *Amperland* 31 (1995): 36–39.

Liebowitz, Ruth P. "Virgins in the Service of Christ: The Dispute over an Active Apostolate for Women during the Counter-Reformation." In *Women of Spirit: Female Leadership in the Jewish and Christian Tradition,* ed. Rosemary Ruether and Eleanor McLaughlin, 153–83. New York: Simon and Schuster, 1979.

Löffelmeier, Anton. "Die Ordnung für den Münchner Stadtoberrichter aus dem Jahre 1560." In *Quellen zur Verfassungs-, Sozial-, Wirtschaftsgeschichte Bayerischer Städte in Spätmittelalter und Früher Neuzeit,* ed. Elisabeth Lukas-Götz, Ferdinand Kramer, and Johannes Merz. Festgabe für Wilhelm Störmer. Munich: Kommission für bayerische Landesgeschichte, 1993.

Lombardi, Daniela. "Interventions by Church and State in Marriage Disputes in Sixteenth- and Seventeenth-Century Florence." In *Crime, Society, and the Law in Renaissance Italy,* ed. Trevor Dean and K. J. P. Lowe, 142–56. Cambridge: Cambridge University Press, 1994.

Makowski, Elizabeth. *Canon Law and Cloistered Women: Periculoso and Its Commentators, 1298–1545.* Ed. Kenneth Pennington. Studies in Medieval and Early Modern Canon Law, vol. 5. Washington, D.C.: Catholic University of America Press, 1997.

Malisch, Kurt. *Katholischer Absolutismus als Staatsräson, Ein Beitrag zur politischen Theorie Maximilians I .* Munich: Kommissionsverlag UNI-Druck, 1981.

Marshall, Sherrin, ed. *Women in Reformation and Counter-Reformation Europe.* Bloomington and Indianapolis: University of Indiana Press, 1989.

Maynes, Mary Jo. *Schooling for the People.* New York: Holmes and Meier, 1985.

McGuire, Brian Patrick. "Purgatory, the Communion of Saints, and Medieval Change." *Viator: Medieval and Renaissance Studies* 20 (1989): 61–84.

Mennell, Stephen. *Norbert Elias: Civilization and the Human Self-Image.* Oxford and New York: Blackwell, 1989.

Miller, Pavla. *Transformations of Patriarchy in the West, 1500–1900.* Bloomington: Indiana University Press, 1998.

Mitterauer, Michael. *Ledige Mütter. Zur Geschichte unehelicher Geburten in Europa.* Munich: C. H. Beck, 1983.

Monson, Craig. *Disembodied Voices: Music and Culture in an Early Modern Italian Convent.* Berkeley: University of California Press, 1995.

Monson, Craig, ed. *The Crannied Wall: Women, Religion, and the Arts in Early Modern Europe.* Ann Arbor: University of Michigan Press, 1992.

Moser, Hans. *Volksbräuche im geschichtlichen Wandel. Ergebnisse aus fünfzig Jahren volkskundlicher Quellenforschung.* Munich: Deutscher Kunstverlag, 1985.

———. "Aufriß zur Geschichte des Münchner Faschings." *Bayerisches Jahrbuch für Volkskunde* (1988): 39–60.

Moser-Rath, Elfriede. "Münchner Volksprediger der Barockzeit." *Bayerisches Jahrbuch für Volkskunde* (1958): 85–102.

Münch, Paul. "Die Obrigkeit im Vaterstand." *Daphnis* 11 (1982): 15–40.

Myers, David. *'Poor Sinning Folk': Confession and Conscience in Counter-Reformation Germany.* Ithaca: Cornell University Press, 1996.

Noble, David. *A World Without Women: The Christian Clerical Culture of Western Science.* New York: A. A. Knopf, 1992.

Oestreich, Gerhard. "Strukturprobleme des europäischen Absolutismus." *Vierteljahrschrift für Sozial- und Wirtschaftsgeschichte* 55 (1968): 319–47.

Om, Anton Freiherr von. "Einkleidung der Prinzessin Maria Anna Karolina im Clarissenkloster zu München (1719)." *Altbayerische Monatsschrift* 2 (1900): 143–48.

Peters, Henriette. *Mary Ward: Ihre Persönlichkeit und ihr Institut.* Vienna and Innsbruck: Tyrolia-Verlag, 1991.

Petroff, Elizabeth Alvida, ed. *Medieval Women's Visionary Literature.* New York: Oxford University Press, 1986.

Petschauer, Peter. *The Education of Women in Eighteenth-Century Germany: New Directions from the German Female Perspective.* Lewiston, N.Y.: E. Mellen Press, 1989.

Puff, Helmut. "'. . . ein schul / darinn wir allerlay Christliche tugend vnd zucht lernen.' Ein Vergleich zweier ehedidaktischer Schriften des 16. Jahrhunders." In *Geschlechterbeziehungen und Textfunktionen. Studien zu Eheschriften der Frühen Neuzeit,* ed. Rüdiger Schnell, 59–88. Tübingen: M. Niemeyer, 1998.

Rabb, Theodore K. *The Struggle for Stability in Early Modern Europe.* New York: Oxford University Press, 1975.

Raeff, Marc. *The Well-Ordered Police State: Social and Institutional Change through Law in the Germanies and Russia, 1600–1800.* New Haven: Yale University Press, 1983.

Rall, Hans, and Marga Rall. *Die Wittelsbacher in Lebensbildern.* Graz: Verlag Styria, Verlag Friedrich Pustet, 1986.

Rapley, Elizabeth. *The Dévotes: Women and Church in Seventeenth-Century France.* Montreal, Kingston, London, and Buffalo: McGill-Queen's University Press, 1990.

Rebel, Hermann. *Peasant Classes: The Bureaucratization of Property and Family Relations under Early Habsburg Absolutism, 1511–1636.* Princeton: Princeton University Press, 1983.

Reinhard, Wolfgang. "Zwang zur Konfessionalisierung? Prolegomena zu einer Theorie des konfessionellen Zeitalters." *Zeitschrift für historische Forschung* 10 (1983): 257–77.

Roeck, Bernd. "Bayern und der Dreißigjährige Krieg." *Geschichte und Gesellschaft* 17 (1991): 434–58.

Rogg, Matthias. "'Wol auff mit mir, du schoenes weyb.' Anmerkungen zur Konstruktion von Männlichkeit im Soldatenbild des 16. Jahrhunderts." In *Landsknechte, Soldatenfrauen und Nationalkrieger. Militär, Krieg und Geschlechterordnung im Historischen Wandel,* ed. Karen Hagemann and Ralf Pröve. Frankfurt am Main: Campus Verlag, 1998.

Röhrich, Lutz. *Lexikon der sprichwörtlichen Redensarten.* 3d ed. Freiburg, Basel, and Vienna: Herder Verlag, 1974.

Roper, Lyndal. "Luther: Sex, Marriage, and Motherhood." *History Today* 33 (1983): 33–38.

―――. *The Holy Household: Women and Morals in Reformation Augsburg.* Oxford: Clarendon Press, 1989.

―――. "Blood and Codpieces: Masculinity in the Early Modern Town." In *Oedipus and the Devil: Witchcraft, Sexuality and Religion in Early Modern Europe,* 107–24. New York and London: Routledge, 1994.

―――. "Will and Honour: Sex, Words, and Power in Augsburg Criminal Trials." In *Oedipus and the Devil: Witchcraft, Sexuality and Religion in Early Modern Europe,* 53–78. New York and London: Routledge, 1994.

―――. "Exorcism and the Theology of the Body." In *Oedipus and the Devil: Witchcraft, Sexuality and Religion in Early Modern Europe,* 171–98. New York and London: Routledge, 1994.

―――. *Oedipus and the Devil: Witchcraft, Sexuality and Religion in Early Modern Europe.* New York and London: Routledge, 1994.

Rösner-Zimmermann, Sylvia. "<Maria Ward> Vorkämpferin einer 'Emanzipation' der Frau in der Kirche." In *Aus Schwaben und Altbayern: Festschrift für Pankraz Fried zum 60. Geburtstag,* ed. Peter Fassl, Wilhelm Liebhardt, and Wolfgang Wüst, 203–17. Sigmaringen: Jan Thorbecke Verlag, 1991.

Rößler, Hans. *Geschichte und Strukturen der evangelischen Bewegung im Bistum Freising (1520–1571).* Nuremberg: Verein für Bayerische Kirchengeschichte, 1966.

Rublack, Ulinka. "Wench and Maiden: Women, War, and the Pictorial Function of the Feminine in German Cities in the Early Modern Period." *History Workshop Journal* 44 (1997): 1–21.

―――. *Magd, Metz' oder Mörderin. Frauen vor frühneuzeitlichen Gerichten.* Frankfurt am Main: Fischer-Taschenbuch-Verlag, 1998.

Ruggiero, Guido. *The Boundaries of Eros: Sex Crime and Sexuality in Renaissance Venice.* New York: Oxford University Press, 1985.

Safley, Thomas M. *Let No Man Put Asunder: The Control of Marriage in the German Southwest: A Comparative Study, 1550–1600.* Kirksville, Mo.: Sixteenth Century Journal, 1984.

Schattenhofer, Michael. *Beiträge zur Geschichte der Stadt München. Oberbairisches Archiv* 109, no. 1 (1984).

―――. *Die Mariensäule in München.* Munich: Schnell und Steiner, 1970.

Schellhass, Karl. "Band II: Felician Ninguarda als Nuntius 1578–1580." In *Der Dominikaner Felician Ninguarda und die Gegenreformation in Süddeutschland und Österreich 1560–1583.* Rome: W. Regenberg, 1939.

Schepers, Elisabeth. *Als der Bettel im Bayern abgeschafft werden sollte: Staatliche Armenfürsorge in Bayern im 16. und 17. Jahrhundert.* Regensburg: F. Pustet, 2000.

Schilling, Heinz. "Between the Territorial State and Urban Liberty: Lutheranism and Calvinism in the County of Lippe." In *The German People and the Reformation,* ed. R. Po-Chia Hsia, 263–84. Ithaca and London: Cornell University Press, 1988.

————. "Die Konfessionalisierung im Reich." *Historische Zeitschrift* 246 (1988): 1–45.

————. "'History of Crime' or 'History of Sin'? Some Reflections on the Social History of Early Modern Church Discipline." In *Politics and Society in Reformation Europe,* ed. E. I. Kouri and Tom Scott, 289–310. Houndmills, Basingstoke, Hampshire: McMillan, 1987.

————. "Die frühneuzeitliche Formierung und Disziplinierung von Ehe, Familie und Erziehung im Spiegel calvinistischer Kirchenratsprotokolle." In *Glaube und Eid. Treueformel, Glaubensbekenntnisse und Sozialdisziplinierung zwischen Mittelalter und Neuzeit,* ed. Paolo Prodi, 199–235. Munich: Oldenbourg, 1993.

Schmeller, Johann Andreas. *Bayerisches Wörterbuch.* Munich: Oldenbourg, 1983. Reprint of the second edition by G. Karl Fromman, Munich, 1872–77.

Schnabel-Schüle, Helga. "Vierzig Jahre Konfessionalisierungsforschung—Eine Standortbestimmung." In *Konfessionalisierung und Region,* ed. Peer Frieß and Rolf Kießling. Constance: Universitätsverlag Konstanz, 1999.

Schnell, Rüdiger. *Frauendiskurs, Männerdiskurs, Ehediskurs: Textsorten und Geschlechterkonzepte in Mittelalter und Früher Neuzeit.* Frankfurt am Main and New York: Campus Verlag, 1998.

————, ed. *Geschlechterbeziehungen und Textfunktionen. Studien zu Eheschriften der Frühen Neuzeit.* Tübingen: M. Niemeyer, 1998.

Schreiner, Klaus, and Gerd Schwerhoff, eds. *Verletzte Ehre: Ehrkonflikte in Gesellschaften des Mittelalters und der Frühen Neuzeit.* Cologne, Weimar, and Vienna: Böhlau, 1995.

Schröter, Michael. "Staatsbildung und Triebkontrolle. Zur Regulierung des Sexualverhaltens vom 13. bis 16. Jahrhundert." In *Macht und Zivilisation. Materialien zu Norbert Elias Zivilisationstheorie,* ed. P. Gleichmann, J. Goudsblom, and H. Korte, 641–60. Frankfurt am Main: Suhrkamp, 1984.

Schulenburg, Jane Tibbetts. *Forgetful of Their Sex: Female Sanctity and Society ca. 500–1100.* Chicago: University of Chicago Press, 1998.

Schultheiß, Werner. *Die Münchner Gewerbeverfassung im Mittelalter.* Munich: Beck'sche Verlagsbuchhandlung, 1936.

Schuster, Beate. *Die freien Frauen: Dirnen und Frauenhäuser im 15. und 16. Jahrhundert.* Frankfurt am Main: Campus Verlag, 1995.

Schuster, Peter. *Das Frauenhaus: Städtische Bordelle in Deutschland (1350–1600).* Paderborn, Munich, Vienna, and Zurich: Ferdinand Schöningh, 1992.

————. "Hinaus oder ins Frauenhaus. Weibliche Sexualität und gesellschaftliche Kontrolle an der Wende vom Mittelalter zur Neuzeit." In *Mit den Waffen der Justiz: Zur Kriminalitätsgeschichte des späten Mittelalters und der Frühen Neuzeit,* ed. Andreas Blauert and Gerd Schwerhoff, 17–31. Frankfurt am Main: Fischer Verlag, 1993.

Schwab, Ingo. "Zeiten der Teuerung: Versorgungprobleme in der zweiten Hälfte des 16. Jahrhunderts." In *Geschichte der Stadt München,* ed. Richard Bauer, 166–88. Munich, 1992.

Schwaiger, Georg, ed. *Monachium Sacrum: Festschrift zur 500-Jahr-Feier der Met-*

ropolitankirche zu Unserer Lieben Frau in München. Vol. 1. Munich: Deutscher Kunstverlag, 1994.

Scott, James. *Weapons of the Weak: Everyday Forms of Peasant Resistance.* New Haven: Yale University Press, 1985.

Scott, Joan. "Gender: A Useful Category of Historical Analysis." *American Historical Review* 91 (1986): 1053–75.

———. *Gender and the Politics of History.* New York: Columbia University Press, 1988.

Seed, Patricia. *To Love, Honor, and Obey in Colonial Mexico: Conflicts over Marriage Choice, 1574–1821.* Stanford: Stanford University Press, 1988.

Sibeth, Uwe. *Eherecht und Staatsbildung. Ehegesetzgebung und Eherechtssprechung in der Landgrafschaft Hessen(-Kassel) in der frühen Neuzeit.* Darmstadt and Marburg, 1994.

Silverblatt, Irene. "Women in States." *Annual Review of Anthropology* 17 (1988): 427–60.

Simons, Walter. *Cities of Ladies: Beguine Communities in the Medieval Low Countries, 1200–1565.* Philadelphia: University of Pennsylvania Press, 2001.

Soergel, Philip. *Wondrous in His Saints: Counter-Reformation Propaganda in Bavaria.* Berkeley: University of California Press, 1993.

Solleder, Fridolin. *München im Mittelalter.* Aalen: Scientia Verlag; reprint, Munich, 1938.

Sperber, Jonathan. *Popular Catholicism in Nineteenth-Century Germany.* Princeton: Princeton University Press, 1984.

Sperling, Jutta Gisela. *Convents and the Body Politic in Late Renaissance Venice.* Chicago: University of Chicago Press, 1999.

Stahleder, Helmuth. "Konsolidierung und Ausbau der bürgerlichen Stadt: München im 15. Jahrhundert." In *Geschichte der Stadt München,* ed. Richard Bauer, 120–47. Munich: C. H. Beck, 1992.

Stieve, Felix. *Das kirchliche Polizeiregiment in Baiern unter Maximilian I. 1595–1651.* Munich: Verlag der M. Rieger'schen Universitäts-Buchhandlung, 1876.

Strasser, Ulrike. "Brides of Christ, Daughters of Men: Nuremberg Poor Clares in Defense of Their Identity." *Magistra* 1 (winter 1995): 193–248.

———. "Bones of Contention: Cloistered Nuns, Decorated Relics, and the Contest Over Women's Place in the Public Sphere of Counterreformation Munich." *Archive for Reformation History* 90 (1999): 255–88.

———. "Vom 'Fall der Ehre' zum 'Fall der Leichtfertigkeit': Geschlechtsspezifische Aspekte der Konfessionalisierung am Beispiel Münchner Eheversprechens- und Alimentationsklagen (1592–1649)." In *Konfessio-nalisierung und Region,* ed. Peer Frieß and Rolf Kießling, 227–46. Constance: Universitätsverlag Konstanz, 1999.

Strayer, Joseph, ed. *Dictionary of the Middle Ages.* New York: Scribner, 1982.

Stuart, Kathy. *Defiled Trades and Social Outcasts: Honor and Ritual Pollution in Early Modern Germany.* Cambridge: Cambridge University Press, 1999.

Thomas, Yan. "The Division of the Sexes in Roman Law." In *A History of*

Women: From Ancient Goddesses to Christian Saints, ed. Pauline Schmitt Pantel, 83–137. Cambridge: Belknap Press of Harvard University Press, 1992.

Vauchez, André. *La Sainteté en Occident aux derniers siècles du Moyen Age.* Rome: École française de Rome; Paris: Diffusion de Boccard, 1981.

Walker, Claire. "Combining Martha and Mary: Gender and Work in Seventeenth-Century English Cloisters." *Sixteenth-Century Journal: The Journal of Early Modern Studies* 30, no. 2 (summer 1999): 397–418.

Watt, Jeffrey. *The Making of Modern Marriage: Matrimonial Control and the Rise of Sentiment in Neuchâtel, 1550–1800.* Ithaca and London: Cornell University Press, 1992.

Weaver, Elissa B. "Spiritual Fun: A Study of Sixteenth-Century Tuscan Convent Theater." In *Women in the Middle Ages and the Renaissance: Literary and Historical Perspectives,* ed. Mary Beth Rose, 173–205. Syracuse: Syracuse University Press, 1986.

Weber, Max. *Staatssoziologie.* Ed. Johannes Winckelmann. Berlin: Duncker und Humblot, 1956.

———. *Economy and Society.* Vol. 2. Ed. Guenther Roth and Claus Wittich. Berkeley: University of California Press, 1978.

———. *Die protestantische Ethik und der Geist des Kapitalismus.* Ed. Johannes Winckelmann. Gütersloh: Mohn, 1981–82.

Weinstein, Donald, and Rudolph M. Bell. *Saints and Society: The Two Worlds of Western Christendom, 1000–1700.* Chicago: University of Chicago Press, 1982.

Westphal, Siegrid. *Frau und lutherische Konfessionalisierung. Eine Untersuchung zum Fürstentum Pfalz-Neuburg, 1542–1614.* Frankfurt am Main: P. Lang, 1994.

Wiesner, Merry. "Women's Defense of Their Public Role." In *Women in the Middle Ages and the Renaissance,* ed. Mary Beth Rose, 1–27. Syracuse: Syracuse University Press, 1986.

———. *Working Women in Renaissance Germany.* New Brunswick, N.J.: Rutgers University Press, 1986.

———. "Gender and Power in Early Modern Europe: The Empire Strikes Back." In *The Graph of Sex and the German Text: Gendered Culture in Early Modern Germany, 1500–1700,* ed. Lynne Tatlock, 201–23. Amsterdam and Atlanta: Rodopi, 1994.

———. "Ideology Meets the Empire: Reformed Convents and the Reformation." In *Germania Illustrata: Essays on Early Modern Germany Presented to Gerald Strauss,* ed. Andrew C. Fix and Susan Karant-Nunn, 181–96. Kirksville, Mo.: Sixteenth Century Journal, 1992.

———. "War, Work, and Wealth: The Bases of Citizenship in Early Modern German Cities." In *Gender, Church, and State in Early Modern Germany,* 114–30. New York and London: Longman, 1998.

———. *Women and Gender in Early Modern Europe.* Cambridge: Cambridge University Press, 1993; reprint, 1998.

———. "Having Her Own Smoke: Employment and Independence for Single-women in Germany, 1400–1750." In *Singlewomen in the European Past,*

1250–1800, ed. Judith M. Bennett and Amy Froide, 192–216. Philadelphia: University of Pennsylvania Press, 1999.

Wiesner-Hanks, Merry. *Christianity and the Regulation of Sexuality: Regulating Desire, Reforming Practice.* London and New York: Routledge, 2000.

Winkler, Maria Theodolinde. *Maria Ward und das Institut der Englischen Fräulein in Bayern von der Gründung des Hauses in München bis zur Säkularisation desselben. 1626–1810.* Munich: Druck und Kommissionsverlag Carl Aug. Seyfried und Comp., 1926.

Wogan-Browne, Jocelyn. *Saints' Lives and Women's Literary Culture c. 1150–1300.* Oxford: Oxford University Press, 2001.

Wright, Mary. *Mary Ward's Institute: The Struggle for Identity.* Sydney: Crossing Press, 1997.

Wunder, Heide. *'Er ist die Sonn', sie ist der Mond.' Frauen in der Frühen Neuzeit.* Munich: C. H. Beck, 1992.

———. "Herrschaft und öffentliches Handeln von Frauen in der Frühen Neuzeit." In *Frauen in der Geschichte des Rechts: Von der Frühen Neuzeit bis zur Gegenwart,* ed. Ute Gerhard, 27–54. Munich: C. H. Beck, 1997.

Zarri, Gabriella. "Pieta' e profezia alle corti padane: le pie consigliere dei principi." In *Le sante vive. Profezie di corte e devozione femminile tra '400 e '500.* Turin: Rosenberg e Sellier, 1990.

———. "Le sante vive." In *Le sante vive. Profezie di corte e devozione femminile tra '400 e '500.* Turin: Rosenberg e Sellier, 1990.

———. "Ursula and Catherine: The Marriage of Virgins in the Sixteenth Century." In *Creative Women in Medieval and Early Modern Italy: A Religious and Artistic Renaissance,* ed. Ann Matter and John Coakley, 237–78. Philadelphia: University of Pennsylvania Press, 1994.

———. "Gender, Religious Institutions and Social Discipline: The Reform of the Regulars." In *Gender and Society in Renaissance Italy,* ed. Judith Brown and Robert C. Davis, 193–212. London and New York: Longman, 1998.

Index

Note: Page numbers in italics indicate figures.

Women (*continued*)
  and sexual relations with soldiers, 105
  single, 64, 70
    honorable single women, 172
    "masterless" women, 76
    and place in society, 66
    as prostitutes, 84
    social service and honor, 150
  as threats to Church, 75
  and Tridentine reform of marriage
    promise, 43–44
    response to restricted options, 44
  widows, 65, 81
  and work as teachers, 153, 167, 169–70
Women and education
  changing notions of appropriate female
    education, 164, 172

education for upper-class women, 153
Enlightenment views of, 166–67
female teachers, 156
  and social mobility, 169
Mary Ward and the Institute of English
  Ladies, 150–51
  and Latin and access to public sphere,
    154
nature of female education, 153,
  166–67
  and class distinction, 164–66
  and domesticity, 172
Women's history, 7–8
  and domestication of women, 174
  and Weberian paradigm, 181–82n. 31

Zuchthäuser, 72, 175